CITIES
OF THE
DEAD

CIVIL WAR AMERICA
Gary W. Gallagher, editor

Contesting the Memory
of the Civil War in the South,
1865–1914

The University of North Carolina Press Chapel Hill & London

CITIES
OF THE
DEAD

WILLIAM A. BLAIR

Designed by Eric M. Brooks

Set in Dante by Keystone Typesetting, Inc.

Manufactured in the United States of America

The paper in this book meets the guidelines
for permanence and durability of the Committee on
Production Guidelines for Book Longevity of the
Council on Library Resources.

Library of Congress Cataloging-in-Publication Data

Blair, William Alan.

Cities of the dead : contesting the memory of the Civil
War in the South, 1865–1914 / by William A. Blair.

p. cm. — (Civil War America)

Includes bibliographical references and index.

ISBN 0-8078-2896-3 (alk. paper)

1. Reconstruction. 2. Memorials—Political aspects—
Southern States—History. 3. Power (Social sciences)—
Southern States—History. 4. Political culture—Southern
States—History. 5. Group identity—Southern States—
History. 6. African Americans—Southern States—
Anniversaries, etc. 7. Southern States—Politics and
government—1865–1950. 8. United States—History—Civil
War, 1861–1865—Monuments. 9. Southern States—Race
relations. 10. United States—History—Civil War, 1861–
1865—Influence. I. Title. II. Series.

F215.B625 2004

973.7′6—dc22

2004007402

08 07 06 05 04   5 4 3 2 1

For My Father

■ ■ ■

WALTER BLAIR
who always encouraged

CONTENTS

PREFACE

Roughly a decade ago, I was researching a related project on national identity when I came across a newspaper item about an Emancipation Day celebration. The year was 1866. Former Confederates in Hampton, Virginia, were angered by the event, which featured black soldiers marching in the streets. The controversy turned violent when someone fired shots. Further digging into newspapers yielded other problems over ceremonies—times, for instance, when federal authorities censored aspects of Confederate Memorial Days. They prohibited veterans from wearing uniforms and stripped the buttons from the clothing of those who did. Speeches about the war were forbidden. On Union Memorial Day in 1869 at Arlington, the former home of Robert E. Lee, soldiers prevented southern women from decorating the graves of Confederate soldiers who had been buried on the grounds. It was apparent that bitterness remained after the war and that something as seemingly harmless as a public celebration—or the placing of flowers on a grave—provoked strong reactions, including life-threatening ones. As controversial as the Civil War has been and still is today with disputes over the Confederate flag, their intensity pales in comparison with the nineteenth-century clashes over commemorations of the conflict.

Since that first discovery, I have hunted for the meaning behind these ceremonies, especially how they revealed the struggles over politics and power in the postemancipation South. Memorial Days and Emancipation Days seemed to offer a way to learn the sentiments of various contending groups, revealing the positions of people who normally do not leave a written record. I thought, for instance, that I might learn more about African American political strategies during a time before much of the South had established black newspapers. The parades contained public associations and clubs that sent a message about political positions or the ambitions of the marchers. It seemed reasonable to conclude that if persons attended civic ceremonies, they found the message and reason for holding the event compatible with their own interests. Their interests may have differed from those of the speaker at times, but common people attending the commemorations of the Civil War and emancipation had to share at least basic premises with organizers or they likely would have stayed home.

I found, however, that far from being merely windows into people's attitudes, the new invented traditions of the Civil War *were* politics and power. They were politics in a way that does not happen today; the lines between election rituals and festive celebrations blurred in the nineteenth century. Public rituals drew crowds to listen to partisan speeches at a time when oral tradition was very important and literacy was still something to be achieved among African Americans emerging from enslavement. Political mobilization depended on outdoor rituals, processions, torchlight parades, and other activities characteristic of nineteenth-century America. They were power in a way that does happen today; they reflected who can declare their history and rituals as the official version. The post-emancipation South, however, provided an electric atmosphere for this power display. The ceremonies emerged as a nation redrew the boundaries of freedom and citizenship, the result of the emancipation of 4 million enslaved Americans. The use of public space, such as letting women decorate Confederate graves at Arlington or black men carry weapons in a parade, would define citizenship, with repercussions extending into the twentieth and now the twenty-first centuries.

It might be good to announce what this book does not do, so readers expecting otherwise can place the volume back on the shelf. I am not primarily interested in the construction of memory, although the concept serves as an important background of this study. Memory has become a cottage industry in the historical profession, with numerous scholars exploring how people define their past and their character using history that has been distorted to suit current needs. I am more interested in how that past was used than in describing how it was constructed. I also did not pursue religious symbolism in the ideology of black or white ceremonies. African Americans during Emancipation Day ceremonies did argue that freedom came because God had intervened in human affairs; however, they more often used secular arguments when calling for the expansion of rights. They deployed demographics and other scientific evidence compatible with the progressive era. I also did not look at statuary, other material culture, battlefield preservation, veterans' reunions, historical societies, or any mechanism beyond the invention of traditions. For better or worse, I tried to remain focused on Emancipation Days and Memorial Days, to see what they revealed about the postemancipation battles for power in the South.

While this study does suggest that additional dimensions existed behind racism in the creation of a new Union, I want to make it clear that I saw ample violence, coercion, and racism as factors in sectional reunion. Racism did factor into the equation; it would be silly to state otherwise. Too often, however, we stop at that explanation without seeing the underlying ways racism is deployed, the political factors that drive its use, or the disagreements among people who supposedly think the same because of skin color. These, too, are some of the issues this book tries to reveal.

■ ■ ■

A project that progresses in bits and pieces over roughly a decade and during employment at two institutions incurs the usual number of debts. I want to begin by extending my gratitude to the host of students and friends who helped me with this book. Many joined in the effort to tease out of newspapers the slim bits of evidence that allowed me to make broader conclusions about the significance of the commemorations of war and freedom. At the University of North Carolina at Greensboro, I enjoyed working with Christopher Patterson, Neil Soiseth, Brenda MacDougal, and Brent Rumble. At the Pennsylvania State University, I benefited from the good work of graduate students Barbara A. Gannon, Susan deWeese, Karen F. Younger, Leah Vincent, and Michael Smith. Andrew Marshal, former student and current friend, provided terrific help in finding and securing newspapers from Louisiana and South Carolina through interlibrary loan. Jonathan White went on from his undergraduate work at Penn State to find an advanced degree at the University of Maryland and help a former professor with essential research support. Another good friend, Debrah Ann Poveromo, gave up a portion of her summer vacation to plow through newspapers. For all of these efforts I am deeply grateful. I could not have collected the necessary materials without this assistance.

Institutional support came from several places. An Andrew Mellon Fellowship at the Virginia Historical Society funded research at that magnificent facility. I want to thank Frances Pollard and her talented archivists there. The University of North Carolina at Greensboro also supplied two summers of research support, which advanced the project. At Penn State, Dean Susan Welch and Associate Dean Ray Lombra provided vital release time that enabled me to make progress on this research while working around the needs of the Richards Civil War Era Center. The College of the Liberal Arts and the History Department, led by A. Gregg Roeber, made it possible to acquire materials and gain the services of research assistants.

A number of colleagues have left their mark on these pages, vastly improving them with their insights. Faculty members at UNCG who gave good critical advice included William Link, Phyllis Hunter, and especially Steven Lawson, who commented on a draft of a paper that presented an overview of the contours of black celebrations of the Civil War. Steve also was a model of a department chair who knew how to encourage a young faculty member to remain focused on both teaching and research. Charles J. Holden, now at the St. Mary's College of Maryland, gave me leads on sources and refined my thinking about southern conservatives. At Penn State I have been blessed with talented faculty members, many of whom brought a special expertise to their critique of the work. I especially appreciate the efforts of Amy Greenberg and Sophie De Schaepdrijver, who provided comment for a Civil War era workshop for what has become Chapter 4 of this work. Nan Elizabeth Woodruff read the entire manuscript, sharpening my ideas about African American history and patiently letting me talk my way through much of this effort. I owe a special debt to Mark E. Neely Jr., who read a majority of the chapters and especially raised my consciousness of politics. Even though I have not taken certain of his comments far enough, I prospered greatly from his contribution. I also would like to acknowledge the input from faculty beyond these institutions. This includes scholars who commented on various aspects of the work at three conferences, particularly David Blight, Nina Silber, Gaines Foster, LeAnn Whites, Charles Reagan Wilson, and the anonymous readers for the University of North Carolina Press.

I also need to thank two other friends who left their mark on this book in different ways. Scott Daggs provided the outdoor office that I always wanted, giving me many moments of peaceful contemplation through his artisanship. I thank him for not gloating about finishing his project ahead of mine. Joseph McGinn helped me take advantage of this setting as we spent hours critiquing each other's works during one very memorable summer. He forced me to find answers to very cogent questions. Both men in their own way made this a better book.

Finally, I must thank the person who always bears the brunt of research projects, listening to all of the angst and putting up with hours of misplaced efforts while enjoying few of the rewards. Thank you, as always, Mary Ann.

CITIES
OF THE
DEAD

III

INTRODUCTION

III

This book examines the political implications of commemorating the Civil War, specifically Emancipation Day and Memorial Day in the former Confederate states from 1865 to 1915. These rituals originated and matured in an era when street processions, parades, and various public displays were instrumental both for partisan political activity and for fashioning a new public sphere. The Cities of the Dead, or what nineteenth-century Americans called the cemeteries for fallen heroes, provided places for community leaders to reach mass audiences of like-minded people to reinforce partisan ideals and behavior. The commemorations of war and freedom also were part of the restructuring of public space, declaring who had the right to march in the streets, have graves tended by federal authorities, or have ceremonies endorsed by a president. In short, they helped to define who citizens were and demonstrate how participants struggled for recognition and rights from the national state. Emancipation Days and Memorial Days suggest how leaders tried to persuade their constituencies, illuminating the practical concerns for power that ran alongside racism in shaping the course of reunion and sectional reconciliation.

The study of civic rituals has exploded since the 1980s when scholars such as Eric Hobsbawm demonstrated how they supported new forms of elite rule in the late nineteenth-century West. Invented traditions employed a version of the past constructed to validate regimes and bind people to nations. Although the content of new public holidays was orchestrated by those who controlled the apparatus of state, these commemorations had to maintain "genuine popular resonance" or they failed to attract supporters. American historians have picked up on these concepts, producing rich work that has featured the role of public activity in the structuring of power in the nineteenth century.[1] Running parallel to this literature have been studies by historians of sectional reunion and the Lost Cause, or the southern interpretation of the conflict as the agrarian South conducting a hopeless fight for states' rights against the industrial North. In works that explore reunion and the emerging Confederate traditions, the pendulum has swung dramatically since the 1930s, when racism had little part in the histories of the war and scholars viewed Memorial Days as providing common ground for former enemies to effect national healing. Today, the antipathy of white people against black people provides a central dynamic to reconciliation, with historians showing how black people were pushed off the nation's public stage and commemorations of the war and freedom created points of conflict as well as consensus.

Although scholars have presented the ceremonies of the Civil War as instrumental in creating a national identity, they have only recently identified politics and power as a part of white celebrations. Beginning with the work of Paul Buck, the first generation of studies that examined Memorial Day explicitly denied the use of this event for partisan needs. Memorial days were depicted as occasions with very little political content primarily for reconciling former enemies. According to these historians, rituals provided the means for veterans from both sides to find common ground through recognition of the heroism of soldiers. There was little recognition of the exclusion of African Americans that this reunion involved; celebrations by black people were ignored completely. Partisanship was viewed as the antithesis of reconciliation, something to be avoided in the new traditions.[2] In the last decades of the twentieth century, the literature of the Lost Cause portrayed Memorial Days as cultural elements with little or no political content, as examples of civil religion, or as a means of helping celebrants overcome the loss of the war. The architects of Confederate traditions often have been considered backward-looking sentimentalists, although Gaines Foster has linked one part of the Lost Cause to more progressive individuals who tried to build a New South with the tools of Yankee capitalism. Rarely have the Lost Cause or the ceremonial aspects of the war been identified as one of the tools of a powerful elite, with invented traditions helping to fend off challenges to the rule of former Confederates.[3]

Scholars of black civic rituals have been more sensitive to their contested and political nature. It is hard to miss these implications in African American commemorations of freedom, which offered a striking counterpoint to the ceremonies of the nation-state. Various works, like that of Antoinette G. van Zelm on Emancipation Days, consider the occasions as "highly political events with the potential to elicit violent opposition." They provided an opportunity for black women to become, according to Kathleen Clark, "spirited participants in community affairs" and agents in reshaping the public sphere. When Mitch Kachun looked at the evolution of black freedom celebrations throughout the nineteenth century, he found that black people were creating a usable past to assert their readiness for full political equality in the nation.[4] These and other studies have revealed additional dimensions to the struggle for equality; however, while van Zelm has placed the ceremonies of followers of the Lost Cause in relief against the freedom celebrations of black Americans, the tendency among scholars had been to adopt racial barriers when examining the commemorations of war.

David Blight's *Race and Reunion* overcomes the limitations of prior works by examining not just one set of practices but multiple traditions: Confederate, Union (including black and white people celebrating Union Memorial Day), and African American. Using extensive research to trace the memory of the war among both northerners and southerners, Blight charts three visions of the American Civil War: reconciliationist, which sought common ground between the sections; white supremacist, which denied the role of slavery in the war and excluded a black memory of the conflict; and emancipationist, which conceived of the war as a struggle to end slavery, with black people as central to the conflict. Ultimately, Blight's story is a tragic one that reveals how "the forces of reconciliation overwhelmed the emancipationist vision in the national culture, how the inexorable drive for reunion both used and trumped race."[5]

Despite the impressive breadth of Blight's study, and his appreciation that public ceremonies in the nineteenth century were part of a struggle for power in the nation, there remains a deeper, more complex story to tell about the political role of commemorations. Blight's *Race and Reunion* takes us to a certain point but, understandable in such a sweeping work, does not follow the political trail far enough. It simply is not his purpose, just as memory does not constitute the main focus of this book. Partisan issues appear in his study, but most often they are confined to Reconstruction. While he acknowledges the third-party movements after Reconstruction, he does not show their connection with commemorations—how they caused black speakers to advocate independent party activity because of the betrayal by northern Republicans and how they reinforced a trend among former Confederates to raise the image of the crippled veteran to keep white voters in line. Racism remains the key dynamic for understanding reconciliation and the exclusion of African Americans.

Racism was a large part of how reunion came, but looking deeper into the political involvement of civic traditions uncovers additional factors. The categories of reconciliationist, emancipationist, and white supremacist do not always hold up. There was a great deal more fluidity and more overlapping concerns.

During Reconstruction, southern white people who called themselves Conservatives openly advocated sectional harmony and reconciliation, even as they supported the celebration of Confederate traditions. They promised to allow black voting and even at times encouraged black people to enter their party, yet they did so to solidify regional power by keeping the federal government from interfering further in their affairs. White supremacists in this case adopted a conciliatory position with the government and sometimes asked their colleagues to tone down the display of rebel flags and other symbolism that might awaken sectional hostility. Emancipationists also supported reconciliation with rebels, including noteworthy Radical Republicans such as abolitionist Gerrit Smith and Chief Justice Salmon P. Chase. Here were men who might have been expected to take a tougher stand against rebels because they shared in the emancipationist vision and memory of the Civil War, yet they also worked for reconciliation. And there was, for lack of a better term, a Unionist interpretation of the war. This was held most noticeably, but not exclusively, by veterans who pledged their lives for reunion, may or may not have viewed slavery as the central reason for war, and were in no hurry to reconcile with rebels. For much of the remaining nineteenth century they sounded the alarm against Democrats' regaining national strength, warning that the rebels had caused war and could not be entrusted yet with the control of the government.

Exploring the political uses of freedom celebrations uncovers the enduring faith of black people in politics as a viable solution until the turn of the century, as well as their conflicted views of the Republican Party. Deep into the 1890s, Emancipation Days featured a strong, persistent call by orators for the race to become more self-reliant. At first this self-reliance was promoted as a way for blacks to prove their readiness for full citizenship and deny white people one more argument for discrimination, but as time wore on—and disenchantment with the Republican leadership grew—some orators argued for breaking from the party. Economic and social self-reliance became for these African Americans the way to create an independent voting bloc to enhance their bargaining power. A majority undoubtedly hoped that the strategy would encourage national Republican leaders to increase the commitment to black issues. In this they were disappointed.

While most African Americans nonetheless remained Republican, they did not consistently support the Grand Old Party in local or state elections. Historians, however, have yet to produce an extended analysis of black voting behavior from Reconstruction through disfranchisement. J. Morgan Kousser comes the closest by revealing a significant minority of black support for Democrats in gubernatorial elections of the early 1880s in the former Confederacy.[6] I suspect that a more detailed look at the voting behavior of blacks would reveal them as maintaining one hand on the Republican Party for national elections, while reaching out with the other to find the best possible allies in local and state affairs.

Memorial traditions also reveal another side to the political engagement of white women in the South. This is dramatically true for white women who originated the first wave of Confederate rituals during Reconstruction. With the fuller context of Memorial Days resurrected, we encounter women conducting a range of public activities that sparked commentary from northern journalists and provoked a reaction from the federal government. Women organized marches to cemeteries to decorate the graves of soldiers in 1866, or the first anniversaries of the end of the conflict. More than just simple occasions for mourning, the practices alarmed northerners who saw marches by veterans and speeches by leaders of the rebellion in a broader context of race riots, violence against white Republicans, and the rising strength of ex-Confederates. Disloyalty and resistance to Reconstruction seemed to prosper in the Cities of the

Dead, fortified by memories of the war sustained through the memorial traditions. By 1867, military officers monitored memorial celebrations, banning marches or speeches dealing with political issues. White Democrats could hold meetings indoors, but Memorial Days became one of the few venues for mass outdoor gatherings for public acknowledgment of the Confederacy. Northerners considered the women who organized these commemorations as agitators and accused men of hiding behind women's skirts, leaving it to the fairer sex to preserve sectional bitterness.

Their efforts had an ironic, beneficial impact on the process of reconciliation. Even though the first Confederate Memorial Days were considered to be divisive and harmful for sectional fusion, it was easier to forget this aspect when white people from both sides finally shook hands across the bloody chasm. Confederate traditions emerged through a women's domain; the veteran came only later in the 1870s after federal supervision eased and Redemption gained momentum. It was easier to forget the discord of the early years while stressing the mourning and sentimental aspects of Memorial Day because the holiday had come about through an expansion of white women's domestic responsibilities.

Black women present a more elusive figure in the celebrations of freedom. It is not that they were absent, but they did not leave the organizational trail that white women did. There were few societies comparable to the ladies memorial associations. Black women planned portions of Emancipation Day activities, but they assumed a division of labor according to gender. Freedom celebrations were meant first to reinforce manhood by drawing attention to the black soldiers who had earned citizenship through fighting. African American women did have one function noticeably different from those found in white celebrations: they formed black militia units for ceremonial occasions. For the most part, however, black women claimed for themselves the roles of the white middle class in public processions. They marched as members of Sunday schools, temperance groups, literary societies, veterans' auxiliaries, and various other clubs and associations. This represented a radical statement in its own right, for they had been excluded from public celebrations in the South before the war and were rarely given the privileges granted to white women. Respectability—whether stressed by men or women—served as a form of political agency through which they intended to earn greater rights.

This study ends with the fiftieth anniversaries of the war because Memorial Days and Emancipation Days by that time had undergone profound changes. The height for mass-producing traditions, to use Hobsbawm's phrase, ended with 1914. In the United States, reconciliation had come between white people who had once been enemies. With the Spanish-American War and World War I, Memorial Days expanded in meaning and no longer exclusively celebrated Civil War soldiers. The style of American campaigns also changed: street activity such as torchlight parades and group processions diminished as a part of election rituals. Popular politics declined. Memorial Days remained useful opportunities for candidates to make an appearance, but they shied away from sectional issues, using the occasions, like Woodrow Wilson at Arlington, to stress the common attributes of the American character—at least for white people. With the mechanism of power solidly in white hands, Confederate traditions became the official celebrations in the South, with freedom celebrations relegated to an unofficial or vernacular status by the ruling elite.[7] Freedom celebrations still had a political meaning and support in black neighborhoods; however, the commemorations of Emancipation Days tied to important anniversaries such as the fiftieth year of freedom became a means to reinforce an accommodationist vision of certain black people who discouraged more activist measures for pressing for rights. White governors and other holders of public office bestowed money and other resources on these exhibitions, rewarding the African Americans who reinforced a conservative uplift strategy that recognized white superiority.

The official fiftieth anniversary expositions of freedom lend credence to Hobsbawm's assertion that while powerful people invent traditions for their own purposes, these traditions must tap the sentiments of the public to have validity. Black people in Richmond failed to support an exposition honoring the fiftieth anniversary of freedom, even though Congress bestowed on the event the distinction of a national observance through an appropriation. Although organized by African Americans, the event drew a primarily white audience. This suggests how to consider the popular understanding of commemorative events. Participants rarely left any record of their impressions, forcing historians to interpret the importance of these occasions to the common person. We cannot state unconditionally that all people in an audience shared the same level of support or enthusiasm for a cause as the speaker on the podium. Even good, faithful churchgoers nod off at a sermon now and then—or get angry with the preacher. Yet they would not attend service in the first place if they did not hold core

beliefs in common with the minister. We learn the most about the sentiments of the audience in times of discord—the moments when participation declines or when organizers express frustration at the behavior of the
crowd. The assumption here is that while these ceremonies offer the most
accurate description of the values of organizers, they do provide windows,
however imperfect, into key ideas, concerns, and beliefs of the public they
served.

To find this story—especially to tease out the trends in ceremonies—
required a deep, focused examination of memorial and freedom traditions
over an extended time. To do this, I chose Virginia as the core of the study
for a number of reasons. The state contained a concentrated level of
combat during the war that left thousands of dead within its borders. This
created a great urgency for reburial efforts, resulting in the creation of
either new cemeteries or new sections in established ones. The memorial
associations in Richmond were especially active, organizing one of the
largest reburial campaigns in the postwar South with the transfer of southern dead from the Gettysburg Battlefield to Hollywood Cemetery. This
process was not only conducted by former Confederates. A host of new
national cemeteries—a phenomenon that dates to the Civil War era—
were created by the government immediately after the war. These were
especially prevalent throughout the Old Dominion because of the high
number of casualties from the battles there. Because Richmond served as
the capital of the Confederacy, a number of the cemeteries and the memorial traditions attained a higher degree of symbolism and attracted greater
northern scrutiny than many places in the former Confederacy. Arguably
the greatest heroes of the Lost Cause, Robert E. Lee and Thomas "Stonewall" Jackson, were native sons and were buried in Lexington. Jefferson
Davis's body was dug up from his grave in Louisiana and transferred to
Hollywood Cemetery. Arlington National Cemetery, the former home of
Lee, lies within the state's borders, revealing the shift from authorities
restricting celebrations by Confederates to their creating a section that
honored former enemies.

Virginia also contained movements of regional and national significance. Readjusters—a fusion of Democrats and Republicans—represented
the most successful biracial coalition in the South. Although confined to
the Old Dominion, the effort was watched nationally and provided the
prescription for southern elites to hold off populism. To keep white voters
in line, they raised the color bar, quit talking about economic issues, and

waved the flag of tradition in the form of the crippled veteran. In the 1890s, the Lee statue went up on Monument Avenue in Richmond, drawing perhaps 100,000 people, including surviving veterans from across the South. Richmond also contained one of the leading black newspapers in the country, the *Richmond Planet* edited by John Mitchell. He spearheaded an effort to rally black people across the region to lobby for a national Emancipation Day holiday. In the fiftieth anniversary of emancipation that received the endorsement of Congress and Woodrow Wilson, we can find the disenchantment that many black people felt in the use of the exhibitions to serve the ends of white leaders in tandem with black accommodationists.

To verify that the trends witnessed in Virginia at least broadly described the former states of the Confederacy, in this study I incorporated newspapers from Louisiana and South Carolina and looked elsewhere when circumstances warranted. The latter two states were sensitive battlegrounds during Reconstruction, containing Republican regimes that were among the last to fall. They also cut across a large geographic section of the Deep South, revealing some of the peculiarities of local traditions, especially how these were geared to dates significant for a particular area. I also leaned on the efforts of other scholars of Civil War commemorations, which have become more numerous every year. I am confident that the overall picture holds true, even as I recognize that there are worthwhile differences within the region remaining to be explored.

What do we learn, then, by using these celebrations as the lens through which to view politics and power in the postwar South? We find a hypercharged environment immediately after the war in which every public act was assessed for the precedent it contained and what it announced about the loyalty of the participants. The ceremonies created hostility, sparked violence, and caused northern authorities to limit the public activity of former Confederates in remembering the war. Through these ceremonies, we can see that the end of Reconstruction was only the beginning of independent movements, with biracial coalitions leaving their mark on the South. The celebrations suggest that black people had more problems with the Republican Party than much of the literature of reunion contains. They also suggest that class worries extended to white elites who learned that their patrician demeanor needed the law and disfranchisement to derail cooperation among poorer whites and black people. The African Americans living through these times entertained real hope that politics offered a means of protecting and expanding equality. And we find that the so-called sentimental and reconciliationist stance of President William McKinley contained the desire to lobby southern whites for support of his expansionist goals in the Philippines. We will find racism in sectional reconciliation, but working hand in glove with invented tradition and rational ideas about how to keep power.

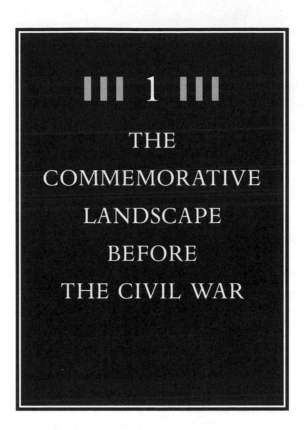

1

THE
COMMEMORATIVE
LANDSCAPE
BEFORE
THE CIVIL WAR

When a writer for *North American Review* looked at the commemorative calendar of the United States in 1857, he bemoaned the lack of a unified holiday. "It is an exceptional trait in our nationality," he noted, "that its sentiment finds no annual occasion when the hearts of the people thrill with an identical emotion, absorbing in patriotic instinct and mutual reminiscence all personal interests and local prejudice." The nation had anniversaries aplenty and even a number of "universal celebrities," "but the dates of their birth, services, and decease form no saints' days for the Republic."[1] It was not as if Americans did not like to celebrate. On the contrary, they headed for the streets at the least excuse to honor just about anything from ethnic background to mechanical skills. This writer mentioned a plethora of local and regional observances, including recognition of Benjamin Franklin in Boston, Pilgrim Day in New England, Evacuation Day in New York, and the victory on Lake Erie in the War of 1812 in Newport. He also reported various social and occupational pageants, such as a march for temperance, a picnic for spiritualists, anniversaries of Henry Clay's birth or Daniel Webster's death, an address by a mechanic to his fellows, and an occasion called Yacht America. Americans before the Civil War had ample spirit for holidays and public commemorations. What they did not have was a unified interpretation of commemorations that honored the republic.

While scholars have more often looked at civic celebrations as a means of forging nationalism, they have begun to appreciate more recently how the same events could divide a populace or serve multiple purposes. In the case of the United States, the limited national observances that existed always contained contested meanings. Before the Civil War, the Fourth of July and George Washington's birthday provided the only civic traditions with a semblance of national coherence. Yet abolitionists used Independence Day to preach the gospel of antislavery. Similarly, some parts of what became the Confederate South quit observing July Fourth by the 1850s or scaled back their activities in a cautious reevaluation of Union. As the war came, Washington's memory furnished Virginians, and by extension fellow southerners, with an ambivalent image that may have reinforced ties to the founding of the republic but also heightened their sense of regional distinctiveness against the escalating assault of abolitionists.[2]

When creating new civic traditions and redefining established ones after the Civil War, Americans black and white drew on important elements of antebellum commemorations. One element that carried over into the postwar world was the use of civic celebrations as a means of practicing partisan politics, with a procession at the heart of civic celebrations. America in the nineteenth century featured the most active street politics in the world, and this practice only intensified with so much at stake after the conflict. Still another inheritance from prewar America was the use of civic traditions in racial discourse, with African Americans employing commemorations of the war to claim the right to citizenship. In doing so, black leaders in the postwar world altered the antebellum posture that featured the revolutionary and international struggles of Africans in favor of stressing black Americans as the true Unionists and consistent supporters of the nation. They also emphasized the need for propriety and respectability, with community leaders trying to curb the more volatile behavior of crowds to conform to middle-class morality. African Americans in particular were keenly aware that their detractors assessed the behavior of crowds in community celebrations to determine whether the race deserved equal rights.

For the ceremonies in the colonial through antebellum period, the streets offered an important venue for a variety of needs, including popular disorders, festivals, and organized political behavior. Persons living in those times understood that these displays reinforced the nature of authority. They were, as scholars have argued, not simply reflections of social behavior but an active means of practicing politics.[3]

■ ■ ■

ROWDYISM, RESPECTABILITY, AND POLITICS

Jacksonian era Americans participated in a variety of street pageantry that linked politics with festival, including torchlight parades, illuminations, pole raisings, and serenades of political figures. Participating in these events signified loyalty to a political party, in the case of a Democratic rally, or an ethnic group, in the case of St. Patrick's Day. These rituals did not include everyone. African Americans, for instance, did not typically observe July Fourth, nor did white persons celebrate the end of the slave trade. Some community leaders on both sides of the racial divide approached events with mixed sentiments. On one hand, they tried to orchestrate celebrations and stimulate the common folk to turn out for a cause. On the other hand, local leaders and members of the respectable middle class fretted over how to keep their own supporters in line. Drunken marchers who brawled with one another and with spectators proved embarrassing, to say the least. As nascent industrialism changed America, an emerging middle class that defined itself in terms of respectability and sobriety increasingly sniffed at the unruly behavior of crowds.

The rituals for civic ceremonies and politics contributed to the problem. They had originated in a plebeian culture that encouraged riotous behavior. The methods of popular disorder and protest of the eighteenth century formed the basis of rituals that Americans in the nineteenth century employed for civic events and political rallies. These included processions, mockery, rough music (banging on pots and other metal), bonfires, effigies, and shaming. Of course, street activity not only involved protest; for many, it was also good old-fashioned entertainment. "For the plebs," one historian has noted, "any tumult was fun, and the suspension of normal rules of social behavior in riots and annual plebeian rituals alike made for grand entertainment." What bears remembering in the American context is that once the old bonds of paternalism faded, the same plebeian rituals became more menacing without the former means of control.[4]

As suffrage expanded, new political parties capitalized on the people's love of spectacle and crowd activity to mobilize voters. The American Revolution had proven instrumental in marrying plebeian culture and what became the rituals of mass politics. Effigies, bonfires, mockery, and rough music folded over into resistance against the British. In New York, residents erected a Liberty Pole to show their defiance. Although activities that involved committees, organizations, and meetings helped forge a common political consciousness, one historian has observed that "it was the persistent use of mobs and street politics that propelled the common man into the political arena."[5]

The heart of any outdoor activity—legal, extralegal, political, or festive—was the procession. These were hardly spontaneous affairs. Community leaders carefully orchestrated them, assigning places in line to make a symbolic statement. Committees of arrangements organized civic affairs, with the leaders authorizing the banners and symbols worn by the marchers and carefully plotting the route to capitalize on symbolic space, such as ending at a candidate's home or the courthouse. The places that groups held in a march mirrored their importance. Public officials usually preceded mechanic societies, temperance groups, or citizens. Political parties naturally adopted the procession as a central procedure for mass rallies, designed to capture undecided voters and maintain discipline within their ranks.[6]

Calling for order is one thing; having it actually occur is quite another, especially if the lords of misrule still retained a hold on the popular mind and racial tensions wracked northern cities. As the antebellum period advanced, associations of the respectable middle class assumed a greater presence in the processions, yet crowds still got out of hand. Even elites who scripted this pageantry grew frustrated at the disorderliness. Violence could serve as part of a crowd's mission, which abolitionists recognized only too well. A mob killed abolitionist Elijah Lovejoy in 1836 in Alton, Illinois, and another chased down and beat William Lloyd Garrison in Boston in 1854. During the Civil War, mob activity often adopted a partisan mission as Democratic crowds attacked Republican newspaper offices, and vice versa.

African Americans shared in the forms of civic celebrations, but discrimination caused their commemorations to run contrary to mainstream events. Negro Election Days, Pinkster Day, and other festivities filled black calendars in the early republic, but these inversion rituals faded in the antebellum period. Black festivals gave way to orchestrated events with processions that celebrated emancipation as part of a revolutionary movement throughout the Atlantic rim. African Americans followed a civic calendar that at times mirrored that of white people and at times countered it. For instance, they observed July Fourth, but not with the same intentions. Additionally, they adopted other holidays that connected them with liberal movements in the Caribbean. As with white celebrations, respectability formed an important part of the message in the civic rituals of African Americans, but with a more pressing concern. Organizers understood that the white community watched these celebrations for behavior that reinforced prejudicial notions of black incompetence. Elevation of the race consequently formed a repetitive theme in the public events of African Americans—a message that continued to sound after the war.

In the South, slavery severely constricted the opportunities for civic participation of African Americans. Although most "holidays" for black people occurred as forms of cooperative, social labor sponsored by masters—like barn raising and corn shucking—slaves co-opted one season for their own use. Before the war, the Christmas season served a dual function in both easing and reinforcing the burden of bondage. The holiday provided customary rest for labor; however, these coerced workers faced their alleged vacation with some ambivalence. Christmas on plantations and throughout the South lasted from as little as three days to the more typical week—sometimes longer, depending on the master. Slaves expected to have free time to pursue their own work or rest from the grueling routine. They also expected gifts and alcohol. Masters used the occasion to play lord and lady, bolstering their sense of racial superiority by delighting in the "antics" of the "servants." Over the years, custom had reinforced these rituals, with masters learning that it created more problems than it was worth to withhold holiday privileges.[7]

For slaves, a more dangerous part of the holiday came toward its end. January 1 signaled the time for the departure of enslaved African Americans hired out under new labor contracts. During the holiday, planters negotiated new arrangements that involved renting or selling a laborer. Although hiring was less destructive than sale to the Deep South, it still had a deleterious impact on families. Planters rented a slave out for one year. Most often this occurred with someone relatively nearby, although even in this case the contract meant separation from spouses and children. Consequently, slaves often called New Year's Day "heart-break day." After the Civil War, a chaplain remembered January 1 as a "day which hitherto separated so many families, and tear-wet so many faces; heaved so many hearts, and filled the air with so many groans and sighs; this of all others the most bitter day of the year to our poor miserable race."[8] The Christmas season—and particularly New Year's Day—assumed a new meaning when freedom came. No more did the holiday separate families. Most black communities held ceremonies to observe the anniversary of Abraham Lincoln's Emancipation Proclamation.

■ ■ ■

CIVIC HOLIDAYS:
JULY FOURTH AND OTHER COMMEMORATIONS

Although July Fourth provided the closest thing to a secular saint's day for the republic, even this holiday had contentious roots. In the early national period, political factions fought over the event. Later in the century, white people who were part of the antislavery movement used the occasion to criticize America for failing to live up to its claim of liberty. African Americans marked the holiday with increasing ambivalence as it became clear that the liberty orators cherished was reserved for white persons. Many African Americans chose another time to celebrate independence, although most of the black community simply took the white holiday off. As the war neared, southern whites shared in this ambivalence. They observed the occasion, but with partisan undertones that paralleled the tensions surrounding the sectional crisis.

Independence Day coalesced as a civic tradition almost immediately upon the colonists' splitting from the British. July Fourth celebrations began during the Revolutionary War in the major seaport towns of Boston, New York, and Charleston. Some historians have seen partisan overtones occurring only later with the advent of the Constitution and awakening differences between Antifederalists and Federalists. This ignores the highly charged political atmosphere of these first occasions: that the rituals poked a stick in the British eye, tried to define the meaning of the war, and demonstrated who supported the patriots' cause. Avoiding these celebrations did not guarantee safety for the opposition, for the absence of persons from these festivities marked them as Loyalists who were fair game for persecution. The first Independence Days featured a combination of orderly celebration and violence, as the plebeian crowd broke the windows of suspected Tories and otherwise harassed the opposition.[9]

These first events established the rituals adopted by most communities. It likely took a deaf person to sleep late. Communities awakened to the booming of cannon, the popping of firecrackers, and the pealing of church bells. The highlight of the day's activities was the militia parade, which usually ended at the muster or fair grounds, where citizen soldiers showed their prowess. The parade wound through the town on an established route that ended at a church, county courthouse, commons, or other site important to the townspeople. The Declaration of Independence was read aloud. Orators reminded the crowd of the sacrifice of Revolutionary forebears and the meaning of the Union. Afterward, the crowd dispersed to eat and drink. Common folk went to taverns or helped themselves to food from the stands that lined the streets. The gentry held dinners with political personages. Massive amounts of alcohol reaffirmed the group's faith in the republic as guests raised their glasses to one-up each other in toasts to the nation.[10]

These celebrations changed in subtle ways that reflected the evolution of American politics and society. They became more overtly political, although not always uniformly so. The extent to which the holidays were spiced with political commentary depended on the historical moment. Additionally, these events mirrored the trends toward respectable associations within communities. Processions contained an increasing presence of civic groups and fraternal associations, some of which openly preached moral positions such as temperance. Independence Day observances thus wore the two mantles of politics and respectability—with neither a perfect fit.

It would be wrong to conclude that Americans always fought over this day and waged warfare in the streets. White people in communities throughout the new nation marked the day fairly peacefully as an enjoyable break from routine—a time for socializing with neighbors and relaxing in the festival atmosphere. Some did not attend the political meetings. Others scarcely noted the day at all. Diaries of farmers suggest that, unless the day held special significance, such as the fiftieth anniversary of independence in 1826, many did not head into town. Yet political contention never disappeared either. Americans recognized the forum that Independence Day offered as the nation stopped to reflect on the meaning of citizenship. While many may have passed the day without thinking about politics—beyond the recognition of the birth of the republic—others seized the time for advancing a cause.

Beginning with the rise of the abolition movement among white people in the 1830s, it became more common for orators at Independence Day celebrations to expound on the limits of freedom in the United States.

Caleb Cushing used his address before the Colonization Society of Massachusetts on July 4, 1833, to wish that the promise of America applied to all the people. He said that Americans gathered because of their love of liberty and that this was the same land where pilgrims had found freedom from oppression. He added, "And would to Heaven that it were so in our whole country: that the curse of involuntary servitude did not still cling to so large a portion of our countrymen, destroying their peace, filling their dwellings with the agonies of perpetual domestic suspicion, subjecting their families to massacre, and hanging its dead weight upon the public welfare." Like many antislavery orators, Cushing stressed the impact of slavery on all citizens—how it weakened free enterprise, eroded industry, and promoted idleness. He reminded his listeners that the Constitution implied that all were born to equal political rights, but because of slavery that ideal remained unrealized.[11]

Black abolitionists repudiated the day entirely. Frederick Douglass in 1852 delivered an address in Rochester, New York, titled "What to the Slave is the Fourth of July?" Throughout he reiterated that the national celebration belonged to white people, not his race. "It is the birthday of your National Independence, and of your political freedom," he observed. He added much later, "Your high independence only reveals the immeasurable distance between us. The blessings in which you, this day, rejoice, are not enjoyed in common. . . . This Fourth [of] July is *yours*, not *mine*. *You* may rejoice, *I* must mourn."[12] Later in his address he indicated that the day was even worse for the slave. "What, to the American slave, is your 4th of July? I answer: a day that reveals to him, more than all other days in the year, the gross injustice and cruelty to which he is the constant victim. To him, your celebration is a sham; your boasted liberty, an unholy license; your national greatness, swelling vanity; your sounds of rejoicing are empty and heartless; your denunciations of tyrants, brass fronted impudence; your shouts of liberty and equality, hollow mockery."[13] A black chaplain made similar comments after the war. According to Henry M. Turner, the national flag was tainted because "every star in it was against us; every stripe against us; the red, white and blue was against us; the nation's constitution was against us; yes! every State constitution; every State code, every decision from the supreme court down to the petty magistrates; and worse than all, every church was against us."[14]

Others noticed another contradiction in two kinds of processions that occurred: the Fourth of July parade and the march of slaves in a coffle. The *National Era*, a black newspaper in Washington, D.C., marveled how the

United States could pay homage to freedom movements overseas while failing to recognize inequality at home. For the Washington procession of 1830 in honor of France, the editor noticed people sporting tricolored ribbons and mixing tricolored flags with the Stars and Stripes. In this person's eyes, however, these processions were marred "by the appearance of another procession, moving in a contrary direction. It was a gang of slaves!" The writer went on: "Think of it! Shouts of triumph, rejoicing bells, gay banners, and glittering cavalcades, in honor of Liberty, in immediate contrast with men and women chained and driven like cattle to market." The editor concluded, "Slavery sticks in its [the nation's] throat, and spoils its finest performances, political and ecclesiastical; confuses the tongues of its Evangelical Alliances; makes a farce of its Fourth of July celebrations, and . . . sadly mars the effect of its rejoicings in view of the progress of liberty abroad."[15]

African Americans formed their own rituals because they were prevented from joining, except as spectators, in the processions and other activities sponsored by the white community. Ironically, the black celebrations were integrated, reflecting the cooperation of white and black abolitionists. Because of the threat posed by the antislavery posture of the crowd, violence sometimes erupted. This was not just the product of lower-class rabble. In an abolition church in New York City in 1834, merchants broke up a July Fourth gathering of black and white people who were listening to a lawyer who had defended fugitive slaves. The mob set the church on fire; the firemen who were called to the scene did little to put out the blaze.[16] This kind of violence was repeated in the South after the war, when African Americans used the day to celebrate their freedom.

One other characteristic of black civic traditions is worth noting. They reinforced themselves as part of an African diaspora that linked them with international revolutions—specifically emancipation through violence in Haiti and through legislation by the British in the Caribbean. African Americans in New York and other communities used July 5 as a form of Independence Day, which also announced their protest against the formal tradition that signaled hypocrisy. During these countervailing celebrations of nationality on July 5, black people freely associated themselves with their African descent. They referred to one another as African or descendants of Africa. Participants gathered in churches to hear sermons that honored the African past, praised the efforts of black Americans in creating the nation, and derided the United States for its lack of liberty.

Antebellum free blacks did mark Emancipation Day, but it was somewhat complicated because of the way freedom had come and by the continuation of slavery in the United States. Not surprisingly, they felt almost more comfortable connecting themselves with abolition movements in the Atlantic world. Emancipation in the North lacked a dramatic, singular occasion that abruptly ushered in a new meaning of freedom. Individual states adopted their own plans and, with a rare exception, did so gradually, with freedom coming for persons born after the law and only when they had achieved a certain age. Black people's observances of emancipation thus usually marked anniversaries of freedom in a particular location, such as New York City. Some also used street processions to commemorate the end of the slave trade beginning in July 1808. But these events were short lived, both because of the white reactions against them and, more importantly, because so many people remained enslaved that the observance seemed hollow. A more important date became the anniversary of the emancipation of 800,000 slaves in the British West Indies on August 1, 1834. The anniversary quickly became a rallying point for black demonstrations that featured prominent speakers for abolition in the United States.[17]

In the South, slaves did not form parades, but scattered evidence suggests that they considered themselves part of traditions of revolutions, similar to northern blacks. A study of Richmond indicates that oral culture kept alive the memory of Gabriel's Rebellion through song and stories in the black community. Free blacks, too, occasionally won the right to insert themselves into white commemorations of the American Revolution. Tom Evans had fought in the conflict and staged a single-man march in Staunton, Virginia. White people encouraged this participation by black people, provided it supported the notion of the faithful slave or offered a sign of ridicule in which white onlookers considered the marcher a child trying to mimic an adult. Free blacks in Salem, North Carolina, commemorated in a different fashion, employing the rough music and burlesque of inversion rituals. In 1836 they awakened the small community between 1:00 and 2:00 A.M. by banging on an old drum, ringing cowbells, and playing pipes. In 1858 free blacks conducted a "burlesque military procession" led through the town by a black band. The mayor and police cracked down on the procession, arresting several of the people they derisively referred to as "patriots."[18]

Black Americans, whether in the North or the South, used a holiday from work for their own ends. A diary left by William Johnson of Natchez, Mississippi, suggests as much. A free black barber, Johnson participated in the spectacle of the white celebrations whenever the occasion warranted. In 1836 he turned out for the large military demonstrations. For the next ten years he continued to take in the parades and accompanying festivities, but in 1846 he used the holiday to go to the racetrack. Part of the reason for his seeking this sport seems to have been waning interest in the town for the spectacle. With "Nothing going on very Lively," the racetrack offered a better diversion.[19]

Ambivalence for the day grew among southern white people as the Civil War neared, but it would be a mistake to think that they rejected the holiday. This posture came after the Civil War as white persons considered Independence Day for black people and Yankees. Before the war, much of the white South held July Fourth celebrations, but with an increasingly sectional flavor. Some viewed the time suspiciously because of the agitation by abolitionists.

This agitation was nothing new. John C. Calhoun had introduced sectionalism into the July Fourth toasts of the 1830s, but the sectional tone sounded more frequently after the Mexican War. In 1851 the residents of Greenville, South Carolina, turned the holiday into an antisecession rally with an estimated 4,000 people attending. In 1858 Jefferson Davis delivered a speech onboard a steamer from Washington to Boston, in which he declared, "This great country will continue united." Robert Barnwell Rhett used his speech on July 4, 1859, in Grahamsville, South Carolina, to propose the creation of a southern nation. In neighboring North Carolina, a newspaper editor in the early 1850s noticed a growing sectional tone in observances throughout the South even as he claimed a declining interest in the Fourth in the region. "Thousands of preachers and orators at the North will avail themselves of the opportunity to instill hatred to the South and her institutions. . . . We cannot, therefore, look forward to the influence of the day with the same hopeful feelings that used to animate us on such occasions."[20]

A final aspect of antebellum civic traditions worth noting concerns the increasing presence of women as caretakers of historic memory. Virginia's women became instrumental in saving the plantation of George Washington. It had decayed until, in the 1850s, the owner tried to sell it. Many in the country balked at this prospect, although the homes of other Revolutionary founders had suffered similarly. Washington's home had become a shrine for the nation, with tourists brought to the estate by steamboat excursions. Despite this, Congress refused to purchase the site. Through the Mount Vernon Ladies Association, women pressured the General

Assembly of Virginia into establishing an agreement that kept the mansion quasi-public and quasi-private. The charter passed by the legislature recognized the authority of the ladies to incorporate as a legal entity and manage the plantation. The women demonstrated not only great energy but also business acumen. They convinced Edward Everett, the most renowned orator in the country, to give speeches and write essays, donating his fees to the association. Through this, they raised more than $69,000 for the restoration of the home. The organization to save Mount Vernon hinted at what would follow the Civil War, when women increased their public activity through commemorative rituals.

After the war, Americans black and white reached for the established rituals for commemorating nationhood. They added new wrinkles by honoring the dead in cemeteries established either through local means by former Confederates or with federal funds in the case of new national cemeteries. The processions had a familiar feel to them. Organizers assigned places in line, picked routes, and selected orators. But the battle for public space contained strikingly new elements. The marching of black veterans in the streets of the South suggested the revolutionary upheaval that faced former Confederates. The change in social relations—and especially a shift in allegiance to a national authority—was reflected in the commemorative traditions of the reunited nation. African Americans observed the national Memorial Day and July Fourth as holidays; the latter contained deep significance as a day of liberation and not just as a commemoration of the birth of nationhood. White Confederates, however, rejected the day as a "Negro holiday."

The ceremonial landscape of the American republic before the Civil War—and throughout American history, for that matter—featured civic traditions that sometimes created unity and sometimes announced differences. Many elites attempted to forge a national identity through various traditions marked especially by July Fourth. Sectional politics entered the picture later in the period, with North and South claiming they honored the true values of the republic. Intraregional problems also beset the invention of traditions, with some of these difficulties class-based and some racial. While many holiday observances passed peacefully enough, contention in the streets marked many of the events in the newly forming republic. Soon this friction worsened as people implicitly and explicitly understood that these ceremonies did not merely reflect the social arrangement within communities but created new meanings for power in the postemancipation world.

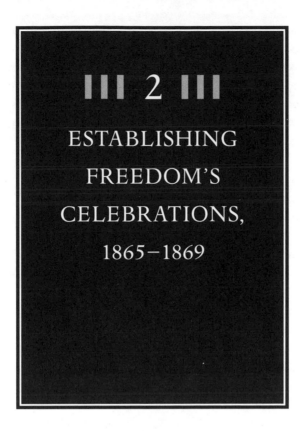

III 2 III

ESTABLISHING

FREEDOM'S

CELEBRATIONS,

1865–1869

In the spring of 1866, the Civil War had been over for a year, but the wounds had by no means healed. That much became clear as the black residents of Hampton, Virginia, gathered on the first anniversary of freedom. They marched on April 9—not the date of the Emancipation Proclamation but the surrender of the Army of Northern Virginia. Black veterans paraded in the blue uniforms of the United States while carrying weapons like the ones that had helped to bring down the Confederacy. The event angered former Confederates; its correspondence with a tragic day seemed to mock their sense of loss. It was a volatile time in the South, with civil authority uncertain and the struggles to define new boundaries among various groups overlapping into a battle for public space, where violence served as the mediator. Someone attacked the procession of black veterans as it wound through the streets. That night, white mobs roamed the area, and sniper fire missed the Union commander who had authorized the ceremony. The episode caused a Republican newspaper editor to sputter indignantly, "Are we to be forbidden to hold national celebrations in our own country, lest we offend the enemy?"[1]

Residents of the postwar South understood that the commemorations of war represented not simply ceremonies of unity and healing but potentially divisive rituals with political consequences.[2] Whoever appropriated the public realm signified that they held power in the shifting context of the postemancipation world. Those who controlled the nation-state determined who the enemy was or which celebrations represented "their country." In this situation, every public act contained additional meaning as it was scrutinized for affirmation of a particular cause. The federal government demanded loyalty as a qualification for restoration of political rights to ex-Confederates—if not wartime faithfulness to the Union, then proof that they accepted the United States as the sovereign authority. One measure of that loyalty came through public symbolism, including the commemorations of war and freedom.

With Republican politicians serving as orators during these formative years, freedom celebrations often resembled political rallies, and the opposition just as often interpreted them that way. The festivities surrounding Emancipation Days and Independence Day provided occasions for the mass assembly of people when the entire community, whether black or white, enjoyed release from work or greater freedom of travel. Especially during the two years immediately after the war, black people in the South had to use these and other festive occasions for mobilizing and announcing their public positions. They had no official standing as voters and were not considered part of the electorate. Civic commemorations provided black people with one way to profess support for the Union and press the case for political rights.

On the surface African Americans appeared to be allies of the national government, or at least the Republican portion. Easy to miss, however, is that a consensus about these events did not exist and that the delineation of three commemorative traditions does not quite capture the complexity of the situation. The postwar world featured more than an emancipationist, a reconciliationist, and a white supremacist interpretation of the war. We should add to the list the Unionist. But even these advocates of reunion did not always favor conciliation with rebels.[3] It was possible for them to think of new coalitions being built with white Unionists without coddling the people who had led the rebellion. Nor did reunion mean accepting the Confederate version of history or absolving the rebels of the blame for bringing on the war.

During the formation of freedom celebrations, differences between the freedpeople and white Republicans remained secondary to the formation of a new order. Similarly, the divisions among black people remained muted, even though there were different ideas about how far to push a revolutionary agenda and collaborate with white people. There were also small concerns with how to celebrate freedom, with black leaders worried about the lack of decorum shown by the plain people, some of whom continued customary habits of displaying less than proper behavior. Scattered in the fields of initial unity germinated the seeds of later problems.

■ ■ ■

ORIGINS OF EMANCIPATION DAYS

That southerners faced a different world after the war became strikingly clear with the fall of Richmond. In a gesture rife with symbolism, black troops were the first to march into the streets of the Confederate capital. The Army of Northern Virginia had to abandon the city on April 2, 1865. The following day the residents who remained saw the 36th U.S. Colored Troops occupy the town. Union officers and soldiers hugged one another as they realized that they had triumphed. Black men and women greeted the liberators with expressions of exultation. Later, the soldiers cheered when a provost marshal had the U.S. flag hoisted over the state capitol that had also functioned as the home of the Confederate Congress. Amid the smoke of the charred capital a new day burned itself into the memories of both black and white residents. African Americans would remember April 3 as a day of freedom, while Confederate southerners would recall the sting of defeat and the humiliation that came from having order maintained by former slaves.[4]

One consequence of the occupation that no one could appreciate at the time was how it complicated the problem of deciding on which day to commemorate freedom. No armistice called a halt to the fighting. The Civil War ended only as various Confederate armies surrendered: at Appomattox Courthouse on April 9, in North Carolina on April 26, and in the Trans-Mississippi region on May 26. The Emancipation Proclamation also left an ambiguous legacy because there were two versions: the preliminary proclamation of September 22, 1862, and the final proclamation of January 1, 1863, which liberated slaves wherever federal soldiers advanced. Freedom came differently and at various times to the enslaved in the South. Black people in Richmond argued that their emancipation dated to the evacuation of Confederate soldiers in early April. Others, like the slaves in Galveston, Texas, did not learn of emancipation until June 19, 1865, weeks after the war ended. Black and white people experienced triumph or defeat on various dates, many of which were determined by local rather than national circumstances.

Celebrations of freedom predated the end of the war, especially in Union-occupied portions of the Confederate South. Sometimes the crowd became violent, although in this case the jubilance of African Americans caused the disorder. As the Emancipation Proclamation took effect in 1863, an estimated 500 African Americans marched down the main street in Norfolk to the fairgrounds. They tore down and trampled Confederate flags then moved on to the city's cemetery to burn Jefferson Davis in effigy.[5] More often, however, the ceremonies were peaceful. On the Sea Islands, soldiers and civilians gathered at Camp Saxton on January 1, 1863, to honor the day when the proclamation took effect. Supervised by Major General Rufus Saxton, the event featured the 1st South Carolina Regiment of black troops, commanded by abolitionist Thomas Wentworth Higginson. White officers had put together the commemoration, with civilians "of every complexion" gathering from throughout the countryside. Although black people had not organized the affair, they added their voices in an extraordinarily moving moment. After Higginson accepted a flag from a visiting minister, he turned to address the crowd but was interrupted as African Americans spontaneously broke into "My Country 'tis of Thee." They sang verse after verse, and the colonel prevented anyone from stopping the singing. To the army officer who had been one of the financial backers of John Brown's raid, the gesture had been electric. Higginson later wrote in his journal that the singing "made all other words cheap, it seemed the choked voice of a race, at last unloosed."[6]

These events contained the elements that became the standard for black celebrations of freedom in postwar communities. Prominently displayed were the U.S. flag and other symbols of the nation. Religion had a presence, as an important minister addressed the crowd or the events were centered within black churches. For a decade or so after the war, the crowds at freedom celebrations, although predominantly black, were racially mixed. While a procession was not held in the Sea Islands commemoration, the proceedings featured drilling by the 1st South Carolina Regiment, giving black soldiers a prominent part in the commemoration. The crowd listened attentively to the reading of the Emancipation Proclamation and sang songs that resonated with the progress of freedom. In addition to a tune that expressed loyalty to the nation, the crowd also broke into "John Brown's Body," in recognition of the bloody side of the abolition movement that had condoned violence. John Brown remained an important figure in many black celebrations even beyond the nineteenth century. Finally, the occasion ended with a feast, with the main banquet attended by officers and important black leaders. Thus they used the ingredients of Independence Days, including a parade or military drill, displays of national symbols, readings of key documents, feasting, and orations that reminded listeners of the importance of liberty.

While using the conventions of antebellum civic rituals, freedom celebrations in Virginia and throughout the former Confederacy signified a revolutionary departure. Black people now formed the centerpiece of public commemorations. They carried weapons when their former masters could not. They marched in uniforms that announced their martial abilities and their role in their liberation. They wholeheartedly adopted Independence Day as a holiday without the reservations of antebellum free blacks or the former Confederates who openly criticized the celebration. They honored Lincoln, formed Lincoln Clubs and Union Leagues that served as Republican Party organizations, and placed these groups in their processions. Missing from the Sea Islands Emancipation Day were the marchers from fraternal groups, mutual aid societies, and benevolent associations that formed the important institutions within black neighborhoods. Taken as a whole, these groups and the black soldiers proclaimed the competency of black people to care for themselves and remain loyal to the United States.

With Reconstruction, African Americans adopted a new civic calendar, and Independence Day became a black holiday in the South for at least a decade. African Americans quickly understood that July Fourth signified loyalty to the nation. A minister who addressed an Emancipation celebration in Augusta, Georgia, reminded his congregation about how the nation's birthday had been a time of bitterness. The Fourth of July, he said, "had no claims upon our sympathies. They made a flag and flew it to the heavens, and bid it float forever; but every star in it was against us; every stripe against us; the red, white and blue was against us; the nation's constitution was against us; yes! every State constitution; every State code; every decision from the supreme court down to the petty magistrate; and worse than all, every church was against us; prayer and preaching was against us—enough to make us fall out with God himself. And why was it? We had always been loyal."[7] Throughout the South in the summer of 1865, black southerners took to the streets. Most often they held a procession that ended with a reading of the Declaration of Independence and a speech that underscored the special freedom they now had achieved. The day retained its festive mood, too, ending with picnics or barbecues.[8]

Ex-Confederates fumed at these events. Instead of freedom, the anniversary reminded these southerners of their subjugation. A Richmond editor noted, "Such anniversaries are fraught with nothing but sad and bitter memories." In his view, the fate of the South resembled what would have visited the American colonists had they not beaten the British. He claimed that southerners had been taxed without their consent, "that our State Governments and Legislatures have been arbitrarily suspended; that our town have been burnt, and our sea coasts ravaged by foreign mercenaries; that our laws have been nullified . . . ; that our people have been tried and punished by illegal tribunals; that domestic insurrections have been incited by false doctrines, and that our petitions to Congress for redress have been derided and laughed at."[9] White southerners believed that northerners and southern blacks perverted the original intent of the Declaration of Independence. "We will let him [the freed slave] have the anniversary of the Emancipation Proclamation all to himself, and lend him the Square for a day to do honor to his freedom," a Richmond editor noted, adding, but "the ringing of the liberty bell on Independence square, July 4, 1776, in no way intoxicated Cuffee with visions of Liberty and Equality before the law. That Declaration of Independence was altogether a white man's affair." He concluded, "The Declaration of Independence was the work of a Virginia slaveholder, and a host of mighty Virginians sustained its indignant protests with sword and pen."[10]

Former Confederates did not totally ignore the holiday. Similar to the way black people before the war used white events to suit their own needs, some neighborhoods still held excursions and picnics, but without paying homage to the nation. In the Shenandoah Valley of Virginia, Staunton's white residents gathered to hear music played by the Stonewall Band, a reminder of the South's chieftain. Still others took advantage of the time to work on the elements of the Confederate tradition. The members of the Hollywood Memorial Association in Richmond, for instance, organized men to tend graves of fallen Confederates or to raise money for reburying their dead.[11]

Other public occasions were transformed in meaning, especially the Christmas season, when the celebrations of black people proved that they were freer than they had been in the antebellum period. African Americans no longer faced the grim prospects of being hired out or sold.

Throughout the South, January 1 became an important date for remembering the Emancipation Proclamation and reinforcing the ongoing struggle for rights. It remained one of the linchpins of black civic rituals well into the twentieth century, receiving periodic support as a possible national holiday.

The initial community ceremonies after the war had strong roots within one of the most important institutions beyond the family: the black church. Many of the first Emancipation Days held around the South on January 1, 1866, either began in a church or featured a prominent African American minister delivering the address. The events were constructed to highlight the most respectable elements of the community, reinforcing that African Americans were a Christian, civilized people able to support themselves and who valued frugality, industry, and sobriety. At the thanksgiving meeting at the Baptist church in Hampton held on December 7, 1865—the anniversary of when freedom came to the area—black celebrants pledged to abstain from alcohol and formed a temperance committee.[12] While temperance did not dominate the subsequent celebrations of freedom, the movement against liquor appeared in processions via temperance societies and various religious groups. The first Emancipation Days featured the Good Samaritans, the Sons of Bethel, the Sons of Abraham, and other groups whose names contained biblical allusions. Sunday schools also could be found. In addition were secret societies, so called because they had kept their membership confidential before the war. Also included were mutual aid societies that helped members weather an economic crisis, illness, or burial of loved ones. Trade and laboring groups marched in the processions as well as the more familiar organizations such as the Masons and Odd Fellows.[13]

Although black leaders naturally wanted to highlight respectable features of their people as proof of their readiness for citizenship, they had additional reasons to stress decorum. White people, northern or southern, examined every action by the freedpeople for confirmation of the race's capabilities. There was concern that former slaves would not exhibit the discipline necessary for work or orderly behavior without the iron hand of masters. During Reconstruction, white authorities anxious to maintain peace in an explosive environment cracked down hard and enthusiastically on black celebrations that became even a little unruly. Some seem to have targeted black activity more than white. One representative of the Freedmen's Bureau shook his head over the swearing, fighting, drinking, and horse racing that accompanied the Confederate Memorial

Day in Winchester, Virginia, in 1868. He noticed that no one tried to police the behavior, adding, "had the colored people indulged in a like manner, on a similar occasion, on the Union dead, the County Jail could not contain their numbers."[14] African Americans repeatedly tried to re-assure neighbors and officials that they neither were inclined toward re-bellion nor desired to resist authority as their detractors had alleged. They stressed whenever possible the peacefulness of their assemblies. A news-paper for black people in Augusta, Georgia, felt compelled to describe the persons who crammed into the Springfield Baptist Church there on Janu-ary 1, 1866, as "a decorous audience."[15]

The exhortations did not always work, revealing the conflicted senti-ments that existed among African Americans about the proper forms of celebration. Throughout early American history, crowd behavior often became destructive or violent. Members of the white middle class were no less frustrated than black leaders over the behavior of the people they referred to as the rabble, but the struggles for power in Reconstruction added an extra dimension to public violence. In 1865 African Americans in Alexandria, Virginia, paraded through the streets on Christmas, banging drums and brandishing weapons in an exuberant display of freedom. In response, white men walked into a tavern frequented by black people and picked a fight. Several white people were wounded from gunfire, and two black people were killed. The white press charged that African Americans had not employed the usual behavior for such occasions but appeared to be "asserting their equality with the whites."[16] Black people continued to display forms of festive traditions that scholars identify as an inversion ritual. When a society prohibits people from a public activity, the re-stricted groups can resort to mimicry. African Americans in the North, for instance, had carried on Negro election days in which they chose a king or governor in a mock election ritual. In the postwar South, it was not unusual to find black people employing January 1 and July 4 commemora-tions for an emotional release. Some rode backward through towns on mules; others conducted raucous marches while tooting on tin horns. Black leaders tried to discourage this burlesque style, but without much success.[17]

Politics was never far from these occasions, even in the addresses of ministers. Black churches provided a safe harbor for political organization and for community members to discuss freely what to do about their situations. A chief concern of African Americans after the war was how to lay claim to citizenship. Orators such as one in Augusta, Georgia, in 1866 offered a possible course that reinforced the importance of civic traditions. At Emancipation Day ceremonies in August, the Reverend Henry M. Turner began his oration by addressing his "Fellow Citizens" and indicating "we have assembled to-day under circumstances, unlike those of any other day in the history of our lives. We have met for the purpose of celebrating this, the first day of the New Year, not because it is the first New Year's day we ever saw, but because it is the first one we ever enjoyed." He added, "The first day of January hitherto, was one of gloom and fearful suspense. The foundation of our social comforts hung upon the scales of apprehension and fate with its decisions of weal or wo [sic] looked everyone of us in the face, and dread and forebodings kept in dubius agitation, every fleeting moment that passed. But to-day we stand upon no such sandy foundation. Uncertainty is no more the basis of our existence; we have for our fulcrum the eternal principles of right and equity."[18]

Indicative of this motivation for citizenship, a black organization appeared in Emancipation Day parades that had not existed in the South: the political club. African Americans may not have enjoyed suffrage, but they nevertheless formed associations that voiced a political agenda. Portions of the Confederacy that had been occupied by the Union had a head start on this form of organization, but it did not take long for the rest of the South to catch up. Union Leagues were one of the best-known forms of this activity. Created in the North, Union Leagues began as Republican patriotic clubs, also known as Loyal Leagues, to garner support for the Lincoln administration and discredit the Democratic opposition. The leagues supposedly kept their membership confidential, shrouding themselves with oaths and rituals resembling secret societies such as the Masons. After the war, the league movement progressed into the South, taking hold first in the regions that had been anti-Confederate or had substantial black populations. Their meetings passed resolutions that showed a united front on issues such as easing restrictions on travel and the southern Homestead Act that redistributed land. When suffrage became a reality in 1867, national Republican leaders naturally used the clubs to recruit African Americans in the South and conduct registration drives.[19]

Processions during Emancipation Days suggest that African Americans and white people were using leagues for political efforts well before 1867. When the first Independence Day celebration took place in central Georgia just months after the war's close in 1865, a formerly secret Union League Club staged a parade in Macon. One historian has called this gathering the largest in the region held by African Americans to that point. The societies that appeared in these parades did not always adopt the name Union Leagues but sometimes chose variations on the theme. A march in Richmond, for instance, featured a group that displayed a banner proclaiming, "Union Liberties Protective Society, organized February 4, 1866." The same march included a club called the Union Sons of Liberty.[20] Abraham Lincoln was a popular figure. It was not unusual for African Americans, like the ones in Bayou Sara, Louisiana, to form Lincoln Clubs to honor the memory of the president and provide meetings for discussing issues relevant to Reconstruction.[21]

African American women participated in these public affairs, although their involvement was not so pronounced. Men controlled the contours of Emancipation Days and July Fourth observances. They set up the speakers, selected the groups for procession, planned the route, assigned the places in line, and formed the majority of the marchers. Women attended but primarily as observers who cheered their menfolk on. That they could perform this role at all was a striking departure, considering they had been prevented from doing even this much under slavery—a fact that did not go unnoticed. Former Confederates saw them along the sidewalks and mingling in the town squares, eagerly consuming the speeches of the orators. Instead of considering this behavior as no different from that of their own wives, ex-Confederates more typically used this as evidence of the deteriorating morals of black women, who, in their opinion, had no business being in such places.[22]

While women did not take the lead in Emancipation Day celebrations, they formed auxiliaries to male associations, providing support for the political clubs. As in Confederate activities, there was a sexual division of labor with freedom celebrations. Men supervised the meetings in church halls and established the procedures for commemorative events. Women, however, helped with the planning and conducted fund-raising. Additionally, they were aware of the impact their presence had on redefining public space and were undoubtedly delighted that their participation raised comment. They also occasionally presented opinions in newspaper columns about their condition under freedom, reflecting their new reach into the public sphere. A woman name Anna, for example, took advantage of the freedom celebration in Hampton on December 7, 1865, to relate in a newspaper what the day meant to her. She indicated that women had an even greater right for thanks than men because women's lives under slavery had been more abject and had given the peculiar institution "its deepest dye." With the shackles gone, she believed that African American women were closer to equality with white women than African American men were with white males. She saw women of both races suffering from similar disabilities before the law, and she reinforced the vital role that women had reserved for themselves in teaching children so that the race would gain in knowledge and refinement.[23]

African American women also did not form memorial associations or other corporate entities to bury the dead because they did not need to. Black celebrations did not suffer from the same restrictions as Confederate observances, and the Cities of the Dead did not provide one of the only venues for staging public expression of the wartime experience. Additionally, the government provided funds and labor for burying the dead, which eliminated the need for extensive reburial campaigns. Federal authorities—both military officers and white leaders of the Republican Party— also assumed leadership roles in the Decoration Days at national cemeteries emerging in the South during 1868. The organization of Memorial Days and Emancipation Days came under the auspices of black fraternal associations or special committees formed for the purpose. Although women helped plan the events, the hierarchy of responsibility followed well-established channels, with women serving on committees such as those responsible for decorations and illuminations. They might sit on a financial committee or help with fund-raising; however, they were not in positions of authority similar to those of white women in Confederate celebrations. Black commemorations of freedom and war did not contain quite the same dynamic as the rebel civic rituals in which women had to take the lead and then sparked controversy for doing so.[24]

Within their broader context, the commemorations of freedom represented only one event in a sea of public activity geared toward gaining equality. The same organizations and leaders appeared in a host of assemblies, church halls, marches, and town squares. "In the spring and summer of 1865," according to historian Eric Foner, "blacks organized a seemingly unending series of mass meetings, parades, and petitions demanding civil equality and the suffrage as indispensable corollaries of emancipation." Although it did take place in the countryside, this activity was most noticeable in urban areas where the fraternal and secret societies existed.[25] Former Confederates consequently viewed Emancipation Days as one part of a wider movement—a range of public behavior that appeared one short step from causing disorder and only a few more steps from revolutionary upheaval. Add to this the context of national Reconstruction and the federal scrutiny of loyalty in communities, and one can understand why violent backlash accompanied some public rituals. One city's experience offers a good window into how these facets—federal intervention, black activity, and attitudes of former Confederates—came together during what African Americans liked to call "the surrender."

■ ■ ■

CELEBRATING THE SURRENDER

In a reminiscence written in the twentieth century, Marion Goode Briscoe, a black woman from Mecklenburg County, still grew animated about the ending of the Civil War. When she mentioned the day Robert E. Lee and Ulysses S. Grant signed the terms that disbanded the Army of Northern Virginia and ended the war in the eastern theater, she exclaimed, "The ninth of April was a day that always made my heart nearly burst with pride." More than sixty years after the war—and after many of these commemorations had begun to fade—another black woman, Mrs. May Satterfield of Lynchburg, Virginia, proudly remembered the day of what she simply called "the surrender." She asked her interviewer from the Works Progress Administration, "You know when dat was?" Without waiting for an answer, she added, "Ninth of April."[26] It should come as no surprise that this anniversary retained such power for so long. For many of the enslaved, the surrender of the Confederate army represented the moment when freedom came. The Emancipation Proclamation had placed slavery on the road to extinction, but the surrenders constituted a more personal time of liberation for those who lived beyond the reach of the Union army.

Perhaps nothing showed the bitter divide that remained more than observances of the surrenders. Chance placed the time for the events in the spring of 1866 during a critical moment as Reconstruction took a Radical turn. Congress had begun to challenge President Andrew Johnson's lenient approach and passed protection for the freedpeople in the form of the Civil Rights Act. The law empowered national authorities to bring suit against violators and allowed cases to be heard in federal courts. Additionally, the surging street activity by black people was alarming—especially because the processions in freedom celebrations contained black veterans carrying weapons. Confederate celebrations were not allowed a similar privilege. The government refused to allow former enemies to carry guns or wear uniforms to honor their war dead, but black people suffered from no such liabilities. By the first anniversary of the surrender, former Confederates had witnessed a Congress increasingly defying the president, passing measures that threatened the power of white people and giving more rights to African Americans. Black people were obviously resisting efforts to return them to the status quo, despite the use of black codes. The inflammatory nature of public symbols was intensifying. Then former rebels in Virginia learned that former slaves planned a new round of commemorations that marked the death of the Confederacy.

In Richmond, April 3 became known as Evacuation Day, a title that resonated with festivities in the early republic that had commemorated the withdrawal of British troops during the Revolution. Word leaked out that African Americans intended to march in parades to celebrate their deliverance from oppression. It also became known that they would carry weapons. One Richmond editor sputtered, "The 3d April is indeed no time for rejoicing of anybody here. It was a day of gloom and calamity to be remembered with a shudder of horror by all who saw it, whether it be the Federal soldier, or the resident, whether white or black." The columnist strongly hinted about the possibility of economic coercion should African Americans stage the activity. "It is not their interest," he wrote, "and should not be their disposition, to insult the people amongst whom they live, and upon whose kindness and friendship they must depend for employment and success in life."[27] Employers leveled more direct threats to fire workers who participated. Terrorists also struck. Two days before the event, someone burned down the second African Baptist Church, location of a school for the freedpeople and a key meeting place for the persons coordinating the emancipation procession. A northern black minister in Richmond said he overheard white people vowing to "wade through blood before the niggers shall celebrate that day."[28]

The enthusiasm of black people for these observances mystified even northern white people. In fact, the 1866 celebration of Evacuation Day in Richmond eclipsed the first commemorations of the Emancipation Proclamation, at least as outdoor, communitywide functions. Republican organs such as the *New York Times* were caught off guard. While sharing in the emancipation sentiment, its readers did not necessarily have African Americans at the center of their concern. Moderate Republicans believed that emancipation was an important part of the war, but they were interested in how slavery's end honored the example of Lincoln and the party. It seemed strange to them that black people could not observe a perfectly good holy day of freedom—one created by a white man who also happened to have been their party's leader.[29] Similarly, former Confederates claimed they understood the impulse behind recognizing emancipation on January 1. But by celebrating the fall of the Confederacy when they already had a holiday commemorating their freedom, black people gave the impression that they deliberately wanted to rub salt in the wounds.[30]

Perhaps most alarming to ex-Confederates was the obvious delight among black people in seeing veterans march in their uniforms while shouldering muskets. The symbolism here could not be missed. Carrying weapons stressed the role of these men as liberators and indicated difficult times ahead in subjugating them. It was hard for former masters not to consider this gathering as containing ominous potential. On the other hand, the impression that these marchers made on the black community was remarkable. They brought out the pride of African Americans, causing chests to swell for a long time. Marion Briscoe remembered these festive occasions:

> Early in the morning, the colored people would be collecting in groups, men on fine horses, with sashes of various colors draped over their shoulders and under the opposite arm and tied in bows with streamers flying. They carried swords, guns, or muskets. Many of them were officers, each of whom commanded a number of men. They rode galloping alongside of them, calling out orders. This army stretched all the way from the village to the colored college a mile away. Throngs of people stood on the roadside admiring them. Bands played stirring marches. The men on horses reached eight abreast across the road; and with the prancing horses, flying colors, music, and loud cheering of the crowds, it was something never to be forgotten.[31]

Ironically, the army in which African Americans had fought tried to stop the commemoration. Major General Alfred Terry, who commanded the region that included Richmond, asked Ulysses S. Grant for permission to quash the event. He had received pressure to intervene from the mayor and the governor, a Unionist who had presided over a loyal government of Virginia during the war. Authorities were more concerned about keeping order and winning the hearts of the defeated Confederates than recognizing a procession of the people who been true Unionists. Grant gave Terry the authority to stop the march. At least one newspaper in Washington also called for stopping it. Former Confederates believed that these warnings from national officials had caused African Americans to think better of their plan. There may have been some truth to the impression; it is possible that some persons in the black community actually did back down, at least for a moment.[32]

African Americans, however, were not to be denied, although they tried to address some of the concerns by toning down the celebration. Young men in the community had been among the most vociferous in favor of keeping the celebration. On March 27, African Americans held a mass meeting in Richmond, announcing that they would go ahead and that they would do so with "procession, speeches, &." They placed an advertisement in a local newspaper and added that the public should "feel assured that the feelings of all good citizens will be respected." A day before the event, a broadside dated April 2 appeared: "NOTICE: The Coloured People of the City of Richmond Would Most Respectfully Inform The Public That They Do Not Intend To Celebrate The Failure Of The Southern Confederacy, As it has been stated in the papers of this City, but simply as the day on which GOD was pleased to Liberate their long-oppressed race."[33] The white press also suggested that the original plans called for trailing the Confederate flag in the dust and marching with effigies of Jefferson Davis and Robert E. Lee that would have been burned after the procession reached its destination. It is difficult to corroborate this story, which may have been a rumor. It also may have been true; the behavior would have been consistent with the Norfolk procession of 1863. In either case, the rumor itself suggests the heightened tensions of the moment and that the black community modified its observance to undercut those who wanted to stop the march.[34] Ultimately, Terry backed off without confronting the group, and the procession went on as planned.

The opposition grumbled at the changing fortunes. One editor observed, "It is to be regretted that a proceeding so indiscreet—so little calculated to encourage kindly relations between the whites and the blacks— a jollification on the saddest of days, and that a day really not appropriate to the object of a celebration—should be resolved upon." However, this writer did advise other disappointed citizens to rest easy because he claimed the whole day came about through the agitation of "silly persons." After all, white paternalism counseled that black people were friendly unless duped into acting otherwise.[35] Others sniffed at the handbill that African Americans circulated to reassure white people that it was freedom, and not Confederate defeat, that they commemorated. Detractors argued that April 3 was not even the day the war had ended. "The simple truth," one correspondent maintained, "is that the *authors* of the celebration, smarting under that social exclusion which *properly* confines them to colored associates, contrived the whole business as a punishment of the people who have too much self-respect to consort with them." In other words, white northern Republicans were behind this effort, not faithful black people. No matter what the leaders said about this event, ex-Confederates believed it marked the burning of Richmond. The same Petersburg newspaper referred to the event as the "conflagration procession."[36]

When the day arrived, the festivities followed what was by now becoming the standard form of celebration. Unlike the gathering on January 1, it was more of a civic than a sacred ceremony, although not devoid of religious symbolism. This time the procession began at the fairgrounds rather than a church. The marchers demonstrated the vibrancy of fraternal and other associations in the black community and the importance of these civic occasions for grassroots mobilization. The parade began around 11:00 A.M., led by a carriage drawn by one white and one bay horse. While this may or may not have been an intentional comment on a new day of racial integration, it was interpreted as such by the opposition. Estimates numbered the procession at between 1,500 and 2,000 people, with perhaps as many as 15,000 spectators. A black minister counted 163 African Americans on horses and roughly fifteen black societies. Toward the front of the procession—just after the buggy and a group of mounted men—came a banner that spoke for the overall parade: "Peace, Friendship, and Liberty with all mankind." Temperance societies marched with Christian associations, fraternal societies, labor organizations, and political groups. Most of these associations designated their members through stars, badges, and large initials indicating their names: Rising Christians, Humble Christian Benevolents from the Chesterfield Coal-pits, Teamsters Star of the East, Reform Sons of Love, Young Sons of Zion, Miller's Mechanics, Loving Tree of Life, Union Sons of Liberty, and Union Liberties Protective Society. The Sons of Love and the Sons of Jacob were mutual aid societies that helped members in times of sickness and provided burials.[37]

After winding through the streets of Richmond, the procession ended at the state capitol that just twelve months before had been the site of the Confederate government. Black marchers now spilled into the space in a gathering that would have been illegal a short time ago. Many were aware of the significance and the need to show decorum. As they gathered near the governor's house, an African American told the group to "'have them-

selves, and show dey wur worthy with to be trusted of their freedom."
The orator convinced former Confederates that an additional motivation
lay behind the ceremony.

The Reverend James W. Hunnicutt, the principal speaker, made the
affair into a mass meeting on how to deal with Reconstruction. A white
man born in South Carolina, he edited the leading Republican newspaper
in the state, the *Richmond New Nation*. He was a mercurial figure, indicative of the complicated loyalties created in the pressure of war and
postwar struggles. As the war began, Hunnicutt had been editor of a
newspaper in Fredericksburg, Virginia, but he was forced out of business
because of his outspoken sympathies for the Union. He had remained
Unionist throughout the conflict and became a leading Republican. Like
so many persons in the party, his primary concern was not black rights. He
had argued against secession because it would lead to the very thing most
southerners hoped to avoid: the end of slavery. But in the postwar world,
even this individual who did not naturally sympathize with African Americans understood that he had to court their support to rebuild the South.

In his address on that first Evacuation Day in Richmond, Hunnicutt
attempted to find common ground with his listeners by suggesting that
black and white people shared a bond as southerners. This connection
resulted from their being born in the same region, not from any other
qualifications or ethnic traits. This was the same criterion used by the
Civil Rights Act and the subsequent Fourteenth Amendment to designate
a citizen—birth within a certain territorial boundary. Hunnicutt played on
the notion that black people enjoyed citizenship as Virginians, giving
them a natural alliance with white persons. He had more in mind than
just building a political party. African Americans enjoyed the freedom to
travel that had been denied them under slavery. This concerned business
owners and planters who wanted to stabilize the labor pool by preventing
migration from the region. If black people emigrated, Hunnicutt asked,
what would become of the land they had cultivated? "My home is in the
South," he claimed, adding, "your home, my 'fellow-citizens,' is in the
South,—in the South we have lived, and in the South we must die."

At the time, Hunnicutt recognized that there were limits to what this
citizenship could mean for African Americans. This Republican representative of the new order was not "one of those men who clamored for that
which could not be had." When the crowd pressed him to explain, he left
this position ambiguous, merely stating that he favored the "freedom of
the Negro without compromising the freedom of the white." For now,

Hunnicutt was not willing to press for black suffrage. Like many Republican organizers in the South, he walked a tightrope. Although he later became more outspoken for black voting and instrumental in bringing blacks into the party, this was not the time to alienate potential white supporters. According to his prescription for the postwar South, African Americans should accept gradual change in social and political status; they would earn additional rights through steady, hard work that would win them the respect of the white community.[38]

Even though Hunnicutt's message in 1866 advocated keeping black labor in place and controlling the pace of change, his speech nevertheless disturbed Confederate Virginians. Although southern, he did not hail from the state and had shown himself to be suspect politically during the war. Ex-Confederates considered him an interloper and a foreigner—the people blamed for stirring up unrest in the South. This was an extremely common theme among white persons after the war, many of whom professed that the natural harmony between capital and labor would prevail were it not for the meddling of outsiders. Hunnicutt, however, presented a second disturbing trend in his talk when he constantly referred to the assembled African Americans as "fellow citizens." One newspaper correspondent indicated that he uttered the phrase sixty-three times in a thirty-minute speech. To consider former slaves in this light opened the door to political equality. Citizenship gave black people a basis for claiming the right to serve on juries and to vote. After all, many African Americans met two of the major criteria for voting in America: they were old enough and they were men. If birth meant they were citizens, then why not have the franchise? Even if unsuccessful in opening the door to party politics, citizenship conferred the right of African Americans to gather in mass meetings protected by law, even if they did so on a day that celebrated the defeat of the Confederacy.

Small wonder that the editor of the *Petersburg Daily Index* took offense at the *Boston Advertiser* for claiming that the celebration in Richmond was the right of citizens who deserved to mark "the downfall of treason and the establishment of the constitution." The editor charged that the celebration did not mark the day of freedom, which to him was January 1, but commemorated the burning of the city and the slaughter of Confederate soldiers. He added, "But the Boston *Advertiser* ought to know that Negroes are not 'the citizens of Virginia,' and that though they were, the destruction of her capital and the slaughter of her children is hardly a proper subject for *celebration*."[39]

The Boston newspaper was not the only northern journal defending freedom celebrations as the right of loyal men and women, no matter if they hurt the sensibilities of ex-Confederates. The *New York Times* abandoned prior reservations about the celebrations. Its columnists tended to side with former Confederates when it came to having a peaceful reunion without the need for long-term occupation. According to the moderate position, Reconstruction could be mediated through the electoral process and not force, giving the governments greater authenticity. This did not mean conceding to former rebels in every case. For the emancipation celebration in Richmond, the editor believed that southern whites had to endure the "negro commemorations." While the remembrance of the surrender offended former slaveholders, according to the *Times* there was no help for it because ex-Confederates had to atone for their sins against the government. "The future will necessarily be full of painful reminiscences of their gigantic crime in the rebellion," the newspaper noted. "Besides, we do not see that they have any right whatsoever to take offense at the negroes' celebration of their day of freedom."[40]

Having little recourse other than to let surrender day take place, former Confederates did their best to diminish it. They dismissed the event by attacking the size of the marches and suggesting that the occasion lacked support from black people. Yet even these editors estimated the number of the marchers at 1,000 to 1,500, corroborating the count of their rivals. They claimed, however, that the procession represented only a small percentage of the total black population in Richmond. Yet they had to deal with the fact that the spectators may have amounted to an additional 15,000 people. A white editor countered this by asserting that many in the community could not recognize the black faces in the line, alleging that marchers had come from elsewhere. "Where, then, did the mass come from?" he asked. "Many [were] idlers from the interior, many, doubtless, imported from Washington and elsewhere expressly for the occasion."[41] If an accurate claim—and it is likely that nonresidents attended the event—then opponents of the celebration praised the occasion with faint damnation. They unwittingly acknowledged the importance of an event that drew people from outside the city and amassed a crowd of potentially 20,000.

Violence did not mar the affair in Richmond in 1866, but it did not remain absent for long from public rituals. Within a couple of weeks, a black procession in Norfolk ended in a shootout that left two white people dead, several severely beaten (one of them a city watchman), a black youth bayoneted in the stomach, and a number of other persons wounded. The confrontation occurred on April 16 as African Americans demonstrated in support of the passage of the Civil Rights Act over the veto of the president. The procession bore a striking resemblance to the one in Richmond a couple of weeks earlier. An estimated 1,000 persons gathered for the march. Included were the usual community groups. Once again, cavalry and infantry led the parade while carrying arms.[42]

Eventually, the concern that black activity would get out of hand taxed the limited patience of the military authorities charged with keeping order. During the July Fourth celebration in Richmond, black marchers wound through the streets and stopped before the home of Burnham Wardwell, a noted Radical. Once again, ex-Confederates objected to black men carrying weapons. Additionally, black militia companies paraded and drilled almost nightly in the city. Tensions grew to the point that General Terry prohibited all drills—whether by African Americans or ex-Confederates. Only the groups that secured permission from the governor could conduct military displays. The white press hailed the ban on the "negro drills which have caused such nightly disturbances in this city, and were so full of danger." The columnist claimed that the celebrations of African Americans were intended to cause disorder. "Those of the 3d of April and 4th of July were well calculated—especially the first named—to provoke collisions. It was a severe trial to which to subject a people."[43]

The order resulted in fewer firearms appearing in Emancipation Day parades, yet it lessened neither the fervor for the activity nor the effectiveness of the occasions for political mobilization. As Reconstruction took a more radical turn in the year ahead, national Republican figures joined local ones in using the mass meetings of Emancipation Days as one means to promote the use of the ballot among African Americans.

■ ■ ■

POLITICAL RALLIES, 1867–1869

Freedom celebrations became a more overt part of the political process with the passage of the Reconstruction Acts in March 1867. This legislation stripped the former Confederate states of their governments, set up five military districts throughout the South, and forced states to reconstitute public offices on the basis of black suffrage. Emancipation Day and July Fourth celebrations provided opportunities for Republicans to deliver political addresses and reach a large audience of new voters. Speakers reminded their listeners that African Americans had aided in their liberation, but they also stressed the importance of the Republican Party as an agent for expanding rights. They reiterated the reasons why the party of Lincoln gave African Americans the best choice for their future. From a vantage of more than a century, it may seem odd that Republican leaders felt they had to court black voters, yet the situation dictated this precaution. A little more than a decade old, the Republican Party was barely an adolescent, with leaders concerned about its existence without antislavery as a cohesive force. With a white majority in Virginia and many southern states, every vote mattered. Under these circumstances, freedom celebrations functioned increasingly like political conventions at the community level and revealed the underlying power concerns that fostered the illusion of reconciliation.

Within the Republican Party differing opinions existed about whether to reach out to former Confederates or concentrate only on African Americans. Chief among the reconciliationists was Francis Pierpont, governor of the state. An antisecessionist, in 1861 he had established a state government in Alexandria that was recognized by the Lincoln administration. After the war, Pierpont extended the olive branch to his former political enemies. To him, the war had resolved the main issues of contention by destroying slavery and rendering obsolete state sovereignty. Men of goodwill, he believed, would renew their leadership of the state as the freedpeople returned to agricultural labor. In part, this was a practical strategy: he needed support from more than former Unionists for his government to survive. He restored political rights to former Confederates and succeeded so well that when the dust settled after the elections of June 1865, most of the offices were held by the people who just months before had fought against the U.S. government. Other Republicans favored less conciliation with former rebels than cooperation with the people who had remained loyal. These men, many of whom were antisecessionists, promoted disfranchisement of secessionists and the franchisement of black people. Some of these men were northern transplants—not the carpetbaggers of the postwar stereotype but northerners who had settled in the antebellum South. Among them was Burnham Wardwell, a native of Maine who became a leading Radical and joined native southerners such as John Minor Botts and Hunnicutt in the Republican Party. Not all of them were thrilled to have black voters. Botts, for one, considered African Americans untrustworthy because he believed they could easily be led astray. Botts and others like him became Republicans because of Whig, anti-Democratic sentiments.[44]

Former Confederates found themselves similarly divided over the extent of reconciliation to adopt. Some rejected this course outright. They remained unreconstructed rebels who hated the Yankees, rejected the Fourteenth Amendment, fought against black suffrage, and stayed with the Democratic Party. Another, more pragmatic strategy appeared in various parts of the South in a movement referred to as the New Departure. Although the men of this persuasion referred to themselves as conservatives, they used the term to designate a moderate and not reactionary position. Conservatives attempted to steer a course between the Radical Republicans and the traditional Democrats. They recognized the need to accept the reality of the war and to cooperate with moderate men of the North for two reasons: (1) to attract resources that could help the South economically and (2) to limit the extent of social change. Conservative thought came down to a simple proposition: well-positioned, moderate white men of good character made the best rulers.[45]

In Virginia the Conservative movement brought together former Whigs, antisecessionists, and conditional Unionists who shared animosity toward Democrats and Republicans. They wanted white home rule but differed from their more traditional colleagues because they acknowledged the need to accept black suffrage. By doing so, party leaders hoped to prove they were moderates who could be entrusted with the fate of black people in the South. Through this stance, they hoped to avoid further disfranchisement of white people, which a clause in the proposed new constitution for the state promised to achieve. The strategy worked. Conservatives found a sympathetic northerner in President Ulysses S. Grant, who would not force the state to adopt stricter disfranchisement clauses for white people. Virginia's Conservatives subsequently maintained enough votes to win the elections and avoid a Republican government.

The movement appeared in other parts of the South. Tennessee had perhaps the next-strongest manifestation of the New Departure. Other states included Mississippi, Texas, and Missouri, but the Conservatives never achieved the same political success in these areas, partly because they were co-opted by moderate Republicans. The Conservative idea had an appeal that kept recurring, however. None other than P. G. T. Beauregard, a Louisianan and a former general in the Confederate army, said that of the two strategies facing the white South—either resistance or submission to the federal government—he opted for the latter, adding that it was better to control the black vote than to try to eliminate it. In this fashion, he claimed, "we shall defeat our adversaries with their own weapons."[46]

One more factor underscores that racial identity did not always create unity of political strategy. There were conservative black people who made it appear plausible that Republican hegemony over African Americans could be broken. This element within the black community is often hard to find, but it surfaces now and then. Lynchburg, Virginia, apparently contained such a group, and in April 1867 its members circulated a flier inviting key members of the Conservative ranks to address them. Conservative black men did the same in other cities, apparently to sound out persons who, like them, found it difficult to support either established party. The Richmond meeting sparked controversy among black people, causing one of the organizers, Wyatt Lewis, to publish an address to his "colored fellow-citizens." In this document he explained the rationale behind the effort. "If we are citizens and freemen in truth," he wrote, "surely we ought to be allowed the right of freely judging who are our real friends among the many professed ones bidding for our favor." He and his colleagues believed it wrong to follow parties or vote for candidates solely because of race. How could they expect to conduct fruitful relations with employers and merchants, they asked, when African Americans impugned the character and honor of these same businessmen? More to the point, black conservatives envisioned long-term interests being hurt if black people did not forge some sort of coalition with the white men who ended up in power. "In Virginia the colored race is in a minority," Lewis reminded readers. "To band them together is to force the white race into a counter combination, in which event our race must certainly be outvoted." He added that he wanted a new constitution that provided for free public education and obliterated racial distinctions before the law. "We cannot secure these most desirable and most vital and priceless objects by forming ourselves into a minority party of colored men, and forcing the white majority to vote us down."[47]

Whether sentiments like Lewis's created real concerns, the situation remained fluid enough that party spokesmen toured the South, reminding listeners that the Republicans represented the party of Lincoln, which had brought freedom. From Pennsylvania came Speaker of the House Charles Gibbon to address an assembly at the African church in Richmond. He said that Republicans "had raised the Negro from the state of slavery and made him free, and it had placed the ballot in his hands." But Gibbon also had a more pointed warning: "If you wish to consult a rebel . . . concerning the purchase of a horse, do so. . . . But never consult a man who has fought against this country concerning your vote."[48] Senator Henry Wilson of Massachusetts traveled to Petersburg to wave the bloody shirt. In no uncertain terms he said that the war had come because of *"human slavery in America."* He told the largely African American crowd that they were now as free as he was and that they should treat the ballot box as sacred. "Go for liberty and the men who will be true to liberty. Go for the preservation of the ballot-box, and the men who will freely concede the ballot to you."[49]

Emancipation Days provided important mass meetings for disseminating the Republican message. On April 3, 1867, the second anniversary of the evacuation of the Confederate army, African Americans gathered in Richmond again. The same black organizations marched, although this time a carriage containing prominent white Radicals Hunnicutt and Wardwell led the way. The next carriage contained other notable white people; the presidents of the participating black associations followed. Behind them came the mutual aid societies and benevolent groups. Near the back was a group of five- to twelve-year-old schoolboys. Weapons were less noticeable, a result of the ban by Union military authorities. Some of the marchers wore uniforms, but they were homemade rather than government issue. Although firearms were restricted, sabers dangled at the sides of young men. The entire display—with white people in the lead and less overt military posturing—seemed to be organized to calm white fears about black social upheaval. Yet the messages in this celebration, although less threatening physically, may have proven even more worrisome to former Confederates.

This time the orations blatantly dealt with political matters, and the celebrants were exhorted to support the Republican Party. Hunnicutt spoke first. He reminded the crowd that many did not appreciate a celebration on this day, and that most white people thought that African Americans should confine their festivities to January 1 in honor of Lincoln's proclamation. "I maintain," he added, "that not the proclamation, but the bayonets of General Grant brought us salvation." Before then, most African Americans in Virginia had been slaves. "If the Southern Confederacy had succeeded you would never have known freedom." He urged the members of the crowd to register to vote and to support the party that had freed them. "The Federal sword freed you, and Congress enfranchised you. Every man who votes for a rebel votes for the whipping-post, the chain-gang, and for a tax of ten or twenty dollars on every cabin. The Southern Confederacy is lost; don't you help to regain it."

The next speaker, an African American named Lewis Lindsay, reflected the ambiguities within the African American community. Although Lindsay was a known Radical, Confederate observers thought that he sounded less vitriolic than Hunnicutt. Lindsay urged African Americans to remain quiet and to wait until they got to the ballot box to declare their political preference. He then counseled the audience not to vote by race, but to discern which white men had remained loyal to the Union: "Then vote for a good man without regard to color; but whatever you do don't cast your vote for a rebel." One of the black marshals, W. J. Fuller, took a more Radical position. He reminded his listeners that the black race was on its way to "legislative halls and offices of trust." Nothing could stop them. Then he added, "My friends, vote for the man who will bring you into his parlor, who will eat dinner with you, and who, if you want her, will let you marry his daughter." This, of course, touched the worst fears expressed by the white majority, who had no desire for what they termed social equality.[50]

The commemorative pattern of the postemancipation South had been permanently altered in conformance with the political struggles throughout the South. Separate commemorative traditions had emerged. (The Confederate side of the story is detailed in Chapter 3.) Black people took to the streets on a number of occasions, but the most important tended to be January 1, in observance of emancipation, and whatever local anniversary commemorated the coming of freedom through contact with the federal army. African Americans in Richmond continued to observe April 3 until energy finally waned toward the turn of the century. January 1 grew in importance, although the memory of the surrender remained until deep into the twentieth century. African Americans also commemorated Union Decoration Day, although it was clear that the days marking their liberation were far more important. The early ceremonies differed pointedly from white, Confederate rituals. Even with the restrictions of Union officers against carrying weapons, the events were more martial in tone than the ceremonies of the vanquished. Processions also were more prevalent, and there was no attempt by military officers to limit political speech. The ceremonies of freedom did not just look backward or even limit themselves to the current political situation. Marchers in each procession, whether on January 1 or on a different anniversary of freedom, looked to a time when full rights would come. It was a heady moment for many African Americans, who felt the future held tremendous potential, even as they recognized the obstacles that lay ahead.

The careful observer, however, could see troubling signs in these early

commemorations of freedom. No one date served as the day of liberation—a situation that hampered black people into the next century from
finding a consensus for a national observance. Violence by the opposition
and unequal arrests foreshadowed future struggles over the use of public
space. White Republicans were not always in synch with the goals of
African Americans. Some, like Hunnicutt, bolted from the party when
given the opportunity. Additionally, the same tensions that existed in the
white community were prevalent: class differences between the "respectable colored" people and the unskilled workers, agricultural laborers, and
others who made up the common folk. Some black leaders advocated a
less confrontational strategy designed to protect the peace by not stirring
up former Confederates and maintaining good relations with white people in general. For this strategy to work, persons of all backgrounds had to
act in good faith, and the government especially had to protect the interests of the most loyal element within the South. That would not necessarily be the case in the decades ahead.

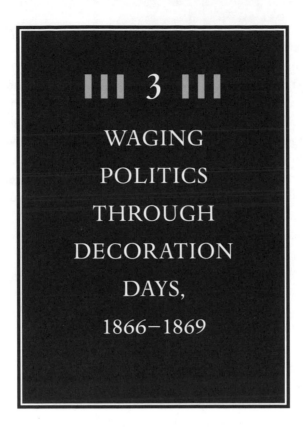

III 3 III

WAGING POLITICS THROUGH DECORATION DAYS, 1866–1869

For former Confederates, a number of shadows darkened the first ceremonies in honor of their war dead. First was the knowledge that those being mourned had fallen in an unsuccessful effort. White southerners had to accept the sacrifice of nearly one-quarter of their seventeen- to fifty-year-old men, many of whose bodies lay in unmarked graves far from home. Another shadow was cast by the ceremonies in which black people marched through the streets carrying guns as symbols of their agency in winning freedom. Still another element darkening the Confederate valley of sorrow was the federal government and its policies concerning commemorations of the dead. Graves of federal soldiers were dug, marked, and tended with government monies in newly formed national cemeteries. No federal arm was raised to gather the southern corpses that often lay nearby. Additionally, various generals prohibited expressions of Confederate sentiment. By 1867 this had resulted in new prohibitions on memorial celebrations that meant conducting the occasions without parades or speeches.[1] To the former masters of the Old South, it appeared as if they did not have the liberty of the freedpeople in creating public occasions for remembering the dead.

Scholars more recently have appreciated the power implications behind the ceremonies for the dead, but they have overlooked the extent of intervention by federal officials in Confederate traditions and the impact that the neglect of southern dead had on the defeated. Northerners expected to forge reunion with their enemies and were in many ways remarkably lenient with the men who could have been considered traitors to the nation. Despite indictments, no Confederate officials underwent a trial for treason. Union authorities, however, expected capitulation to the government and acceptance of national symbols by the vanquished. Officers often prohibited public display that smacked too much of honoring the rebellion: the waving of Confederate flags, the wearing of military uniforms, or the honoring of the southern cause in public addresses. Reconciliation in the five years or so after the war was to be a one-way street, with the defeated accepting the terms of the victorious.

Interference with their public rituals added to the sting of Reconstruction for former rebels, especially because of the contrast with the ceremonies of emancipation and the creation of government-funded cemeteries. But it also created an irony. The emerging Confederate commemorations in the postwar South assumed a more solemn tone because officials banned the behavior that seemingly kept treason alive. This has allowed historians of Memorial Days such as Paul Buck and Gaines Foster to stress the role of these commemorations in helping the process of reunion or allowing the Confederate psyche to heal. The pattern of Memorial Days has steered observers then and now to interpreting the ease with which ex-Confederates acquiesced in defeat.[2]

Despite having to style their rituals according to federal tastes, former Confederates still found the Cities of the Dead useful as places for resistance. For more than a decade, and possibly for more than two, the dominant motivation behind Confederate commemorations was to maintain a sectional identity that defied complete assimilation within the Union. Ex-Confederates could not conduct open warfare in their ceremonies, but even the watered-down versions contained more points of conflict than consensus with the government. More to the point, the celebrants of Decoration Days fell into patterns that reflected the political alliances of Reconstruction. Union Decoration Days became branded as Republican Party events by the opposition, who saw them as belonging to scalawags, carpetbaggers, and southern African Americans. Confederate Decoration Days, on the other hand, attracted former southern Democrats and Whigs who tried not only to keep alive the Confederate past but to use that memory as one of the bases for political unity.

■ ■ ■

ESTABLISHING THE CITIES OF THE DEAD

As former Confederates instituted memorial customs in the spring of 1866, a number of elements came together to generate controversy around cemeteries and reburials. Political winds had turned against white southerners, who were increasingly on the defensive and limited in their ability to find a public means for Confederate expressions. Black codes and other problems in the former Confederacy made northern moderates more receptive to radical measures for the region. The actions of white southerners raised concerns that they were attempting to restore the antebellum status quo. Public displays of all kinds—including those of commemoration and mourning—received intense examination for what they revealed about the desire to accept defeat and embrace the government.

The Civil War had turned a variety of public actions into statements about loyalty and disloyalty. From the moment that Union troops entered Confederate communities even before the war ended, military officers carefully monitored public activity. Loyalty oaths might attest to political fealty, but the treatment of the national flag and other behavior provided a visible manifestation of a person's heart. One of the first acts by occupying troops was the restoration of the national flag. During the conflict, federal military officials took the issue so seriously that in New Orleans they executed a man who tore down the ensign. After the war, Union authorities sometimes provoked ex-Confederates by flying the U.S. flag in a prominent place and forcing the population to walk beneath it. Provost marshals did this in Charlottesville, Virginia, placing guards in a public square to block residents from stepping off the sidewalk. The commanding general in Charleston, South Carolina, followed suit by posting a U.S. flag over the route for a firemen's parade and ordering the marchers to tip their caps to the banner.[3]

Anyone who needed proof that these symbols remained controversial in the politically sensitive year of 1866 only needed to look at a meeting of Unionists in Winchester, Virginia. Intimidation after the war was not only aimed at black people but included white residents who supported the

North and especially the Republican Party. When a group gathered for a political rally in a fire hall in May 1866, the captain asked the men to take down the Stars and Stripes that hung in the window because it might create too much controversy and possibly spark a violent backlash. According to the local Republican newspaper, the incident demonstrated "conclusively the state of feeling among a considerable class of our citizens when the flag of our Union must be hauled down for the purpose of conciliating those who have sworn to support it and the Government it represents and talk so lordly of their loyalty and spirit of submission."[4]

It should go without saying that former rebels could not march in mass assemblies with weapons, but another restriction might not at first be so obvious. Early on, rebel uniforms were expressly prohibited. In one of his first orders after he assumed office, President Johnson considered them to be contraband of war. On April 29, 1865, the president issued an executive order that removed restrictions on trade in the former Confederacy but specifically mentioned "gray uniforms and cloth" as one of the exceptions. Union officials recognized the danger uniforms contained for perpetuating the memory of the rebellion and nurturing potential resistance. They ordered private firms that had been contracted to make uniforms to turn over their stock of gray and twill cloth. Throughout the South, Union military officers in charge of occupation supported the ban and issued edicts against wearing the gray. A Union captain in Clark County, Georgia, used Johnson's order to state, "On and later than the 3d day of June, any person found upon the streets or in any public place dressed in the uniform of an officer of the so-called 'Confederate Service' will be arrested and tried for misdemeanor before the Provost Court." As was typical, the order made allowances for soldiers who had been left destitute and had no other clothing. The captain explained: "Those who cannot obtain citizens clothes must take from the gray cloth all military buttons, trimmings or insignia of rank." The occupying forces summarily stripped buttons with the Confederate seal from clothing. In protest, former rebels covered the buttons with crepe or black cloth.[5]

The federal government, meanwhile, exacerbated the hard feelings by turning cemeteries into contested ground that highlighted the divide that remained between former foes. Throughout the South, many of the bodies of Union and Confederate soldiers lay where they had fallen, often in shallow or mass graves. Within a year after the surrender, the government began to collect the bodies of the nation's soldiers and reinter them in national cemeteries. Congress authorized the funds for this task, and throughout the South in early 1866 neat new cemeteries started to appear. Work began in February around Richmond, Virginia, where numerous prisoners had been buried at Oakwood and Hollywood cemeteries, as well as on Belle Isle. Next, the quartermaster's corps fanned out to Cold Harbor, Seven Pines, Hampton, Glendale, and Fort Harrison. At each place, the workers created new burial grounds divided into orderly sections with individual markings for the graves. Eventually at least seventeen of these sites were established within the Old Dominion—a figure that represented 20 percent of the eighty-three cemeteries scattered throughout the country in 1904.[6] These Cities of the Dead contained only the loyal soldiers who had fought for the Union. Government bureaucrats did not concern themselves yet with corpses of those who had fought for the Confederacy.

Ex-Confederates noticed this fact and quickly concluded that the new cemeteries signified that they were second-class citizens within the new nation. The burial of only Union dead proved to them that northern officials intended to subjugate the Confederate South rather than place the region on an equal footing with the North. Editors reminded readers of this fact, using the federal slur on the Confederate dead to gain support for reburial activity. "The 'Nation's Dead,' as our stricken opponents are called," one editor commented, "are abundantly cared for by their Government. We, it is true, poor and needy, have to contribute to the magnificent mausoleums that enshrine their crumbling relicks. The nation contemns our dead. They are left in deserted places to rot into oblivion."[7]

The phrases are quite telling in this case. The writer refers to "their Government" and not "ours" when mentioning the United States. He also noticed whom the nation considered to be its dead: only Union soldiers. Another correspondent in Norfolk echoed these sentiments, noting that since the end of the war the people of the North had been honoring their dead by erecting stately monuments and designing beautiful cemeteries. "But as the splendid shaft rises above the Northern dead, how sad and painful to think of the unmarked ground that holds the ashes of those dearest to us; how cruel the words of Henry Ward Beecher . . . pointing his finger to the neglected mounds around our hospitals and in our fields, and asking, 'Who shall comfort those who sit by dishonored graves?' " This particular writer was hardly unique in attempting to play on the regional pride of white southerners to goad them into caring for the rebel dead.[8] If they could not have the bodies of their loved ones buried by the government, then ex-Confederates at least could tend to their own graves and find ways of memorializing these men.

The ceremonies quickly adopted a fairly uniform look throughout the former Confederacy; however, organizers chose dates that were important locally. No single day became the logical choice for holding commemorations in Cities of the Dead. Spring made the most sense for scheduling, both for practical reasons concerning mourning customs and because of the cycle of war making. Weather from April through June brought to bloom the requisite flowers for decorating graves. Additionally, spring contained anniversaries of important battles that had taken place during this time. Armies tended to camp during the winter and launch a new campaign in better weather. The battles that inevitably followed claimed their share of soldiers, including some of the most prominent heroes of the Confederacy. Stonewall Jackson died on May 10, 1863, and J. E. B. Stuart on May 11, 1864.

People invariably adopted dates of the greatest local significance. Some in the Deep South, such as Louisianans, used the anniversary of the surrender of Joseph Johnston's army in North Carolina on April 26, 1865. Charleston, South Carolina, observed the battle of Secessionville in early June. The common denominator was to select the anniversary that blended Confederate pride with a sense of loss. For many, this meant the death of Stonewall Jackson. Throughout the South, early Decorations Days in some way touched on the death of this general, but even the importance of Jackson did not present a consensus on the date for Memorial Days. Richmond residents celebrated Decoration Day twice, with different cemetery associations conducting the ceremonies on May 10 and various dates surrounding May 30.

Confederate observances in the spring of 1866 featured traditional mourning customs organized by women and rituals conducted by men that promised anything but reconciliation. Very aware that the North watched closely, speakers walked a fine line in trying to ease the sting of the war—and current circumstances—while not appearing too inflammatory. They repeated time and again that they had accepted defeat, pledged loyalty to the Constitution of the victors, and did nothing political in honoring their dead. Yet they did not allay fears. Northerners believed the seeming compliance masked underlying discontent. There was too much emphasis on Confederate soldiers, too many martial themes, and too much denial that the ceremonies contained political commentary. A close examination of the Richmond celebrations and a few others throughout Virginia illustrates why northerners at the time did not see them as attempts for reconciliation but as evidence that the rebel spirit persisted.

On May 10, two observances took place in the former capital of the Confederacy that illustrate the dual functions of mourning and resistance performed by these civic rituals throughout the white South. The Oakwood Memorial Association sponsored a Decoration Day to capitalize on the memory of Stonewall Jackson. At the same time, the Hollywood Memorial Association held an event to remember the Richmond Light Infantry Blues, one of the first militia units that responded to the call for troops in 1861. Later in the month, Hollywood served as the site of an important Decoration Day that drew thousands to a location that contained important symbolism for the South.

On the surface, the rituals seemed innocent enough and wholly in line with established customs in Victorian America. The Oakwood ceremony began at St. John's Church. Observers noticed that women composed the majority of the audience—surely nothing at odds with standard mourning rituals. Traditional gender roles assigned mourning and religious ceremonies as responsibilities for women. A minister opened the commemoration with the reading of a psalm, followed by a prayer. He spoke of the need to care for the graves of the soldiers who had fought for the Confederacy. Afterward, the usual procession took place. At Oakwood Cemetery, orators urged the audience to support efforts to repair the cemetery and put the graves in order. Many remained sunken or unmarked, serving as a reminder of the poverty of the region and of neglect by the government. Another minister delivered a second speech. All denied that there was anything controversial or political in this occasion and that the government should not concern itself about something so natural and so honored by history and custom as mourning for the dead. One heard tones that sounded somewhat conciliatory, forecasting what became the mantra of the early twentieth century as the North and South buried sectional differences by focusing on the common valor of the men who had fought. "None could object to our honoring the memory of fallen soldiers," proclaimed the Reverend Dr. Norwood of St. John's Church, "for if those who fought against us were here, the bravest and noblest among them would assuredly unite with us in paying respect to the dead."[9]

In another part of town, members of one of Richmond's historic militia units paid tribute to their dead in both Shockhoe and Hollywood cemeteries, employing the closest thing to an outright military display possible under Reconstruction. It was an indication of how the Confederate ceremonies might have evolved had organizers enjoyed the freedom to celebrate as they wished. The ladies, as they called themselves, had little to do with this affair. This event contained more masculine overtones and bore the ritual imprint of July Fourth celebrations from the antebellum period. It was also more akin to the black parades that featured soldiers. The memorial association for the cemetery had postponed its Decoration Day until later in the month, but the men of the Richmond Light Infantry Blues, which had formed on May 10, 1793, used this anniversary to honor members of their unit who had died in the war and, especially, to pay tribute to Stonewall Jackson.

Unlike the event at Oakwood, no church services or ministers started this memorial. Led by a band, a group of three officers and thirty-six enlisted men paraded through the streets of Richmond to the two cemeteries. Because of federal orders, the men could not wear their uniforms, but they sported blue ribbons in their buttonholes "as a distinguishing badge." When they arrived on the Shockhoe cemetery grounds, they began visiting the sites of comrades who had died in Confederate service. Some of the women of Richmond met them and assisted in the decoration of graves, but there were no official ceremonies and no preachers. Then the procession went to Hollywood Cemetery. This was a particularly significant site. The bodies of soldiers from throughout the South lay there, attracting interest from beyond the region. Here the men were interested in honoring the contribution of their own unit to the war, which they did fairly systematically; the band played a dirge as the living placed flowers on each grave.

The militia unit had been among the first to volunteer for Confederate service, and one of its members who lay in the cemetery enjoyed a connection that attracted some interest in Reconstruction. The unit's first captain in the Civil War, O. Jennings Wise, was the son of Henry A. Wise, an antebellum governor of the state and brigadier general. The son had died in the unsuccessful attempt to prevent the Union landing at Roanoke Island in February 1862. The elder Wise was a controversial figure, a slaveowner who had criticized planters for the favoritism they enjoyed in the law. He had set himself up as champion of the underclasses by pushing for expansion of democracy and fighting for the political interests of common white men. His political opponents before the war often called him a demagogue. After the war, he continued to portray himself as the champion of the common people, but he also became a diehard rebel who refused to admit wrong or seek a pardon. During the 1866 ceremonies, Henry Wise was absent for the comments at the gravesite, presumably because of the concern his presence created among federal observers. Had he attended, he would have heard the one and only address of the day—by a minister who regretted that the father had not been there. Wise, however, did not miss the evening's festivities. Held at the Exchange Hotel, the event provided an excellent opportunity for political commentary.

At night the commemoration followed the form of a traditional Independence Day holiday, with the unit holding a dinner at which political personages raised toasts. Among the dignitaries attending were the mayor of Richmond and Henry Wise. Thirteen toasts were delivered in recognition of the original thirteen colonies. The first, of course, honored the Richmond Light Infantry Blues. A majority of the remainder praised the heroes from the war, those who continued to resist federal authority under Reconstruction, and the noble women of the South for their service in the conflict and tending graves. The group acknowledged the "southern press," by which they meant non-Republican newspapers; Robert E. Lee, "soldier, patriot, citizen, and Christian"; Stonewall Jackson "the only unconquered General"; Virginia, "right or wrong"; the Lost Cause; the Conquered Banner, "fold it up tenderly"; and Jefferson Davis, "the illustrious prisoner!—bearing in his own person the imputed crimes of his people." Davis endured two years in prison while northerners debated whether to try him for treason. Other Confederate leaders also were indicted, but instead of imprisonment these men suffered travel restrictions.[10]

Henry Wise fell into this category and made the most of the fact on this festive occasion. The crowd toasted him as a "political prisoner" because he had been disfranchised and his movements restricted. Never one to miss a chance to speak, Wise claimed that northern authorities had told him that he was not a prisoner because he could travel freely within the confines of Virginia. Because he could go no farther, Wise nonetheless still felt constrained. He then praised the performance of the Blues and the southern army, claiming that the cause "must not be spoken of as lost" because the cause involved "civil and constitutional liberty, which must, and will be victorious throughout the United States." For Wise and at least some of his listeners, the struggle against the federal government continued on a different field of battle.

To Radicals and uneasy moderates within the Republican Party the proceedings smacked of outright disloyalty or, at the least, demonstrated an unwillingness to put to rest the sentiments that had fed the rebellion. It was one thing to place graves in order and mourn the dead, but quite another to honor the people who had led the armies that had killed so many Union soldiers. Orators boasted of the qualities that had made Jackson a feared, respected general. First and foremost he beat Yankees, although speakers and writers did not put it quite this crassly. Instead, they highlighted his abilities as a "warrior" whose "name was a terror to his enemies." Because the general had died midway through the war, he wore the perfect mantle of a martyr for the South. He had died undefeated, as the Confederate sun reached its height. He represented to his admirers the best of southern civilization by being a teacher and exhibiting a sober character (he did not drink liquor) that was extremely pious as well. Also during these occasions, no southerner expressed remorse for having conducted the war. To the contrary, the editor of the *Richmond Times* noted, "The sublime exhibition of popular feeling in this city on the 10th of May is a proclamation to Christendom that although obedient to the Constitution and laws of the dominant party, *our sentiments, affections and sympathies are unconquered.*" Like many at the time, he claimed he would obey the law but would not give his sympathies to the Union.[11]

There were other indications in those first ceremonies in Richmond that Confederate sentiments remained alive. One was the participation of military figures who only recently had laid down arms. Although ministers led the Oakwood proceedings, even there the final orator of the day was Raleigh Colston, a former general who had been a colleague of Jackson's at the Virginia Military Institute in Lexington. His brief address stressed the loyalty of the enlisted man to the Lost Cause. "Whatever may be said against our late Congress, our leaders, or our newspapers, nothing could be said against the rank and file of the army." That he spoke at all on a topic that promoted the rebel fighting man could have been seen by northerners as a problem. Then there were the soldiers of the Richmond Blues marching to Shockhoe and Hollywood. They had not worn their uniforms, true enough, but they marched as a cohesive unit, mourned for men who had recently killed northerners, and sounded like Confederate sympathizers during the toasts.

Even the ministers seemed potentially subversive. At Oakwood, the Reverend J. E. Edwards reminded his listeners that wartime suffering had created a special bond among southerners. He particularly highlighted the sacrifices of soldiers and civilians, including the women of the South who succored the wounded and said the final prayers over the dead. The soldiers who lay in the graves had come from all corners of the Confederacy to defend the capital. He added that "the blood of the people of every southern State has been mingled together; they were comrades on the march and in camp; were one in thought and one in purpose." He added, "The South is now united by a band of graves—a tie that can never be sundered." In another portion of the state on the same day, residents of Charlottesville gathered for a similar ceremony in honor of Jackson. A young woman noted in her journal, "It was a solemn scene; the vast concourse of loving friends assembled to do honour to the memory of the dead." She then quickly added a comment that showed how mourning could overlap with current political fortunes: "I almost wish I was dead, & in the grave with them, when I think of our state of degradation."[12]

Other developments in that first spring after the war warned northerners that vestiges of the rebellion lingered. In Richmond the biggest celebration of the first anniversary of the end of the war occurred on the last day of May, with the ceremonies organized by the Ladies of the Hollywood Memorial Association. This Decoration Day combined elements from the two that had occurred on May 10: the sentimental aspects of the Oakwood event and the soldiers from the visit to Hollywood. This time, more of the community turned out, and an estimated 20,000 people flocked to the cemetery. Many stores closed—except those owned by Republicans or black people. Even former Unionists seemed to cooperate by shutting down their businesses, although some may have done this to avoid repercussions. One proprietor had conducted business on May 10 in defiance of the Oakwood celebration because he had "no respect for rebels living or dead," but his store was closed on this occasion. It is unclear whether he had suffered reprisals, but the people who were against the celebration appear to have kept their feelings to themselves.[13]

Troublesome were the blatant military expressions that appeared throughout the city. Storefronts displayed portraits of favorite generals draped in black crepe. Veterans clustered on street corners wearing their old gray uniforms, albeit stripped of the forbidden symbols of the Confederacy. The color, according to one newspaper account, was "dearer still to their hearts than all the gauds and pomp of tinsel and embroidery which had passed with them." While some veterans may have been destitute—and thus allowed to wear the gray, according to government provisions—it is hard to believe that a majority of the men did not have any other clothing. Soldiers also formed the procession to the cemetery; civilians found their way to the site however they could. Many members of the

Ladies Memorial Association, who had organized the affair, apparently made the half-mile trip by carriage but not as a part of a formal march. Sunday school children marched with their teachers, but they, too, proceeded on their own in the general flow of civilians to the City of the Dead.

The day clearly belonged to the Confederate Army of Northern Virginia. Beginning at 8:30 A.M., between twenty and thirty military organizations from the war gathered at assigned places throughout the city. These groups included longtime militia units such as the Richmond Light Infantry Blues along with a heavy representation of artillery batteries such as Purcell, Otey, and Letcher. Members of the 1st Virginia Regiment were there, as were cadets from the Virginia Military Institute. These organizations marched separately from their assembling points to a rendezvous at Grace Church. Here the various units, led by two local notables with military titles, combined into one line behind a military band. The veterans of the Army of Northern Virginia, many wearing their gray uniforms, paraded once again.

At the gravesites, the emphasis on military units and war heroes continued. Organizers had planned for neither ceremonies nor speeches because of the sensitivities of government authorities, but the gathering nonetheless sent a strong message that the Confederacy lived in the hearts of the people. Singled out were the graves of prominent Confederate heroes: J. E. B. Stuart; Joseph Davis, the president's son who died in an accidental fall during the war; Henry Wyatt, reputed to be the first regular soldier to die for the Confederacy at the Battle of Big Bethel in early June 1861; and numerous other local heroes. Stuart's grave drew particular attention. Organizers had created a niche of evergreens and flowers at the foot of the gravesite. On a pedestal in front of the niche rested a bust of the general, lent for the occasion by artist Edward Valentine, a native of the city who later created the sarcophagus for the Lee Chapel in Lexington. Stuart's head rested eight feet off the ground facing south and was framed by an impressive flower display. On the plinth, in letters of box leaves, appeared the words, "Stuart—dead, yet alive—mortal, yet immortal." The grave became one of the mandatory stops for the crowd.

Once the military companies arrived, they made the rounds of various sites. At Stuart's grave the entire assembly bowed heads and listened to the band play dirges. After a few similar tributes to other comrades, the soldiers broke into their own discrete units to visit the graves of more personal acquaintances. They made sure that the gravesites were appropriately decorated, dressing those that had been neglected even if the soldiers buried there were not part of their organization. Members of Pegram's Battalion, for instance, noticed that the graves of three soldiers from South Carolina had been overlooked. They remounded the sites and strewed them with flowers. Members of the 1st Virginia Regiment, about 150 strong, wore rosettes of red, white, and blue while led by a colleague carrying a cross of evergreens "instead of the battle flag which they had borne with honor for four long years." Units left the grounds individually, without a final grand procession.

The pattern of the Richmond celebrations was repeated elsewhere. Ladies memorial societies in Petersburg, Winchester, and Charlottesville— to name a few—organized the cleanup of cemeteries, set dates for decorating graves, and collected and distributed flowers. Processions, when they existed, consisted of some combination of the ladies organizations, Confederate veterans, and institutions important to the community, such as military bands, fire companies, and Sunday schools. More to the point, the soldiers gathered in clearly identifiable companies and regiments from the war. Once in the cemetery, the men paid tribute to their comrades, whose exploits were either mentioned aloud or remembered in newspaper reports. Banners typically appeared with messages that honored heroes or characterized the cause for which they died as resistance to tyranny. Sometimes orators gave addresses. One minister at ceremonies at White Sulphur Springs mouthed the usual denial that the proceedings contained anything disloyal, but he also observed that "we are not ashamed of the cause for which these gallant soldiers fought and died." He stated, "We retract nothing, recant none of our principles; but in giving up the cause we only feel that 'all is lost save honor.' "[14]

Republicans, especially Radicals, refused to accept the claims that the celebrations contained no political content. In every march of former soldiers in their old uniforms and regiments, and in every gathering that honored rebels as heroes while cherishing the cause for which they had fought, northerners saw an obstinate group of people who threatened the hard-won achievements of the conflict. Even moderate Republicans were concerned. Governor Pierpont of Virginia considered the festivities at Hollywood Cemetery an indication that treason remained alive. Periodically, reports surfaced that a Confederate flag had been spotted. William D. Harris, an African American who heard about the flag-waving, became alarmed when he saw for himself that more than one had been raised. Harris believed that if the behavior continued, the Confederate feelings would "get larger, until our political elements are again overspread and blackened sending forth war, blood, and death." The *New York Times* also noticed that the "southern" spirit grew through the memorial associations that conducted these events. According to the *Times*, the organizations had begun with good intentions, but they had become "nothing more than potent political engines in the hands of the most unscrupulous Democrats."[15]

Small wonder, then, that by the middle to the end of the summer of 1866 federal authorities in the South had more tightly circumscribed expressions of Confederate sentiment, even in the ceremonies for the dead. Processions in many cases were banned on Decoration Day. Raleigh residents could not march to their Cities of the Dead for roughly five years after the war.[16] New Orleans experienced proscriptions even against fundraising for monuments. Major General Philip S. Sheridan broke up associations that raised money to support the widows and orphans of Confederates or to construct monuments. The prohibition included public appeals for funds as well as concerts, exhibitions, and collections for such purposes. The order caused the Ladies Confederate Memorial Association in New Orleans to drop "Confederate" from its name.[17] Sheridan's was only the first wave of such actions to wash over the South. The following year witnessed a host of federal officers enacting similar restrictions.

■ ■ ■

THE POLITICAL GOES UNDERGROUND, 1867–1869

By the time the second series of Decoration Days arrived, the Reconstruction Acts had reestablished military occupation of the South that, among other things, further restricted memorializing the rebellion. The acts passed in March 1867 disbanded the state governments, carved the former Confederacy into five districts ruled by military authorities, and compelled officers to begin registering black men to vote. Federal officials did not halt the anniversaries of emancipation, but they eliminated weapons in parades as a means of easing tensions in communities. Confederate observances faced more severe restrictions. Throughout the South, military officers quashed processions, speeches, rallies, and virtually any sign of the rebellion. In Memphis, Tennessee, Union captain C. A. M. Estes warned the mayor on April 25 that Decoration Day would not go on as planned. He asked the official "to prohibit any procession, speeches, or public demonstrations, in order to prevent military interference, and to confine the arrangements to simple acts of mourning for deceased relatives in the customary manner." Similarly, former Confederates in Raleigh, North Carolina, went without a procession when they commemorated Jackson's death on May 10, 1867.[18]

Frustration with their situation sometimes caused ex-Confederates to lash out violently. Symbols of the United States became a target, especially as African Americans more vigorously pressed for their rights. When rioting occurred in Charleston, South Carolina, over the use of streetcars by African Americans in late April, a white man named Stephen Calhoun seized the opportunity to mutilate a U.S. flag. He was arrested for this act but escaped prosecution after publicly expressing his regret and attributing his behavior to being carried away by the excitement of the moment.[19]

Where Decoration Days were concerned, both sides to a certain extent participated in a give-and-take relationship as they negotiated the features of the rituals. The prescriptive measures on the part of the military were not uniform but varied throughout the South, and even within states, depending on the officers in charge and the situation within communities. Military authorities had wide latitude in interpreting what constituted signs of Confederate sentiment. They almost never banned outright all Decoration Day activities but usually expressed concern over certain elements. No one was prepared to prohibit entirely the right of people to mourn for their dead. On the other hand, former Confederates and ladies memorial associations understood that they had to balance their desire to retain Confederate sentiments and to portray these feelings in a way that did not provoke further federal intervention. What resulted were ceremonies that historians have interpreted as mourning rituals without political meaning, yet the commemorations assumed this form because participants were forced to abandon a more inflammatory style. The first celebrations in 1866 had shown that, whenever allowed, a more militant display occurred at these events in the form of veterans marching in their regiments. Even when they knew they were under the microscope, some southerners in 1866 still waved the Confederate flag, displayed portraits of their generals draped in bunting, and asserted in public speeches—some by leading figures in the rebellion—the righteousness of their war against the United States.

Richmond again provides a useful place to see the grassroots impact of the changes in these celebrations after the Reconstruction Acts of 1867, as well as a point of contrast with other regions of the South. The large gathering at Hollywood Cemetery at the end of May took place once again, although attendance was down from the preceding year and the symbolism was more muted. Not as many businesses closed. An observer noticed that the streets did not have the air of a Sabbath, although major mercantile establishments had shut down for the day. Members of the Hollywood Ladies Memorial Association appear to have understood the limits of federal patience. Their leaders announced in newspaper columns before the event that no processions would take place and no speeches would be delivered.[20] Under these circumstances, the military commander of the district looked the other way and allowed the mass decoration of the graves on May 31. This was not the case everywhere. Earlier in May, federal authorities in Lynchburg had stepped in to prevent H. Rives Pollard, a newspaper editor, from delivering a speech titled "Southern Chivalry." Similarly, Lynchburg's Decoration Day had no procession or organized celebration because of "military rule" in the South.[21] By the time the Hollywood celebration occurred on May 31, ex-Confederates had an idea about what actions would elicit military intervention.

It should come as no surprise, then, that the second Confederate Decoration Day at Hollywood Cemetery differed dramatically from the first. There was no procession or soldiers in recognizable organizations. People began streaming to the cemetery around 10:00 A.M. but without an apparent, orchestrated order. They walked as individuals or in groups, with arms full of flowers and other material to decorate graves. More businesses remained open than in 1866, and estimates placed the crowd at 15,000 to 20,000, or perhaps 5,000 fewer than the preceding year. The grave of J. E. B. Stuart still commanded attention, but it did not have the bust of the officer or an elaborate niche. No band played dirges and no men gathered in their former military units. In fact, one newspaper account specifically commented that few men attended, adding that the majority of persons there were women and children. The efforts of the ladies—especially in managing to have the affair at all—were not lost on male community leaders. Writing to a friend, a Richmond man noted that the Hollywood Memorial Association had held its Decoration Day in 1867, but he added, "I have heard of no unpleasant occurance, but if the management had not been under the control of the Ladies, [a] thousand bayonets would have bristled to prevent the celebration."[22]

A representative from the New York Times approved of the celebration, indicating that people watched these kinds of events closely for signs of reconciliation. The reporter reminded readers that Confederates had been denied a resting place in the national cemeteries. The newspaper favored allowing former rebels to tend their dead and to hold mass celebrations, as long as the occasions did not drive a wedge deeper between the sections. Any hint of Confederate arms or of speeches that dredged up controversial views was not condoned. The Decoration Day at Hollywood sounded the perfect tone. The report noted, "The work was done silently, decorously and without a word of anger. Orations in eulogy of the dead were expressly forbidden by the managers of the 'Memorial Association.'" In a different column the newspaper applauded the wisdom of the local commander, John Schofield, for allowing the event to take place. "This nation can certainly afford to permit the indulgence of affection and sorrow on the part of the Southern people toward their sons and brethren who perished in a worse than fruitless cause. Grief is always sacred, and nothing could possibly have a worse effect upon the sentiments and temper of the people of the Southern States than military interference with the discharge of its sacred duties." Schofield's handling of the affair, according to the newspaper, encouraged reconciliation and served as a model for other military leaders.[23]

In general, the policies of military officers forced the Cities of the Dead to become public spaces dominated by women's groups and with minimal symbolic representation of living Confederate veterans. Responding to the pressure, the ladies memorial societies steered the ceremonies in a more neutral direction by firmly stating in newspaper columns before events that they would allow no marches, speeches, or behavior that broke the solemn mood of the day. In Staunton, Virginia, a minister presiding over the service on Decoration Day verified their control when he announced "at the request of the members of the 'Ladies' Memorial Association,' that the services would be of a strictly religious character, and that it was their earnest wish that no demonstrations inconsistent therewith would be made, and requested the audience to refrain from indulging in demonstrations of applause."[24] Under the circumstances, it was better to tone down the proceedings than to have none at all.

Wherever supervising officers were either less vigilant or more sympathetic to the vanquished, a different spirit asserted itself in the Cities of the Dead. In Atlanta, citizens made their way to the cemetery without an organized procession but, once there, filed by a portrait of Stonewall Jackson and, nearby, a miniature flag fashioned from flowers. An observer recognized it as "the old Confederate flag that our soldiers rallied and died under."[25] In Virginia, participants respected the wishes of the Ladies Memorial Association in Staunton to avoid demonstrations, but a careful eye could spot Confederate sentiments in the festivities. First, there was a procession, with John B. Baldwin as the marshal. During the war he had served in the Confederate army and as a representative in the Confederate Congress. Members of fire companies also held a place in the march. Seemingly an innocent representative of an important community institution, one of these companies consisted primarily of men "whose members have heard the roar of the guns in every battle fought by the army of Northern Virginia." Residents who looked upon the marchers knew that they had been comrades in arms during the recent conflict. Once at the cemetery, the procession confronted a decoration of evergreens in honor of Jackson.[26]

The third wave of anniversaries, in 1868, provided a turning point for ex-Confederates. The continuation of Decoration Days suggested that the celebrations could become a lasting tradition. Not everyone had expected Decoration Days to last. Numerous obstacles existed, especially the lack of money in the South for building monuments or caring for graves. Inventing new traditions drained precious funds for other needs. Then there were internal divisions. Some white people had become Republicans, and others differed over the best way to cope with the political circumstances—from outright resistance to reconciliation. Editors wondered if the plethora of observances on different days would sap the strength of the ritual, and they recognized that celebrations geared to local anniversaries kept various regions of the South apart. Intervention by the U.S. military, of course, made staging mass gatherings for political goals difficult.

A column about the celebrations in Petersburg in 1868 shows the contrast with the first memorial events. The celebrations of June 9, 1868, did not feature the same rituals of the first Memorial Day in 1866. "On the former day there was a regular procession of ladies, military organizations, schools of the city and others," the columnist wrote. "Yesterday, the people, without organization met in the Old Church Yard. Then we had speeches—yesterday we had none; but notwithstanding this no diminution of interest was observed—no diminution in the attendance, no scarcity of flowers." Like many colleagues across the South, this columnist pressed for a consensus on celebrating Decoration Days. Local interests created almost as many different days for celebrating as there were cities and towns. This writer, however, also measured the importance of the observance, indicating that the "South has now no lot or part in the Fourth of July, and will, it is hoped, never celebrate it again until our Lees and our Jacksons, instead of being stigmatized as 'rebels,' shall have a place alongside of Washington and Jefferson, and Henry." The column continued: "With the heel of the oppressor on our necks, we have no use for a day of rejoicing now, but rather for a day of mourning and humiliation; and until we recover our own, let these memorial days be sanctified in the hearts of every true son and daughter of Virginia and the South."[27]

The year 1868 also featured creative attempts to use Confederate Decoration Days for promoting candidates for political office. The stakes were high, since important local and state elections were held that year. African Americans were now voting. Democratic politicians were unable to make the same use of commemorative events as Republicans, but they tried to capitalize on the exposure that these mass meetings allowed. Decoration Day in Staunton, Virginia, featured a prominent spectator, James A. Walker of Pulaski County. He was a former Confederate general who had served with Stonewall Jackson during the war and had commanded the famous brigade of the same name. Additionally, he had local connections, having been born in Augusta. It was clear from the newspaper account, however, that he had an additional reason for attending Memorial Day in his native area. He was running for state attorney general on the Conservative ticket. It was important for him to attend the ceremonies that attracted constituents.[28]

While former Confederates could not commemorate the war in the manner that they wanted, they did hold other meetings that expressed their contempt for Reconstruction and the new governments. Members of the Conservative Party of Henrico County, near Richmond, used the anniversary of Jackson's death to hold a mass meeting to adopt resolutions to counteract the elections and the new state constitution. They were worried about black suffrage and about white superiority in general. Judge W. W. Crump came right to the point. He asserted that the people had assembled "to consider how best to prevent our subjugation. An absolute despotism, more complete than that in any country upon the globe, was hanging over us, and yet we asked rather to live under this than to have to submit to that awful domination with which we were threatened. We would rather have the sword and bayonet over us than this proposed Constitution." He continued by saying that "universal suffrage had been conferred upon the black race, but the most restrictive measures had been imposed upon the white people. A constitution of abominations, more obnoxious than in any other State in the South, is proposed for Virginia." He and his compatriots were convinced that the new laws would elevate black people to a host of local offices because the requirement for an ironclad oath of loyalty during the war proscribed most white people. The committee as a whole adopted four resolutions. The last indicated that the members believed they needed to protect African Americans from loss of life, liberty, or property, but they were "not willing to surrender the government and control of this country, bequeathed to us and our race by our revolutionary ancestry."[29]

That no one stopped this meeting sheds light on the values of the military officers overseeing Reconstruction and what was acceptable behavior within nineteenth-century political culture. Certain kinds of meetings were condoned, no matter how objectionable the content. It was appropriate to gather inside a hall and pass resolutions. Such had always been the rituals of participatory democracy. Plus, military officers sometimes shared the perspective of ex-Confederates on Reconstruction. Schofield had refused to release funds to finance the elections in Virginia because he was convinced that the constitution would result in bad government because the ironclad oath would disqualify the most competent men. He was a moderate Republican who was unsure of the competency of black people for holding public office. The other person who supervised military Reconstruction, General George Stoneman, was a Democrat.[30]

The same leeway was not granted for events in public spaces, which contained greater potential for conveying messages of dangerous protest beyond the control of normal political operations. If Confederate symbolism appeared in inappropriate ways, neither Schofield nor Stoneman prevented military subordinates from stepping in. In Norfolk, Virginia, officers at the U.S. navy yard took umbrage at a window that the rector of the Trinity Church had given as an Easter present to the church. The window contained the names of the congregation who had died in the late war, but the caption explained that the window honored those who had died "during the invasion of the United States forces." The church was shared by U.S. military personnel, who did not appreciate being referred to as invaders. The day after the gift was presented to the church, officers from the navy yard visited the vestry and ordered the window removed or else they would shut down the yard and throw all of the civilian laborers out of work. The church complied, but the incident sparked a reaction. "Thus, like Ireland," wrote one editor, "the South must wait to write the epitaphs of her heroes when the land becomes free."[31]

By 1869 the first Decoration Days celebrated by former Confederates had assumed a fairly uniform pattern. Because of federal military supervision, expressions of the Civil War had become constrained and references to heroes were introduced surreptitiously. No soldiers marched openly as part of their units, although they did so as members of a band or a fire company. Processions were noticeably absent, or they seemed to honor the institutions of middle-class decorum symbolized by ladies memorial societies, pastors, and Sunday schools. Some newspaper editors and community leaders were concerned that no specific date consistently presented itself for commemorating the sacrifice of soldiers. At least for the moment, the Cities of the Dead wore a widow's black garb of mourning rather than a veteran's gray uniform.

■ ■ ■

UNION DECORATION DAYS

When the Union began to observe Decoration Days in 1868, the ceremonies touched a sore in former Confederates who interpreted these activities as anything but an attempt at reconciliation. In fact, the first celebrations of the Union dead appeared to drive the sectional wedge deeper, even though many northerners may have intended nothing of the kind and, for the most part, hoped for peaceful reunification. The political context fostered suspicion on both sides as people worked their way through the uncertainty that the Reconstruction Acts had left. Black suffrage had become a reality, and new constitutions not only expanded rights but also threatened to limit participation in government by former Confederates. Union Decoration Day in the South heightened the anger of former rebels by unintentionally flaunting well-tended federal cemeteries and displaying an alliance of white and black people in the Republican Party.

On the other side of the commemorative divide, northerners were not ready to believe that the former rebels had embraced the new Union. While most wished for reunification with forgiveness, others did not think it was time to clasp hands across the bloody chasm—the common metaphor of reconciliation in the 1870s and beyond. Too much had happened for everyone to forget so easily. It would be wrong to assert that no reconciliation characterized the five years or so after the Civil War; however, as the Union commemorative events illustrate, there were limits to what northerners accepted for how people defined the conflict and the cause for which their comrades had paid the ultimate sacrifice. They wanted to protect a Unionist memory of the war—a memory that did not so easily forget the culpability of a slaveowning oligarchy that had nearly divided the nation.

Union Decoration Day started in earnest in 1868, after General John A. Logan exercised his authority as commander in chief of the Grand Army of the Republic (GAR), a Union veterans' organization, to order members to decorate the graves of Union dead on May 30. Later in the century, when reconciliation became a theme for both sections, the wife of the general claimed that he had gained his inspiration from the ceremonies held by southern ladies. It is possible that he did. It is also difficult to trace the origins of this ritual, which borrowed from standard mourning customs. Decorating the graves of the dead was not an unusual practice. If all it took to win the honors of being the first was to have a group of individuals decorate graves, then most communities could claim bragging rights as the originator of Decoration Day. If, however, it took more than individuals but an entire community, then Confederate celebrations appeared before the national event. But even they had a precedent. As David Blight has shown, one of the first Decoration Days involving Union graves in the South was conducted by black South Carolinians and northern abolitionists who offered "the first collective ceremony, involving a parade and the decoration of the graves of the dead with spring flowers." As many as 10,000 persons gathered on May 1, 1865, to decorate the graves of more than 200 Union soldiers who had died in a prison converted from a planters' race course.[32]

Union Decoration Days, nonetheless, contained features that made them distinctive. For one thing, they took place in conquered territory with the bodies of soldiers lying on what had been enemy ground. Additionally, the Union celebrations drew together various regions in one national day of commemoration—something that frustrated the organizers of both Emancipation Days and Confederate Decoration Days. They had the stamp of authority of the government, which recognized the veterans who had saved the nation. That same government declared a holiday for its employees, releasing them from work so they could support the new ceremony of nationhood. Of course, the organizers of Union Memorial Days could do whatever they wanted, without military officers looking over their shoulders. Soldiers attended Union commemorations as weapons-carrying regiments that staged reviews. Speakers used the occasions to declare what the war had been about. The government also gave the northern Cities of the Dead resources that made the graveyards tasteful showpieces. Architects hired by the government designed these sites of mourning, and they did a splendid job. The cemeteries often were laid out in circular patterns, with the Stars and Stripes perpetually flown on a mound at the center. Graves were prepared uniformly, with similar markings. The atmosphere was solemn, organized, and respectful. None of this was lost on the southern people, who were having difficulties rebuilding the South, much less raising money to rebury the Confederate dead.

On May 30, 1868, the first Union memorial celebration in Richmond took place at the national cemetery on the Williamsburg Road, just a couple of miles below the city. There were many more national cemeteries in the vicinity, but this one was the closest and contained the bodies of between 6,000 and 7,000 soldiers. Apparently there was no procession. The crowd of roughly 3,000 people gathered at the cemetery around 11:00 A.M. The press sympathetic to former Confederates indicated that most of the people were African Americans; only about 400 were white. It was important whom they identified as part of the ceremony: federal officers and spouses, newly appointed city officers, and prominent Radicals. The participants decorated each grave with flowers and a tiny Union flag that waved in the wind. A minister of the Northern Methodist Church opened the ceremonies with a prayer. Then another chaplain delivered the oration. The address honored both sides by focusing on the valor and patriotism of the citizen soldier. The speaker also hoped that the custom of decorating these graves would last. Throughout the day, the band of the 11th Infantry, which was stationed in the region, played funeral dirges. It was a solemn ceremony without an obvious attempt to inflame the sensibilities of the former Confederates.

Yet it did just that—at least according to the mainstream Richmond newspapers. Correspondents focused great attention and descriptive detail on the cemeteries. They stressed the splendor of the Union Cities of the Dead, highlighting the money and labor that the North enjoyed in establishing these national cemeteries. Moreover, Congress had provided for these funds from money collected, in part, from the South. Confederate bodies remained untended by that same government. They also noted the exclusive nature of the ceremonies, and that they broadcast the alliance that existed among northern transplants and native, southern Republicans, black and white. The composition of the crowd raised concerns that the affair was designed to reinforce the political coalition that had formed. The *Richmond Dispatch* could not resist observing, "Of course it was not expected that our people generally would join in the tribute, as Logan's order was couched in words libelling us and insulting our own noble dead."[33]

The newspaper also raised a question that struck at the heart of the problem in creating new national traditions that eventually were to bring together formerly warring factions. "How is it that we see here two sets of people in the same community paying separate honors, under different names, to the dead? Animosities and prejudices should be buried with the dead." The column criticized national leaders who "raise up monuments to sectional strife, and hand down to posterity the passions which have rent the nation and desolated the land." It added that a "wise Government would have sought to bury animosities in the grave—would have gathered the dead, the honorable and brave dead, of the civil strife within the same enclosures, and marked them with the same care." Another newspaper saw this display as a blatant attempt to reinforce political identities. The *Richmond Examiner and Enquirer* characterized the GAR as "a political organization, similar, we are told, to the Loyal Leaguers." All told, the report indicated that the federal holiday appealed to the northern people who resided in the vicinity "and those who are identified with them in social and political feelings."[34] Louisiana residents had a similar perspective concerning the political nature of the ceremonies. One newspaper equated the day with a Unionist memory, indicating that it honored the dead "who gave their lives in vindication of the sovereignty of the Union." The item added that Union Decoration Day there was associated with "the Republican portion of our community."[35]

One part of the proceedings brought out the sanctimonious delight—as well as the racial bias—of these observers of the first Union Decoration Days. To ex-Confederates, the day lacked decorum. "The solemnity of the exercises," reported the *Dispatch*, "was much marred by the cries of cake, lemonade, and peanut-venders, who made the most noisy efforts to dispose of their wares." The newspaper also referred to a "prominent colored Republican of Richmond" as taking part in these pursuits. The vendors, however, characterized the behavior of crowds for most public holidays in American history. While there was reason for solemnity, there was also cause for joy; they were celebrating liberation. For African Americans in general, Union Decoration Days were not the main event on the commemorative calendar. Black people did make up a majority of the celebrants, but Emancipation Days were more prominent and popular events within the African American community.

Even in this most divisive of times parts of the Union Memorial Days contained references to reconciliation, with themes that became prominent later in the century. Ministers at the first Union Memorial Day in

Richmond appreciated the bravery of soldiers on both sides, foreshadowing how white people came to view the war. Chaplain Manly at the national cemetery on the Williamsburg Road dwelt on the "patriotism and valor of the citizen-soldiers of the Union, averring that the world had never seen the like."[36] Although the chaplain referred to northern soldiers, his approach left room for former Confederates to join. Periodically throughout the North appeared references to Union Memorial Days in which Yankees decorated the graves of rebels. Post 19 of the GAR adopted an openly conciliatory approach for its celebration in 1868. "Wishing to bury forever the harsh feelings engendered by the war, Post 19 has decided not to pass by the graves of the Confederates sleeping within our lines, but to divide each year between the blue and the gray the first floral offering of a common country. We have no powerless foes. Post 19 thinks of the southern dead only as brave men."[37]

Southerners, however, were not convinced that true reconciliation was coming. Too much distance remained between the former enemies. The political situation had not stabilized, and to many these events—however well intentioned—seemed geared to instigating rather than calming sectional animosity. Such was the opinion of Robert E. Lee. As early as 1869, veterans from both sides gathered at Gettysburg to begin marking with granite monuments the positions held by divisions of the opposing armies. Few high officers from the Confederate side attended. Lee was invited but declined the request. He cited other commitments but in the process gave his real reason. "It is wisest, moreover," he explained, "not to keep open the sores of war, but to follow the examples of those nations who endeavored to obliterate the marks of civil strife and to commit to oblivion the feelings it engendered." Lee obviously believed these events exacerbated sectionalism.[38]

Union soldiers were not unanimous in their desire to bury the past. An incident occurred at the ceremonies in 1869 at Arlington National Cemetery that revealed that many were not quite ready to forgive their enemies. Arlington, the home of Robert and Mary Custis Lee, had been confiscated during the war and, in 1864, turned into a cemetery. Within its grounds lay the bodies of Confederate soldiers, many of whom had died while in prison or receiving treatment in a Washington hospital. Over these graves—marching directly over the mounds rather than between them—patrolled a small squad of four enlisted men and a sergeant in the U.S. marines. They were commanded by a lieutenant who created a scene when a woman threw a small bouquet of flowers on top of a Confederate grave. The officer picked up the flowers, tossed them to the ground, and crushed them underfoot. When a crowed gathered, he shouted, "D——n you, get away from here, every one of you, or I'll make you. Guards, come up here and disperse this crowd." Later, as other women placed flowers on the graves, the soldiers escorted them from the cemetery.[39]

Who allowed this to happen is not known. Blame fell on various people, from the secretary of war to the superintendent of the cemetery. Regardless, the marine guard obviously enjoyed public support. Members of GAR Post No. 1 defended the guard, explaining that "while we hold no malice against the dead who fell attempting to haul down our flag, and thereby endangering the nation, we will not divide the honors by decorating the Confederate graves, and thereby taint the character of those who sacrificed their lives 'that their country might live.'" The statement added that the members would not want to wound the wives, sisters, and orphans of the Union dead or insult the comrades who had fought under the Stars and Stripes.[40] The guard was present again in 1871 for the Memorial Day proceedings at Arlington. As before, they screened members of the public who wanted to decorate the graves of Confederate dead. Once again they raised some controversy by preventing women from putting flowers on rebel graves.[41]

Northern opinion was divided over the incident. On one side were people who thought the soldiers had acted egregiously and created a problem where none had to exist. But the Arlington episode indicated that it was still too early for reconciliation. One correspondent wrote Supreme Court Chief Justice Salmon P. Chase—who had publicly spoken in favor of a more conciliatory posture with the South—to explain why it was not a good idea to let Confederates decorate the graves at Arlington. "We strew flowers, therefore, on the graves of our comrades and prevent their being strewn in the National Cemeteries at the same time on the graves of such Rebel dead as may be buried therein, not because we cherish any feelings of hate or desire to triumph over individual foes, but because we seek to mark in this distinction & manner the feelings within which the Nation regards freedom and slavery, loyalty & treason, republican principles and those of a slaveholding oligarchy." The writer suggested that the veterans were ready to forgive former Confederates, "but we will never consent by public national tribute to obliterate the wide gulf which lies between the objects, motives and principles for which we fought, and our comrades died, and those for which the rebel armies banded together, and for which their dead now lie in numerous graves."[42] This reasoning formed an important counterpoint to both the reconciliationist and emancipationist visions of the war. This veteran indicated that forgiveness was possible, even to be encouraged, yet the nation in his view was not ready to use national sites to honor the men who had tried to wound the country.

The refusal to let women decorate graves at Arlington created indignation among ex-Confederates. One newspaper editor called the situation a disgrace to the GAR. The circumstances at Arlington seemed to make a mockery of Grant's slogan in his inaugural: "Let Us Have Peace." Instead of promoting healing, the Union appeared to be more interested in keeping wounds open through dishonoring the dead.[43] Propagandists did their best to promulgate this image. James Ryder Randall wrote a poem that won wide circulation in the South for its depiction of Yankee meanness. He had gained attention for creating the lyrics to the second-most popular song during the Civil War, "Maryland, My Maryland." Sparked by a riot between soldiers and civilians, the words composed in 1861 had castigated Lincoln and Union authorities for their tyranny in Baltimore. Randall used some of that imagery—especially to characterize northerners as mercenaries and barbarians—as his stanzas retold the indignity visited on women who wanted to honor not North or South, but only their dead. The key passage noted the confrontation of the women:

> Between their pious thought and God
>   Stood files of men with brutal steel;
> The garlands places on "Rebel sod"
> Were trampled in the common clod,
>   To die beneath the hireling heel.
>   Facing this triumph of the Hun,
> Our Smokey Caesar gave no nod,
>   To keep the peace at Arlington.[44]

Despite opposition to Confederate traditions on federal grounds, the government's hand was softening on commemorations in general. The political situation was stabilizing. By the end of the decade, elections had been held, and in many places Republican governments had begun their administration. The fears subsided that Confederates might rise up again or help a foreign power in a war against the United States. Black people appeared to be protected by new laws and constitutions as well as access to the ballot. Decoration Days continued for a short while as affairs of mourning organized by women. Here and there throughout the South, however, a new aggressiveness emerged in some of the speeches that dotted these occasions. The speakers foreshadowed themes that came to full flower around the turn of the century. And they laid out the terms for reconciliation between the sections.

A speech by William C. P. Breckinridge reveals this aggressive posture. Delivered at ceremonies in 1869 at Battle Grove Cemetery in Cynthiana, Kentucky, the speaker boldly stated that the North, not the South, had caused the Civil War. Slavery had no part in the conflict's origins. Two civilizations had grown at unequal rates next to each other until "the time came when submission or separation were the alternatives." He portrayed the North as the aggressor, suggesting that "prior to any act of resistance, the South was deliberately, fiercely, insultingly thrust from share in the government which, with threats and maledictions, was seized to be used against her interests, her property and her honor." The Confederacy, in his view, had fought for independence from a tyrannical government. According to Breckinridge, that same government was treating its former foes unfairly. With great care, the northern government gathered the bones of the fallen and placed them in national cemeteries with monuments. He added what became the terms of reconciliation:

> If they be heroes who fell at Manassas and are now gathered in the National Cemetery, surely they who drove them in flight, who captured their artillery, and crushed their resistance, must also be heroes, and their unmarked graves, scattered in mournful numbers over the hills and in the ravines of that memorable battle-field deserve honor at some one's hand. . . . I utter what I believe [is] the universal feeling of the South: never will the graves of our dead be left undecorated by us until a common government and a united people treat all the dead alike.[45]

Years later a president would heed that statement and seek a juncture with the South by promising that the government would assume the burden of care for Confederate graves. But that day had not arrived. More turns lay ahead on the road to reconciliation.

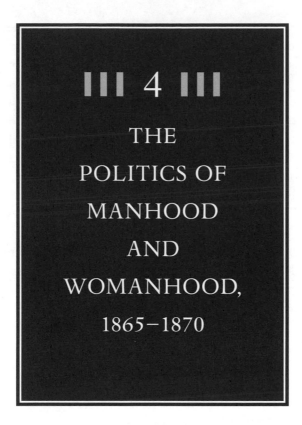

III 4 III

THE POLITICS OF MANHOOD AND WOMANHOOD, 1865–1870

When viewing Confederate Decoration Days during Reconstruction, northern commentators often reached the conclusion that their former male enemies hid behind the skirts of women. Periodicals suggested that the events served as thinly disguised political rallies for the Democratic Party and that men let their women organize a ritual that allowed the rebel spirit to thrive within a mourning cloak. Incensed editors of the Confederate press sloughed off these allegations, claiming that everyone had the right to care for their dearly departed and that the Cities of the Dead were not places of political controversy. Despite the rebuttal, northerners persisted in identifying women as the purveyors of Confederate sentiment who helped prevent the wounds of disunion from healing.[1] Women who had supported the Confederacy relished being recognized for performing the work of a nation, even if their effort was on behalf of a failed government. Through reburying the dead and commemorating the Confederacy, women did more than simply find a new channel through which to influence public policy. Because of the nervous federal authorities who looked for treason in a variety of public acts, Confederate nationalism had to be expressed, in part, in the domestic world of white women.

The Cities of the Dead created by women provided a means for rebel resistance to continue in a form of guerrilla warfare through mourning, yet the ladies memorial associations conducted this often-acknowledged political effort without threatening the broader contours of male-female relations. Southern white women determined the content of ceremonies, mobilized men to collect and rebury the dead, and raised funds for all of these concerns. Perhaps because federal officials meddled in their affairs, the women believed that they protected the memory of the Confederacy from oblivion. Their efforts earned them the recognition of many southerners—and not a few northerners—as providing the occasions that kept the Confederate past alive. Whenever federal authorities looked the other way, speakers used these ceremonies to reinforce rejection of Reconstruction. The organizers of these events and the ladies memorial societies that administered them, however, had little thought for creating upheaval in gender relations. Drew Faust's characterization of white southern women as a "paradox of progressivism and reaction" aptly captures the position of these elite women who recognized their contribution to a broader cause beyond the domestic world, even as they sought a partnership with men in preserving the world both had known.[2]

By performing their job as caretakers of men, alive or dead, southern women also helped fashion public rituals that sorted out new ideas about men and women. Military defeat and the end of slavery had opened public space to black people; freedom celebrations warned white southerners of the change that had come. African American males marched in the streets; black women filled the sidewalks and town squares as spectators and participants in celebrations of the defeat of former masters.[3] Whoever appeared in public spaces, and under what auspices, testified to the distribution of power at a particular moment. In the simplest terms, the conventions of public behavior determined whether a black or a white man stepped into the gutter to let the other pass on a sidewalk, or if a white man gave way to a black woman. While these are important matters for an individual's sense of honor and worth, more was at stake in the use of public space than whose boots were dirtied. Wars often leave loose ends concerning the roles of men and women. The Civil War had removed a fundamental means of distinguishing the privileged position of white men and women through the ownership of human beings, and it had left white men needing to resolve masculinity with defeat and with their political subjugation to Yankees.[4] Confederate observances showed the limits of what the vanquished accepted and warned of the resistance that lay beneath acquiescence. Under the circumstances, it was small wonder that northerners saw in these events, and in the organizational activities of women, much more than occasions for remembering the dead.

■ ■ ■

ORGANIZED SENTIMENT

Very quickly throughout the postwar South, ladies memorial associations emerged as a vital force in most communities. Organizers characterized their efforts as merely fulfilling the extension of their supervision of mourning. Some women may have believed that they were not doing anything beyond finding meaning for their loss and a final resting place for the dead. But many knew their efforts contained a greater purpose. The associations had an enormous impact on the Confederate past and present. The elite women who ran these organizations mobilized entire communities for their projects and changed the physical face of the South by organizing men to refurbish or establish cemeteries, construct monuments, and stage celebrations that drew thousands to the Cities of the Dead. At the same time, the care of Union bodies by the government touched sores in the Confederate psyche because it signified that the government considered the Confederates who had died as traitors. Ladies memorial associations consequently started with multiple functions: to conduct ceremonies of bereavement but also to ensure that they preserved the idea of Confederate sacrifice when men were constricted in performing this task.[5]

While nearly every town in the South had its memorial association, the more daunting efforts belonged to the regions with the worst battles. Because the grisly pattern of combat meant the grim reaper harvested more rigorously in the eastern theater of war, the more ambitious reburial and cemetery movements occurred there as well, especially in Virginia. Having the most significant heroes of the Confederacy, including Robert E. Lee and Stonewall Jackson, lent memorial weight to the Old Dominion. Other parts of the former Confederacy boasted of cemeteries containing more than local heroes and memorial movements of noticeable consequences as well. Vicksburg, Mississippi, by 1868 contained roughly 2,500 graves representing most states of the Confederacy.[6] Georgia, especially at Marietta and Atlanta, laid early claim as a center for memorial traditions. Numerous physical sites, however, existed within Virginia as places of memorials to great carnage. Eventually, the societies in Richmond conducted an effort that widened the significance of Hollywood Cemetery, with the memorial association reclaiming the bodies of fallen soldiers not only in the region but also from Gettysburg. This reburial campaign did not merely target men who had been from Virginia but included any southerners who had fallen in the three-day battle in Pennsylvania. All told, the corpses of several thousand Texans, Arkansans, Georgians, Virginians, and more were moved to the cemetery. So were more than eighty bodies of men who had been buried at Arlington. This considerable organizational effort involving bodies from a battle that became known as the high-water mark of the Confederacy gave credence to the Hollywood Memorial Association's claim that it managed a sacred shrine for the entire Confederate South.[7]

Although each ladies memorial association had unique elements and celebrated according to local custom, the societies were strikingly similar. Nearly all began in the spring of 1866, or roughly a year after the conflict ended. Women—many of whom were well connected and married to prominent officials, Confederate officers, or officers of cemetery companies—typically met in either a church or a civic place such as a courtroom to form their association. A secretary dutifully recorded summaries of the meetings, which received public acknowledgment in the local newspaper. All developed what corporations today would call mission statements, or an explanation of what they hoped to accomplish.

Now and then words appeared in these statements that showed the women understood that their work had a quasi-official status with a greater significance than fulfilling their capacity as guardians of sentiment. Many stated that they were trying to provide suitable interment for Confederate soldiers—either those who were not in cemeteries or those who had been improperly buried. The Ladies Memorial Society of Petersburg, organized on May 6, 1866, indicated that "a mysterious Providence has devolved on us a duty, which would otherwise have been a nation's pride to perform." The women justified their activity in the public realm based on what they called the "instincts of nature," or the belief that women were more sentimental and innately suited to handle funeral customs. In the case of the Petersburg association, however, the members indicated that their efforts resulted from a civic duty to act responsibly as citizens.

They mentioned that they had to live up to the expectations of the "land of a Washington and a Lee" and understood that they were helping to craft the meaning of patriotism in the postwar South.[8]

Ladies memorial associations employed organized, businesslike methods to conduct their sentimental work. Members selected officers and adopted a constitution or bylaws that set the rules for membership and the procedures for holding meetings.[9] Some, like the memorial association for Oakwood Cemetery, built their membership base from existing church congregations. When the group met in April 1866, it did so at the Third Presbyterian Church and appointed officers to represent the congregations on Church and Union Hills. These featured a range of denominations, including Baptist, Presbyterian, Methodist, and even Roman Catholic. It was clear that the association hoped to use churches to reach the community and enlist support.[10] Once organized, the association needed to raise money for grave markers and acquisition of land. Securing contributions was not always easy, as the South struggled to recover from the devastation of the war. Editors often commented on the dilapidated condition of many graves, blaming the situation on poor economic times rather than a lack of "patriotic" spirit for the Confederate dead. When the Hollywood Memorial Association formed on May 3, 1866, its members needed to collect nearly $500 within a few weeks just to put the graves in order for the first Decoration Day. The number of graves needing attention was staggering. Oakwood Cemetery, for instance, contained some 16,000 bodies.

Women who had supported the Confederacy solicited contributions from acquaintances, through newspapers, and by distributing fliers; they also staged fund-raising events. Membership dues provided a small start, but the annual fees at Hollywood were fifty cents per half-year. Canvassing friends and neighbors provided another source. Additionally, women put on a tableau to try to cover expenses for repairing the graves in Hollywood Cemetery.[11] Other women's groups successfully solicited funds from local government. In 1868 the women at Vicksburg, Mississippi, secured an appropriation of $300 to support their efforts to restore graves of the Confederate dead. Georgia memorial associations in 1868 also made a big push for funding by staging concerts sponsored by what one newspaper termed the "first ladies" of the state. Whatever the method used, the money went directly to the associations for their own direction, without male intermediaries.[12]

When these measures failed to secure enough funds, organizers broadened their efforts by issuing regionwide appeals. In the spring of 1866, the Hollywood Memorial Association of Richmond put together a broadside for this purpose, claiming to be an organization with "neither party, nor section, nor division." The object was to "rescue from the oblivion to which they are passing the graves of the great host which perished in the war and sleep undistinguished in our cemetery." The next passage belied a simple, memorial effort: "Their memory history will transmit from age to age, propounding without number illustrious examples from which the noblest of every age may catch new inspiration." Records from the organization do not show the results from this solicitation, but newspaper accounts suggest that money did come from other parts of the South. The problem was that the Richmond group was not the only memorial association to employ this technique. Throughout the South, ladies memorial associations mounted similar campaigns, often competing to fund projects.[13]

Although the associations performed like male organizations, they walked a tightrope concerning gender roles for a couple of reasons. First, theirs was not a mission to overhaul the roles of men and women but to try to restore positions under assault by northern conventions, black advancement, and free labor in general. Second, women running the memorial associations needed another vital resource beyond money: manpower. Quite literally, this meant male power in two areas that conventions of the day dictated as the responsibility of men: engineers to design project and agents to conduct business and organize heavy labor to disinter bodies, remound old graves, and build new cemeteries. During the organizing meetings, most of the memorial associations invited men to sit in. These may have been spouses of the leaders or important individuals of the community interested in collaborating with the women. Both societies in Richmond selected men to serve as their agents in negotiations with businesses and cemetery companies. In the case of the Hollywood Memorial Association, Francis W. Dawson performed this role. A veteran of the Army of Northern Virginia and a journalist, he boasted in his memoirs to have been instrumental in forming this particular group.[14]

Although men like Dawson may have encouraged the formation of these groups and continued to serve as advisers and agents, women unquestionably made the important decisions. In the early stages of Reconstruction, these decisions had a tremendous impact on the preservation of the Confederate memory and identity, expressed in a wide range of projects that shaped the landscape of the South, as well as its white psyche. Memorial associations organized and directed men in the cleanup and building of new cemeteries. They led campaigns to gather the dead from other states and transport them back home for reinterment. They had monuments erected to those same dead. Each of these projects involved supervision of professional men, especially engineers and lawyers. The Hollywood Memorial Association used Charles Dimmock as its engineer for overseeing the construction of a pyramid of granite that commemorated the Confederate soldiers in the cemetery. He also served as the agent between the association and the male-run cemetery company. Yet he did not act independently. He had to receive authorization for every step of the project from the memorial association and provide progress reports to the female officers.[15]

When it came to the commemoration of the dead, women controlled all facets. The memorial associations decided when celebrations were held, what should be their content, and what tone was appropriate. Women determined the order of procession—if there was one—and selected the orator. The choice of a speaker was very important for the success of a celebration. These were matters that required great care and thought. As historian LeAnn Whites has observed, speakers could make a big difference in the size of a crowd, which stimulated donations for the memorial efforts. During occupation of the South, women generally invited ministers to lead the ceremonies. Whenever the federal officials eased their control, the associations tapped popular officers from the Confederate army or Democratic politicians who led the drive for restoration of home rule. Political and military figures obviously contained great appeal for the crowds.[16]

These business functions required women to negotiate with a host of other agencies and merchants year-round, which gave them a life beyond annual Decoration Days. The memorial associations conducted extensive business in areas typically dominated by males. It was common for the women, working through their male associates, to secure from railroad companies either reduced or free fares for passengers attending these celebrations or special freight charges on headstones, flowers, and tools. They also sometimes won free transportation from express companies that moved the materials to the cemeteries.[17] Someone had to buy land, arrange transportation, and organize the labor for moving bodies and creating graves. The efforts to reclaim the bodies from more distant battlefields such as Gettysburg and the building of monuments involved securing contracts with burial teams, finding carpenters who made coffins, directing engineers in building projects, working with architects for the design of monuments, and hiring masons who did the labor. On

Decoration Days, the memorial associations also had the power to declare a holiday that businesses were asked to respect, especially all "loyal" Confederate shops.[18]

A division of labor quickly sorted itself out that kept gender roles within comfortable areas. Women deferred to men as agents for financial affairs as well as for negotiating contracts and delivering public addresses. They either collaborated with the cemetery companies that were separate corporate entities led by men or used their own agents. In Petersburg the memorial society established a male committee in 1868, resolving that "all contracts for any mode of labor connected with the disinterment, removal, and reinterment of the dead, be referred to the committee of gentlemen who shall see that they be promptly and effectually executed."[19] Men accepted the leadership of the memorial organizations, recognizing the right of women to conduct these commemorative efforts as compatible with their duty as caregivers and as people whose sex suited them for work involving sentiment. Perhaps more fundamentally, women in these associations were viewed as partners with men in efforts to preserve the Confederate past and prevent those who had fought for the Confederacy from being remembered as traitors. Circumstances had put the societies in the right place at the right time. Women from the middle and upper classes had the time, energy, and connections to devote to these projects. Additionally, because of the restrictions on displays of old symbols during Reconstruction, funereal commemorations provided a safe place for preserving the Confederate era. It was difficult for federal officers to stop memorial proceedings as long as orators did not become too outspoken against the policies of Reconstruction.

It was clear that men viewed this work by women as having a public impact—one that was impossible for men to achieve at the time. A periodical called the *Southern Opinion* noted the value of women's memorial efforts for fighting a rearguard action against obliteration of Confederate identity and raising hopes that better days lay ahead. The newspaper applauded the ceremonial efforts of ex-Confederate women throughout the South, saying that the anniversaries to honor the heroic dead kept alive "that nationality and hereditary feeling that our destroyers would systematically crush out." According to this columnist, history was maintained as an ineradicable presence in the long ranks and files of the graves of the fallen, whose stories awaited a future chronicler. Cities of the Dead served as a corrective to the current corrupt government. "Nationality no longer exists, and the Constitution is subverted by demagogues, misrule, plunder, infidelity, and legalized robbery." Even Robert E. Lee acknowl-edged the efforts of women. He avoided attending memorial events and refused to support publicly the erection of monuments because of the inflammatory feelings they could provoke among northerners. In a letter to a former general, he explained that a monument, no matter how welcome for Confederate sentiment, would have the effect of "continu-ing, if not adding to, the difficulties under which the Southern people labor." He added, "All, I think that can now be done, is to aid our noble and generous women in their efforts to protect the graves and mark the last resting places of those who have fallen, and wait for better times."[20]

Some of the concerns expressed in newspapers, however, suggested that men were not always comfortable with relying on women for this endeavor. Discussions about the Cities of the Dead often revealed the challenges to manhood that the new world presented. Newspaper editors and members of the memorial societies made it clear that there were limits to what women should do. When it came to preparing graves and performing labor in the cemeteries, they were to give way to men, whose service in this capacity proved their patriotism and their manliness. An account in the *Richmond Dispatch*, probably written by Dawson, rhap-sodized about the work done by men in preparing the graves before the first Decoration Day in 1866. He had been impressed with the "long ranks of men—the men of Richmond—armed not with musket, bayonet, or sabre, but with the axe, spade, and pick; intent not on the smoke and carnage of war . . . but upon placing the seal of their love and remem-brance upon those whom that war had clasped to the bosom which kills all whom it touches." The columnist added, "In life we tended and nursed our Confederate soldiers; our ladies gave them all the care that the ten-derest solicitude could inspire; but the work of repairing their graves is a work for men, and a work for Confederate men—and it is our duty to carry through a work that we have now commenced."[21]

Columnists such as this one deliberately connected Confederate patri-otism and manliness with the cemetery movement, giving credence to the scholars who claim that women's work aided in the reclamation of white southern manhood.[22] Service in the Cities of the Dead represented one of the ways men declared their allegiance in the struggles of the day and, even though denied muskets, could use other tools to fight the attempts to obliterate the memory of the war. Under the call of manhood, columnists conflated the military valor represented by the dead, the patriotism to honor their sacrifice, and the manliness to fulfill their duty as laborers unafraid to pick up axes and shovels to perpetuate the cause for which men had died and fought. Appeals to manhood in this fashion were cunningly used in Richmond to prod workers into repairing gravesites at Hollywood Cemetery on May 28. After a slow start, an estimated 800 men assembled for the work. The old military companies—such as the artillery units of Otey, Letcher, Crenshaw, and Purcell and the 19th Virginia Militia—helped organize the workforce. The men assembled in their former military units prior to the day to commit members to the cemetery work. Their actions lent credibility to the notion that men did not operate in the sentimental world but served in their former army functions, responding as they had during the war to a new call to patriotic duty.[23]

Another line of reasoning struck at the concern expressed by northerners and southerners alike that men might have a difficult time operating in a world ruled by free labor. Not a few columnists on both sides of the sectional divide raised the prospect that men who had grown up looking upon labor as something done by enslaved African Americans might have a problem embracing work as something of value for themselves. Certain kinds of hard labor in particular had been racially defined in the Old South. In the postemancipation world, southern newspapermen complained of unspecified, unemployed men who lurked on street corners or avoided going into the churches where women conducted the patriotic efforts. "In this city of Richmond," noted the *Dispatch*, "there are at this time hundreds of young men who, either from necessity or inclination, have no better employment than that of sauntering about the streets, lounging on the corners, smoking cigars, and patronizing the billiard saloons. They become wearied of life from having nothing to do." Part, although not all, of the problem could be alleviated by employing these men in the cemetery campaigns. "They do not remember that their youthful muscles can be turned to even better purposes than that of trenching, building winter quarters, or cutting the massive log to supply the blazing camp-fire. But they have now a noble work before them."[24]

Whenever men failed to respond to volunteer levies, editors hoped that, if nothing else, they would prove northerners wrong who said that southerners would not work to restore the South. "It has been said," noted the *Richmond Dispatch*, "that our young men are idle and careless, but we will not believe this of them; and the best practical proof they can give of their industry and regard is to shoulder the spade or pick and march to Hollywood by 3 o'clock to-day."[25] Another correspondent suggested the same thing—that the memorial associations offered a way to prove that southern men valued labor. "We were once rich, and while we had money gave it away like water," remembered a man who signed himself G. A. W. "But we can still work with strong hands and willing hearts, and thus maintain the dignity of labor."[26] Pitching in and raising a few blisters was not only the patriotic, Confederate thing to do; it was also manly.

■ ■ ■

REBURYING CAESAR—WITH PLENTY OF PRAISING

Viewed from north of the Mason-Dixon line, memorial efforts appeared to maintain Confederate resistance through a woman's world. Northern accounts hinted of an emasculated male population that let women carry on the fight to preserve a treasonous past. The problem, however, went beyond merely trying to keep the Confederate story alive. To Radical Republicans in particular, the efforts to commemorate the Confederate soldier had become a means of sustaining treason that could burst out again in further rebellion. Southern women, as Nina Silber has shown, were viewed as having hearts that passionately nourished the rebellion. This also proved the weakness of southern masculinity by highlighting men's failure to assert control over their women. "In both the antebellum and postbellum dialogue," according to Silber, "gender served as a central metaphor in the sectional debate between the North and the South. Implicit in northern men's free-labor ideology, and their free-labor critique of the South, was an understanding of two competing notions of masculinity—one rooted in hard work and moral self-restraint, the other mired in slavery, aggression, and vice."[27]

Most northerners clearly believed that women who had supported the Confederacy kept alive hostility between the two sections and became as tiresome as the Radicals in their zeal. Even the moderate *New York Times* saw cause for alarm in the memorial associations. The editor believed the southern—by which he meant Confederate—spirit grew rapidly through the women's efforts. The organizations had begun with good motives but had become "nothing more than potent political engines in the hands of the most scrupulous Democrats."[28] Controversies occasionally arose in both regions over what to do about the remains of people who had fought for the other side. When this discussion occurred in 1868 within the Union League of New York—a Republican club—the members apparently argued over whether to bury Union and rebel dead side by side. A newspaper editor in Illinois threw up his hands in disgust at the affair. "It should be left to Southern women and Radical politicians," he wrote, "to exhibit such animosities." In essence, he had put these two disparate groups of people together. He considered those who tried to keep the conflict alive as feminine because they failed to exhibit the correct restraint of passions and accept life the way it was. As he put it, harboring bitterness was "unmanly."[29]

What made northerners think this way about these southern white women? After all, women who had supported the Confederate commemorations of war proclaimed (as did their male counterparts) that they did nothing more than what human beings anywhere would do by trying to ensure that friends and acquaintances received a proper burial. Time and again newspaper editors declared the allegations of politics as false and capricious on the part of barbarians who would ask ex-Confederates to go against the tide of decent, civilized human beings in respecting the dead. One editor in particular became incensed at the *Chicago Tribune* when it denounced the ladies of Richmond for strewing flowers on the graves of the Confederate dead. "No matter what we do we are censured," stated an item in the *Richmond Whig*. "If silent, they call us sullen; if cheerful, they call us insolent; and when the women of the South, with that regard for their dead kindred which savages even manifest, innocently and mournfully choose an appropriate day in the month of flowers to decorate the graves of their dead kindred, it is charged that they engaged in an effort 'to keep alive the political feeling of hostility to the Union.'" The columnist added with particular emphasis, "*Political significance is not attached to these funeral ceremonies in the South. They are conducted by the ladies, and it is not the habit of the Southern ladies to form political conspiracies.*" In conclusion, the writer leaned on gender to absolve women of complicity in these affairs: "If the men of the South contemplated treason and 'civil war,' they would resort to other methods than these—nor would they put forward their wives and daughters to do the dangerous work."[30]

A number of persons in the North remained unconvinced. Actions spoke louder than denials. The first Decoration Day ceremonies of 1866, as outlined in Chapter 3, contained considerable numbers of military organizations. Men marched in their former units and surrounded graves of their fallen comrades. Some wore their old gray uniforms, although stripped of military insignia. Merchants displayed portraits of Stonewall Jackson draped in crepe. The memorial associations sometimes scheduled workdays on graves for July 4, creating a tradition counter to the nation's holiday.[31] Whenever they had a chance, speakers at these memorial events emphasized the valor and nobility of the soldiers for the cause while denying that slavery had served as the root of the war.

Even the fund-raising efforts of the memorial associations seemed to promise the continuation of sectional feelings. Fund-raising occurred all over the South, including within the border states that had remained in the Union. In the spring of 1866, women in Baltimore held a Southern Relief Fair that raised more than $3,000. Taking in the fair was Admiral Raphael Semmes, a prominent naval officer in the Confederacy who had helped destroy much of the Union merchant marine. A native son of Maryland, he had just been released from prison and stopped by to bestow his blessing on the proceedings.[32] The following year the women of Richmond held a memorial bazaar for the benefit of the Hollywood Memorial Association. It was an incredibly successful affair that lasted fifteen days, amassed roughly $18,000, and drew participation from most states of the former Confederacy as well as the border states of Kentucky, Missouri, and Maryland. Women and men donated a variety of goods and merchandise. Many were famous, such as Varina Davis, the first lady of the Confederacy, and wives of former generals. At the fair, items were laid out on tables arranged by state. Noticeable were pictures of Lee, Jackson, Davis, and other top Confederates such as Wade Hampton, a former general who continued to wage political wars in South Carolina.[33]

The more provocative incidents dealt with burying the dead. In the highly charged atmosphere of Reconstruction, burials of the dead and funerals became highly politicized. While memorial associations at first stressed that they would tend the graves of Union soldiers in Confederate cemeteries, the trend nonetheless was toward segregation and trying to ensure that good southern boys did not lie next to the enemy for eternity. As the men of Richmond worked to prepare Hollywood Cemetery on May 28, 1866, they encountered the graves of two ex-Confederates buried in the area reserved for Union soldiers who had died as captives. The name of one of the men was not known; the headboard had been marked "Rebel; died June 15, 1865." The second body belonged to a lieutenant from the 49th Georgia who had died in late May 1865. The work details immediately began to disinter the bodies. A sexton at the cemetery at first tried to stop this process, claiming that the soldiers were not really Confederate but had been buried under that name "for reasons which he was not at liberty to divulge." The men would have none of this. They opened both coffins, satisfied themselves that the corpses wore Confederate uniforms, and then reburied the bodies in the southern section. Segregating Confederate from Union dead had considerable private support. Five years after the war, a woman wrote the Hollywood Memorial Association for information about the remains of her son. Mrs. D. B. Comfort of Mississippi wanted to make sure he had not been buried with "the enemy."[34]

The reburial movements occurred in a broader context of white southerners staging public funerals as a convenient excuse for mass assembly. The habit of using burial grounds and funerals to support political positions has existed for several thousand years, exemplified in Pericles' funeral oration over dead Athenians in the Peloponnesian War. Scholarship on South Africa has shown groups digging up bodies to give the martyr a "proper" burial, which provided an occasion for thousands to hear speakers cite the memory of resistance embodied in the dead. Northerners had resorted to the same custom, with President Lincoln using the dedication of the cemetery at Gettysburg—a massive reburial campaign—to deliver one of the most important speeches in American history.[35] Southerners did the same in their first ceremonies honoring the dead under Reconstruction. Marc Antony of Shakespeare's plays—the man who gave the funeral oration over the body of Julius Caesar—would have nodded in satisfaction at the strategy. While the organizers professed they did not wish to overly praise their Caesars at the expense of the new government, they certainly did their best to fan the emotional flames of the crowd as they brought up contemporary political circumstances.

We can see this process at work in the dedication of the Stonewall Cemetery in Winchester, Virginia. To dedicate the cemetery in October 1866, organizers arranged for the reinterment of three former Confederate heroes, witnessed by an estimated 8,000 to 10,000 people. Organizers reburied the body of Confederate cavalry officer Turner Ashby and held a funeral for him, his brother Richard, and another comrade in arms. (A fourth body was made part of the procession but was buried in another cemetery.) It was the crowning achievement of the women in the region, who had bought land, organized a cemetery, enlisted men to perform the labor, and enhanced the notoriety of the occasion through the Ashby bodies.[36]

In many respects, Turner Ashby embodied the qualities that former Confederates—and later in the century many northerners—liked to attribute to the southern soldier. Ashby had been one of the first martyrs, during dark times in the beginning of the war. He commanded cavalry troops under Jackson in the Shenandoah Valley, a theater of war that

contained success against the Union army while southern forces everywhere else were losing during the winter of 1861–62. Ashby died on June 6,
1862, fending off a federal assault on the rear of the Confederate column as
it retreated to Port Republic. He was known for his dash and bravery
under fire but not as a particularly good administrator or disciplinarian. In
fact, Jackson had tried to reduce the size of Ashby's command because the
officer could not control his men, but he backed down when Ashby
threatened to resign. Jackson understood that his subordinate's person-
ality attracted men and created admiration and loyalty among them, even
if he did not hold a tight rein. Historian Douglas Southall Freeman described Ashby as "dark, almost swarthy," suggesting the popular conception of someone from the Middle East. "To romantic Southerners he
looked as if he had stepped out of a Waverley novel." He also had "fierce
mustachios and a beard that a brigand would have envied." News of his
death was carried in the national newspaper of the Confederacy, the
Southern Illustrated News.[37]

Ashby had no reason other than his military career to claim a final
resting place in Winchester. He was born in Fauquier County and spent
most of his life in northern Virginia. When he died, the military interred
his body in Charlottesville at the University of Virginia. His brother Richard, who died in a skirmish in early 1861, was interred at Romney. Turner
Ashby's defense of the Valley was appealing to the women who established the Confederate cemetery in Winchester. They used male emis-
saries—one of whom was a biographer of Ashby—to ask surviving sisters
for permission to disinter the bodies and place them together in the
Stonewall Jackson Cemetery. They suggested that the cemetery was an
appropriate place to bury the brothers because much of their military life
had involved operations in the region. The logic apparently convinced the
sisters, although members of the University of Virginia opposed the move
and at first resisted. Since the family had consented, however, there was
little the university could do to prevent the transfer of the body.[38]

In early October, men dug up the bodies of the brothers as well as two
other comrades and began a long march that contained strong elements
of the Confederate military and suggested the form Decoration Days
would have taken without federal intervention. One procession included
the body of Turner in a hearse pulled by four white horses and escorted by
a guard of honor of approximately sixty members of the Ashby Brigade.
The procession stopped in Berryville, where the coffin was displayed at an
Episcopal church until the other bodies arrived. On October 25 began the

final journey, which included former military officers and local politicians. Henry Kyd Douglas, a former aid to Jackson, served as a marshal. Around Ashby's hearse were a number of cronies, including John Singleton Mosby, a partisan ranger during the war. Filling the ranks were members of the Ashby Brigade, representatives of a Masonic lodge, and citizens in general. Unlike processions for Decoration Days, no special place was reserved for the women who had organized the event. This mass funeral was designed for spectators to remember the Confederate military.[39]

The oration for the day fell to Henry Wise, who invoked memories of the dead to declare opposition to Reconstruction. The former governor first established the attributes of Jackson, reminding listeners that the general had been a staunch Presbyterian and lover of the Union, as proven by his service in the Old Army. The speaker painted a portrait of faithfulness to prove that the survivors of the Confederate cause had not been traitors but people who believed in a principle. If someone with the character of Jackson had enlisted in the southern effort, Wise reasoned, then how could the men who lay in the Cities of the Dead be traitors? "Whenever or wherever enemies shall accuse them [former Confederates] of rebellion and treason," he said, "truth will point to the example and the fact that Confederate revolution was sanctioned by the faith of Stonewall Jackson!" Wise suggested that the revolution had not been discredited by defeat. Echoing a key part of the Lost Cause rationale, he said a people should not accept arbitration by brute force—that a war won by the overwhelming might of the North should not be taken as judgment of the righteousness of the effort. Mere numbers did not overcome moral principle.[40]

Wise used Jackson to convey the stance that ex-Confederates should take concerning Reconstruction, asking his audience, "What in this hour would *he* have us do?" Because Jackson had neither surrendered to the enemy nor faced decisions about whether to seek a pardon, Wise had free rein to interpret the general's positions. Not surprisingly, he believed the general would have rejected a conciliatory posture. Jackson, Wise mused, would not have taken an oath of loyalty or forsaken the cause. He would not have praised proclamations of peace when there was none. He would have demanded the withdrawal of troops from the South, the dissolution of the Freedmen's Bureau, and the restoration of civil rule. Jackson would not have marched arm in arm "with subjugation itself into any convention, to acknowledge as lawful the rapine which plundered all rights of property, and consented to debase his own race to a level of protection with negro blood in *all respects* of *person* and of *property.*" The general also would not have supported black suffrage, knowing full well that to grant such a right also guaranteed personal equality, raising the specter of amalgamation. Wise then offered some of his own opinions on political affairs, reaffirming that state, not national authority should remain the best form of government and calling the creation of West Virginia "the bastard child of political rape."

Other issues that Wise raised concerned the economic recovery that presented real challenges for old and young alike. Here he criticized the conquering government for forcing ex-Confederates to repudiate claims to war debts. Repudiation, he said, was a "demoralizing devil" that "will not discriminate between Confederate or Federal . . . but will devour all." Professing that it was folly to push for recognition of the debts, he could not resist pointing out the injustice of being denied payment for the defense of the Confederacy while having to pay for the invasion and occupation of the conqueror. He also hated paying the pensions of the "hireling" soldiers "out of our unrepresented taxation." Like many, Wise was concerned that young men might give up on the state and look for employment in more prosperous regions of the country. He counseled young men to stay home and embrace hard work. "We must renounce luxurious idleness and not be ashamed to work *at home* and among our friends. Stonewall Jackson was not ashamed to work and by the earnest labor of his own head and hands earned immortality." Wise advised the young men to accept a life of work to repair the South and turn its fortunes around. "Thus work, oh young men, or you are not men. You are not Stonewall men! You are not Virginians worthy of these graves! Work! or you can't be happy."[41]

Before he finished his speech, Wise addressed most of the demands imposed on the Confederate states in rejoining the Union. He did not recognize the supremacy of the national government and refused to support advancement of black rights. He even rejected one of the more moderate requirements favored by most people, including President Johnson, to have no recognition of Confederate war debts. The former governor was something of an extremist and held less sway in the state as the postwar period advanced. Yet his positions obviously had some popular appeal or he would not have been chosen by the memorial association to provide the keynote address for such an important occasion.

Let us return to the question that started us down this path of analysis: why would northerners see the mourning rituals of women as having a political purpose? The Ashby funeral was a ceremonial effort made possible by women. They had originated the idea of a cemetery in Winchester for the Confederate dead, found the resources to establish it, and organized the dedication ceremony for the grounds. They invited white southern men to dig up corpses that had received proper burials, transport them untold miles surrounded by some of the more significant officers of the rebellion in northern Virginia, take these bodies to a place that had no familial connection to the deceased except as a symbol of where they had fought during the war, and bury them in a cemetery named after a chief lieutenant of the rebellion. Then they called on a controversial political figure known for his antipathy to Reconstruction to deliver an address that advocated resistance to the United States based on the memory of the man who was not buried in the cemetery. Sectional mentality was still very much alive in the Cities of the Dead.

If the truth be told, southern men knew how important the women's associations were for keeping alive the memory of the Confederacy and for allowing a form of political commentary. The observation of a Richmond resident concerning the 1867 Decoration Day at Hollywood Cemetery more than illustrates the point. If the affair "had not been under the control of the Ladies," pointed out James Gardner, a "thousand bayonets would have bristled to prevent the celebration." That recognition, however, does not mean that men always appreciated women as the defenders of the Confederate cause. Sometimes frustration was expressed in newspaper columns over sectional bitterness finding its expression through women. A columnist in Norfolk bemoaned the outpouring of feminine poetry intended to immortalize the Lost Cause. The writer beseeched the women, "Come back out of the feminine war-path." For good or ill, according to this writer, the dead were buried; "do not disturb them." He claimed to be tired of hearing poetry that did nothing more than recall the unpleasant past. "Let the editors write what they will," he counseled, adding, "let them fire hot shot, or cold, but don't write poetry to them, 'intended for publication.' " He blamed women for stirring their men up and preventing peace: "The flirt of calico, and a pretty poem dedicated to our 'Lost' or 'Dead' or all of that, makes them mad, and before they are aware of it, they fall to raving, and writing, and fulminating against an indecent Congress, and a God-forsaken country."[42]

Another funeral a few months later caused federal authorities to block ceremonies in Galveston, Texas. The corpse in question belonged to Albert Sydney Johnston, a Confederate general killed in the battle of Shiloh in 1862. He had been buried in St. Louis Cemetery in New Orleans, but Texans wanted to bring his body back to the Lone Star State. Although a native of Kentucky, Johnston had moved to Texas, where he served as a war secretary for the republic before it became part of the United States. The body was disinterred in January 1867 and paraded through New Orleans accompanied by many of the top generals of the Confederacy, among them James Longstreet, Braxton Bragg, Simon Bolivar Buckner, and Richard Taylor. When Johnston's body came to Galveston, citizens there hoped to stage a funeral procession. They published a program that established the pallbearers and the order of procession, which included public dignitaries, judges, newspaper reporters, benevolent associations, and the fire department. When he saw the program, Major General Charles Griffin, in charge of the district of Texas, refused to let the march take place. "Although there is a sacredness surrounding the remains of all deceased persons which makes it exceedingly delicate to interfere with their funeral celebrations," the general stated, "it becomes my duty, owing to the position that General Johnston occupied toward the United States Government, during the latter period of his life, to forbid the funeral procession." Griffin also warned against the ringing of bells or any other popular demonstrations as the body was moved.[43] When the mayor of the city appealed to Major General Philip Sheridan, the commander of the department, he received no satisfaction. Sheridan tersely responded, "I have too much regard for the memory of the brave men who died to preserve our Government, to authorize Confederate demonstrations over the remains of any one who attempted to destroy it."[44]

Not all such ceremonies were quashed, and neither did all northerners condone sanctions against funeral processions. The *Alton Democrat* in Illinois criticized Griffin. In 1868 another funeral for a controversial Confederate officer appears to have taken place without incident. Rebel cavalry officer John Hunt Morgan, a man known for his dashing raids into the North and escape from prison, was moved to his final resting place in Lexington, Kentucky. He had a brother who also died in the conflict, and survivors used the occasion to reunite the men in death. Again the ceremony featured more military symbolism than the typical Decoration Day, with former Confederate officers serving as pallbearers. The determining factors in whether a funeral was shut down were the political sensitivities of the supervising officers, whether political circumstances appeared to be settled, and, as the case with Morgan's funeral, if it took place in a state that had remained in the Union.[45]

One of the grandest reburial efforts conducted by ladies memorial associations was the reinterment of the Confederate dead from the Gettysburg battlefield. Shortly after the war, reports filtered into southern newspapers that indicated that neglect of dead soldiers sometimes bordered on desecration of corpses. A visitor from Mississippi to the battlefield reported that the headboard of a favorite colonel was decaying and would soon totter. Many of the headboards placed by comrades over the dead suffered similarly. The person making the report added, "The field in which many of our Mississippians were buried, is to be used this year as a cattle pasture, and soon all traces of their graves will be obliterated." The letter claimed that plows were turning up the bones of Confederate dead. The columnist made the connection with northern criticism of the way southerners had cared for prisoners of war and Union dead. "Let the fiends who cry out against Confederates for ill-treatment of their prisoners and dead think of this when they charge us with cruelty and fiendishness."[46]

In 1871 the Hollywood Memorial Association dispatched Charles Dimmock to tour the battlefield, report what he found, and provide estimates on the cost of transporting the bodies to Richmond. What they learned shocked them. Dimmock claimed that he found the trench in which lay many of the men from Major General George E. Pickett's division by following a trail of bones "which had been ploughed up and now lay strewn about the surface." He reported that some farmers demanded pay for allowing Confederate soldiers to remain buried on their farms. The *Army and Navy Journal* had corroborated this account with a letter in 1867 that predicted that rebel graves would be obliterated in another year or so. "In very few cases the graves are respected, but as a general thing the ground is cultivated without regard to the remains of the misguided men who lie beneath it."[47]

At least three states became involved in trying to return the bodies to the South, but Virginia claimed the largest number of corpses, collecting roughly 3,000 during 1872. The Hollywood Memorial Association received support from the Virginia legislature with an allocation of $1,000, but the women could not raise enough money to cover all the expenses. Northerners who helped the cause eventually absorbed about $6,000 in expenses. As the first bodies returned to Richmond, the events demanded special ceremonies in which crowds gathered to watch boxes placed on wagons draped in various decorations, which included the Confederate flag. City police led the procession, which featured key military organizations from the war. Also in the procession was General George Pickett leading a band of survivors and members of the Southern Cross Brotherhood, a veterans' association.[48] This time no controversy surrounded the dedication of the Confederate section of Hollywood Cemetery. Radical Reconstruction had been averted; Conservative white leaders controlled the state. Former Confederates were free to do as they pleased with their commemorations of the Civil War.

During Reconstruction, Confederate men accepted a role secondary to that of women in commemorative events, or perhaps one can more accurately say men assumed a partnership with women to conduct a rearguard action against what appeared to be an attempt to obliterate the past. Men had little choice in taking this route. Federal officials had intervened in Decoration Days and reburial efforts enough to allow women to take the lead in mourning. The public realm had become contested space, with many actions still measured for what they revealed about loyalty to the nation. White men claimed certain parts of these civic rituals, stressing patience, service through honest labor in the Cities of the Dead, consistency in political action, commitment to the Confederate cause, and recognition that a different day would dawn. The efforts of elite women to sustain the Confederate past attracted consistent public recognition, especially for how it annoyed federal authorities. But the collaboration with women contained some discomfort for their male allies, and under certain circumstances, bitterness and sectional hostility risked being defined as feminine or unmanly if it became too sentimental. Like it or not, the new Confederate traditions invented after the Civil War rested on a foundation of womanhood. Members of the ladies memorial associations gained a new public presence with a political influence that, while somewhat altered later in the century, would not go away. The fact that these rituals had originated through women's organizations became enormously helpful later when the movement toward reconciliation fondly remembered only the gentle hand that decorated graves instead of rituals that helped forge a consensus on resistance during difficult political times.

■ ■ ■

NOT ONLY MURDER MAKES MEN

In *Black Reconstruction in America*, historian and social activist W. E. B. Du Bois mentioned the importance of military service to African Americans. They fought not only for freedom but also to prove their worth as men and citizens. This was not necessarily a new observation.

Decades earlier, Frederick Douglass and virtually every black writer had asserted the same premise: that rights as citizens would come with the demonstration that African Americans could fight in combat like white men. Du Bois, however, exposed the chilling assumption on which this definition of manhood rested. "How extraordinary," he noted, "and what a tribute to ignorance and religious hypocrisy, is the fact that in the minds of most people, even those of liberals, only murder makes men. The slave pleaded; he was humble; he protected women of the South, and the world ignored him. The slave killed white men; and behold, he was a man!" Regardless of the wisdom of building a society on such a premise, the Civil War nonetheless served, as Jim Cullen has noted, as a "watershed for black manhood," built in part on the performance of black men as soldiers in the U.S. military.[49]

Emancipation Days and other processions of African Americans stressed the new power of the freedpeople, especially through military performance that had helped win the war. Whereas Confederate memorial traditions emerged through a woman's world, black celebrations from the start assumed an assertive, male quality that announced the desire for rights based on fighting for the nation. Gone was the Sambo who fawned before white people. He was replaced by a proud figure that marched through streets in Union blue and, at least in the beginning, carried weapons. Even after bans on weaponry, paramilitary outfits continued as a staple in these events, with sabers, sashes, and uniforms of civic organizations reminding the crowds of the martial abilities of the race. Black women supported these endeavors and announced their own claim for citizenship on the public stage in more subtle, but no less important, forms.

Any composition of masculinity, however, involves more than one characteristic, and the manhood of African Americans was no exception. With due respect to Du Bois, it took more than murder to make a man. A true man in the nineteenth century needed to temper the brutish tendencies of his nature to gain recognition as a civilized being. Black leaders especially stressed this element. The concern shaped the message of many speeches in the postwar South. African Americans reinforced the need to earn respect by demonstrating proper behavior and applying oneself to moral uplift through education and manners. Giving in to passions was not considered manly, according to the code of the northern middle class. Passionate outbursts were a woman's prerogative—or, even more to the point, a trait of children. This is not to say that southern white men never erupted passionately. When provoked, men were supposed to use violence that could end even in death when honor demanded. But in the white man's world of the antebellum South, respectability had been making inroads as a new generation of privileged men signified a sea change in attitudes that favored the image of a Christian gentleman who was more sober and less inclined to violence.[50]

The image of a black man who marched proudly with weapons contained the promise of social upheaval, yet African American orations from the start were more conciliatory than those of former Confederates, promising that no matter how assertive the processions, former masters should have no fears of vengeance. A number of white people were concerned about reprisals by former slaves during the first year after the war. December 1865 in particular was an anxious time for former masters. Orators at freedom celebrations capitalized on the military prowess of black soldiers but usually tried to calm white anxiety. Speakers claimed African Americans had a generous spirit inclined toward forgiveness, and they used this conciliation as another indication of the degree of civilization among African Americans. The Emancipation Day oration of the Reverend Henry M. Turner in Augusta, Georgia, provides an illustration. During the war, he had been stationed at James River in Virginia with a group of black soldiers who had come under attack from the Confederate army. He told his listeners that the men stood their ground against three charges. What made them even more distinctive than their bravery in combat, according to Turner, was how they behaved once the shooting stopped. Turner said the black soldiers scoured the field for the wounded, collected them, transported them back to hospitals, "and treated them kindly." He then drove the point home: "The fact is, we have a better heart than the white people."[51]

Thus the phrase "black manhood" incorporated a number of characteristics. It meant the ability to protect a family by providing subsistence through industrious labor, by acting as duly lawful head of that family, and by serving as a laborer for the nation in the military. It also meant restraint in behavior—a comportment that proved the moral worth of the freedpeople as civilized beings. Brute force alone belonged to animals; civilized men exercised judgment. African Americans argued that the slave had demonstrated a remarkable compassion that revealed a nobler heart than many white neighbors and that made the freedpeople no threat to launch a race war. They were self-reliant, with the skills to make it in the world on their own as long as they had a fair start and suffered from no discrimination. They had been the most loyal element in the South, either through helping the Union military as civilians or by serving in that same army as an agent of freedom. Given the chance, they would be no different from other men, meaning that the goals for advancement were middle-class industry and independence. These multifaceted ideals could come together in a single sentence, as when Turner told his Emancipation Day crowd that the race displayed gratitude "that we, to[o], have a day reckoned in the catalogue of anniversaries, in which we can assemble, rejoice and feel our manhood."[52]

In public rituals black leaders advocated that the freedpeople accept the values of the white middle class. The strategy seemed the best way to achieve progress peacefully, yet the approach proved to be a double-edged sword. On one hand, it encouraged the formation of a black middle class—or what Glenda Gilmore more appropriately has termed the "better classes" or "best men," who enjoyed some community power and economic standing. This self-conscious, class label was not part of the first freedom celebrations, yet most black orators quickly settled on themes of frugality, industry, education, and proper public behavior as important for African Americans. Doing so provided a strong argument for the abilities to vote and hold public office, two of the public functions of men. On the other hand, appealing to racial uplift through certain class markers could limit the improvement of the race as a whole. The bar was set very high, with white people serving as the judges of achievement. If African Americans dressed well and staged elaborate processions, the white opposition decried them as inferior beings who put on airs by mimicking white people—like children dressing up and pretending to be adults. If celebrations featured rowdiness, drunkenness, or festive behavior that did not show "proper" decorum, then the race was perceived as not yet ready to assume the responsibilities of citizenship.[53]

The ingredients for manhood stressed by Emancipation Day orators thus contained a class bias that promised future tensions between black leaders and their constituencies. As the nineteenth century wore on, orations increasingly featured speakers attempting to control the behavior of black celebrants.[54] John Mercer Langston, for instance, was a popular orator at events throughout the Upper South during late 1865 and early 1866. Born a slave in Virginia, he was bequeathed to a family who went to Ohio. There he became an attorney and returned to the South to become a congressman from Virginia. Invited to speak in early 1866 at an emancipation celebration in St. Louis, Missouri, Langston noticed that most of the crowd was "representative, at least only of the upper and middling classes of the colored people." The reason partly came down to money. Organizers held the event in a hall, sent out invitations, and charged an admission of one dollar per person, which was a steep ticket price for the time. Langston's message on this anniversary of emancipation fit his audience perfectly. He "attempted to impress those lessons with respect to education, labor, thrift, forecast, economy, temperance and morality, which are indispensable to fair and permanent progress in freedom."[55] Paternalistic attitudes, no matter the race of the person expressing them, did not always elicit broad public support.

Black women entered the postwar civic ceremonies through a more traditional portal, yet here the conventional proved to be the exceptional. That they were present at all, in the same ceremonial roles as those of prewar white women, was a marked departure from antebellum practices. Their presence itself made a statement that they deserved respect as free people. During the 1860s, African American women marched in parades as members of benevolent societies and Sunday schools that reinforced the striving for moral uplift. They mirrored the activity of middle-class women whether in the North or the South by riding in liberty cars and portraying abstract principles of the nation. In Richmond's Evacuation Day ceremonies, observers commented on women lining the sidewalks and composing a majority of the crowds that gathered to view the procession's arrival to its final destination. Women's volunteer work was essential to these civic ceremonies, but their jobs were making food, wreaths, and banners. A newspaper at the time noticed the irony: "They cannot get along without the ladies, except in the procession."[56]

Women sometimes enjoyed a place in the parade—as long as it was a position that reinforced their charitable and moral nature. The July 4, 1868, procession in Greensboro, North Carolina, offers an example. Military music courtesy of a drum corps led off the procession. Immediately following were two groups of women marchers: the Daughters of Zion and the Union Benevolent Society, both identified as charitable groups within the black community. A white observer estimated that about 200 women marched under the auspices of these groups and that approximately another 100 women were sprinkled throughout the parade without apparent affiliation with either organization.[57] Through such means, black women signaled that they deserved the same treatment as white women and that—in tying their benevolent association to the name of Union—they were loyal to the United States.[58]

This claim on respectability and citizenship played itself out in everyday interactions between white and black people. If a woman was recognized as respectable, men were obligated to act in a certain way—something that black women wanted and that white men resisted. The Confederate press referred derisively to the freedwomen who tried to put on airs like white folks. A Richmond correspondent who traveled to Washington, D.C., in 1866 reported on the outrageous behavior of African Americans who "now verily believe that they are equal in the social scale to the white man." He continued to relate occurrences that would be "shocking in the extreme" to his readers. He cited a streetcar in Washington in which he saw "three strapping negro wenches sitting at ease, and displaying their gaudy paraphernalia of dress, while two *white* ladies in the same car were made to stand up. The street railroad companies cannot prevent such disgusting exhibitions as this." The correspondent attributed the companies' apathy to the fact that they owed their charters to the U.S. Congress, which was influenced by Radical Republicans. The reporter concluded that "those who would endeavour to remedy these evils . . . have now their hands tied, and can scarcely protect themselves from injury or their wives and children from insult."[59] To many former Confederates, the appearance of black women in the public arena—including civic ceremonies—was interpreted as one more sign of political subjugation.

Civic ceremonies such as Emancipation Days and Memorial Days do not reveal all of the public activity of African American women. While they followed a traditional route into freedom's celebrations, black women also took new paths to a variety of mass meetings that demonstrated their keen sense of the political moment. The work of Elsa Barkley Brown has claimed for black women an involvement in public policy that may have superseded that of white women. While this overlooks the ceremonial behavior of white women as political, the point about black political awareness and participation contains great insight. In the immediate aftermath of emancipation, the freedpeople reached decisions more collectively on a variety of matters, including what rights to argue for and what party to support with the franchise. Through records of African American congregations, Brown has found that women participated in the meetings within churches—a center of the black community—sometimes as voting members. At the least, men sought their opinions on a variety of important subjects, such as picking a minister or crafting stances on public issues. While calling this practice "internal politics," Brown argues that the collaboration continued outside church walls, overflowing into mass meetings that debated public policy. African American women crammed the balconies of important political meetings—itself an important gesture that defied past practices—and lent their voices to the proceedings. What appeared to white people as appalling behavior of inferior rabble who could not understand the decorum of such occasions actually was the reverse. These were people who knew the importance of the decisions being made and who made sure that lawmakers knew they were watching.[60]

Anyone who paid attention to the composition of the crowds at mass meetings during Reconstruction could not help but notice that African American women often formed a large portion of the participants. One such meeting in Amelia Courthouse, Virginia, was designed by opponents of the Republican Party as a hearing on why the freedpeople should not so quickly abandon their former masters. A key speaker for the opposition was Colonel F. R. Farrar, known throughout the state as "Johnny Reb" for the content of his speeches. He intended to convince the assembled that they had no fear of a race war and that they should trust the former Confederates instead of the northern Republicans to lead them in these new circumstances. A black man named John Oliver challenged these assertions. He reminded the group, "There are two great parties in this country. One—the Republicans—freed you. They are the friends of liberty. The other is the Democratic, whose principles are in every respect opposed to the spirit of freedom. If the latter is successful, the old state of things will be revived; and all must deplore that as an evil above consideration." The report on the proceedings noted that about 200 African Americans had assembled to hear the remarks, "a large proportion of the assemblage being women of color, who seemed to take an unusual interest in the affairs of the nation." At a similar meeting held near Richmond in April, a crowd of about 75 African Americans gathered to hear the Reverend James Hunnicutt press support for the Republican cause. Of those participants, 50 were females and 25 were males.[61] These statistics reaffirms that African American women had a political consciousness of their own, and that black men recognized that their partners digested and conveyed information that helped them reach decisions on important issues of the day.

The public expression of black womanhood, especially as it concerned the commemorations of the Civil War, differed from that of white womanhood. The civic celebrations of black people suggested that black women followed in the footsteps of middle-class respectability, with the expectation of receiving the deference due to their sex. They equated femininity with religion and morality through their association with benevolent societies and Sunday schools. But theirs was a far more assertive womanhood, too, indicative of their lives, which often required them to perform the work of black men or lower-class white women. Beyond the processions for freedom days, they appeared in public spaces where many white women did not tread, and they helped shape public policy beyond the ceremonial. They also associated themselves with the role of defense that was typically a man's domain. The sensitive political situation during Reconstruction sometimes demanded that guards protect the assembly from intruders who might try to take weapons inside to open fire on the crowd. On a number of occasions, women were encountered patrolling outside while men deliberated inside. By the 1870s, black women sometimes formed ceremonial militia units that drilled with mock weapons so they could march on important occasions, such as Emancipation Day.[62] No equivalent of this behavior existed in the white community. Finally, black women were eager to embrace the Union and prove themselves as loyal citizens—a stark contrast from the Confederate women who brushed past occupying soldiers with averted eyes and who did their level best to perpetuate the spirit that had tried to tear apart the Union.

The remembrances of war and freedom also contained contrasting images of manhood. For former Confederates, the Decoration Day events did not—during Reconstruction—feature men as killers for the nation-state but as patient, civilian laborers who helped women care for the dead and did their best to endure the current circumstances. Women were blamed by the opposition for carrying on political resistance. Black events, on the other hand, prominently broadcast the martial abilities of the marchers, as well as their gentility. The Confederate ceremonies perpetuated hostility toward the Union government, while the black events bound themselves to that government. Ironically, both ceremonies stressed the need of the men to labor. Ex-Confederates wondered whether young men in particular would embrace work as a means of dictating worth in a world that no longer guaranteed the mastery of white gentlemen over slaves. White and black speakers at Emancipation Days underscored the need for black men to prove themselves by showing they could earn their keep. Idleness remained a condition to avoid in either case, although for the white race the existence of loafers would be attributed to individuals with bad morals, while for the black race it was considered the norm that might never be overcome.

Throughout the decades after the war, these definitions had consequences that went hand in glove with setting the limits of freedom. No one at the time knew what might be lost or gained. If African American males were considered men, and especially free men, then these same males argued that they deserved the rights and privileges of a citizen. That included a right to education, a right to sit in jury boxes, a right to choose work as a free person, a right to marry and keep a family together, a right to ride in streetcars without sitting in a particular section, a right to walk down a street and have a white person at least occasionally turn to give easy passage, and a right to live anywhere one wanted. If they were truly women, then African American females should enjoy a certain kind of treatment that included respect for their sex. They deserved a right to have men give way to them on streets, a right to have access to public accommodations, a right to be educated, a right to work—all of this and more, even if they did not have the right to vote. Freedom celebrations announced this agenda and reinforced a common interpretation of these notions in a time when an active street culture still formed a basis for politics.

■ ■ ■

It is significant that Confederate identity took shape in the postwar world through the domestic hands and space of women. Because the politics of Reconstruction had forced commemorations of war into the cemeteries, the Confederacy could be remembered as something less threatening than it might have been, and thus reunion with the North was made easier. Sectional reconciliation would have come anyway, but it might have traveled a more difficult road if the Confederate traditions had emerged through veterans marching with weapons in proud defiance of the nation that had just defeated them. Our own appreciation of these events might be different if the nation today thought of southern whites as having been less inclined to give their hearts to the Union. Filtering Decoration Days through a woman's domain made it easier for people to forget the bitterness behind these early occasions and to recall them as benign rituals of mourning to help a nation heal. It was truly stunning how quickly people were coming to this conclusion. In 1873, for instance, a person touring the South stopped at the memorial ceremonies in Hollywood Cemetery. He observed the monuments, the militia regiments, and the solemn procession of thousands of women in black walking among the graves. Rarely did he hear a speech or see emblems of the Lost Cause. He concluded that the grief had been too deep and the cemetery "too sacred to be associated with the vulgar details of politics."[63] If only he had watched more closely for a longer time.

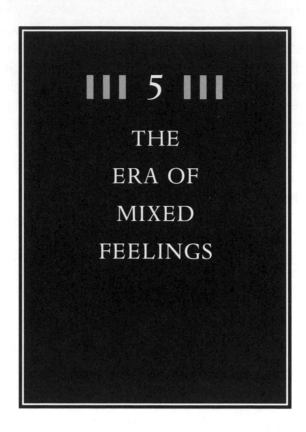

III 5 III

THE
ERA OF
MIXED
FEELINGS

Ten years after the Civil War, people throughout the country noticed a
changing mood between the sections. In 1875 Congressman William D.
Kelley of Pennsylvania returned from a six-week tour of the South convinced that the North had little cause to fear its former enemies. At a
Confederate Decoration Day ceremony in Augusta County, Virginia, the
onetime Radical Republican watched men and women pay tribute to dead
soldiers while accompanied by a band from a U.S. infantry unit. Kelley
heard no taunts, insults, or complaints from the crowd leveled at the
troops—proof to him that military occupation was no longer needed. The
black press acknowledged similar behavior among former rebels. An item
in the *People's Advocate* headlined "Southern Good Feeling" marveled at
southern whites attending the burial of a U.S. naval officer in New Orleans
during 1876. Black men petitioned the governor of Virginia in 1875 to
march in the parade for the unveiling of the statue to Stonewall Jackson,
and the state of South Carolina returned the captured flag of the 54th

Massachusetts, the unit that had helped to prove the combat capabilities of African Americans. The commemorations of war and freedom seemed to symbolize a new spirit among ex-Confederates, with the decoration of graves encouraging both sides to clasp hands across what had been a bloody chasm.[1]

Although newspaper editors interpreted these events as signs of an era of good feelings, the 1870s remained a decade of mixed sentiments. Political and sectional animosities kept wholehearted reconciliation at bay. Former soldiers from North and South may have gathered periodically for reunions, but these were sporadically attended and, in any case, did not prevent Union veterans from opposing ex-Confederates for national office.[2] Former Confederates did show a greater willingness to make peace with the North during the mid-1870s, but the literature of reunion, with rare exception, has overlooked the political reasons behind this stand. Ex-Confederates reached across the bloody chasm to protect their hold on regional power, adopting accommodation so authorities would not have reason to intervene in southern affairs and would let the best white men govern. Some also believed they could not rebuild the South without the help of northern capital. With the centennial in 1876, white southerners began to celebrate July Fourth once again, but it was not because they had become converted nationalists. They used the anniversary to bolster regional instead of national importance. In fact, the 1870s featured ex-Confederates resurrecting the veteran on Memorial Days as part of a resurging sectional pride. Conciliation may have existed, but it masked a greater concern with consolidating home rule than in creating a unified national home.

After 1877 ex-Confederates still had not completely won the battle for power in the South, even with the end of Reconstruction and the symbolic withdrawal of federal troops. Problems continued for white leaders, which C. Vann Woodward noted in his seminal study of the post-Reconstruction era. If black power was held in check and foreign control eliminated, Woodward asked, what would become the basis of white unity? More recently, Michael Perman has observed that the end of Reconstruction may have overturned Republican governments, but it left intact the franchise for black people, which created ongoing problems for Democrats. "Even though the Republicans no longer controlled any of the state governments in the South after 1877," Perman observes, "their party was still part of the electoral system, as were the newly created and mobilized voters." After 1877 the floodgates opened, with independent movements undermining the Democratic Party in most of the former Confederacy. The maneuvering by the electorate contained the worst fears of the white power structure. Several biracial coalitions formed, and one in Virginia mounted a successful challenge for the governor's office. Even Republicans were not exempt from the need to keep their houses in order. Black people at times supported Democratic candidates for governor in a variety of states in the South. There was enough drift from the main parties on the part of both whites and blacks to make post-Reconstruction a time of political fluidity, or what one historian has termed "plasticity," when the "political system as a whole was therefore malleable, mutable, and open to change and reorganization."[3]

Woodward concluded that the redeemers' solution to the problem of post-Reconstruction white unity was a heightened emphasis not only on racism but also on tradition.[4] This had an effect on Civil War commemorations that most scholars have overlooked. With the specter of third-party movements, orators at Confederate Memorial Days increasingly invoked the common sacrifices of white southerners during the war as one basis for unity among classes. Instead of general officers, the common soldier became an important focus. If northern Republicans waved a bloody shirt to oppose placing Confederates in national office, southern white orators unfurled the empty sleeve to remind their constituents that whatever honor ancestors had won through bloody sacrifice would be desecrated by desertion from the correct political cause. This was not the only reason for a shift toward the common soldier in civic traditions, but the crippled veteran provided a compelling image for white Democrats determined to block cooperation between white and black people.

On the black side of the commemorative divide, the political situation caused orators at Emancipation Days to become even more assertive about the need for African American independence. This was not to be confused with an attempt to promote separatism or black nationalism. Speakers simply pressed more urgently the need for the race to prove its self-reliance. Doubts about the Republican Party crept into Emancipation Day addresses, to the extent that Frederick Douglass felt it necessary to remind black people why the Grand Old Party (GOP) deserved loyalty. The 1885 inauguration of Glover Cleveland further underscored the need for black political unity as former Confederates marched in the parade in honor of the first Democrat elected to the presidency since 1856.

■ ■ ■

THE POLITICS OF RECONCILIATION

Even during the time of greatest sectional antipathy, politics served as a two-edged sword for reconciliation. Paul Buck's classic *Road to Reunion* saw partisanship as needlessly holding hostage the consolidation of the nation and the burial of sectional animosities until the 1880s. While true to a large extent, the argument ignores the manner in which politics encouraged reconciliation, even in the most problematic decade immediately after the Civil War. David Blight has been more perceptive on this count, although he has not fully explored this dimension. He correctly notes that most Republicans neither opposed reunion nor shared the goal of Frederick Douglass to "thwart the reconciliationist legacy until the emancipationist legacy could be permanently secured." But he passes over the extent of the political underpinnings for reconciliation sentiment within two influential groups: Radical Republicans (beyond Horace Greeley) and Conservative southerners who at times reached out even to black people to preserve their dominion in the former Confederacy.[5]

Northern white people in general wanted reunification with the white South—urgently and more rapidly than the supporters of the Confederacy. This was the war aim that brought together Democrats and Republicans alike. When Grant assumed office in 1869, he stressed peace between the sections in his inaugural address. Even the many Republicans who championed antislavery often took this position to validate the ideals of free labor and representative democracy rather than because they shared priorities with black people. Many were nation builders who bid good riddance to slavery because it had propped up a planter aristocracy, demeaned the dignity of white labor, held down the wages of working men, limited the advancement of poor white people in general, served as an antiquated and immoral system that prevented the country from achieving its full potential, or made American claims for freedom appear hypocritical in the eyes of the world. Reaching across the bloody chasm to white ex-soldiers had been a continuous part of the northern psyche from 1861 on. A peaceful, reconstructed South provided the capstone of the northern war effort—proof that a democracy could survive.

While northern Democrats who hoped to rebuild their national strength were reaching the fastest and farthest across the chasm, they were not alone. Republicans shared in the desire for a possible coalition with white southerners. The party was not that old, having elected its first president in 1860 on roughly 40 percent of the popular vote. As Michael Holt has argued, the party was founded on principles that made leaders unsure it could survive the Civil War. Republicans had been antislavery and antisouthern since their inception. With slavery gone as a common cause, some Republicans considered a political realignment and the rise of new parties as a logical step, one that may have caused the demise of the antebellum and wartime arrangement. Leaders of the party held varied sentiments about the degree of cooperation to solicit from former enemies, but especially in the first couple years of freedom, when black people did not have the vote, they pondered whether their future depended on reaching across the sectional divide to white people who had been loyal or at least neutral during the war, as well as those willing to accept the congressional plan for Reconstruction. Holt argues that the dynamic within southern politics for the first decade after the war featured "conscious attempts to bring about a realignment that benefited former Whig politicians and programs and prevented a polarization of politics along racial lines."[6]

Even the hard-liners in the party—or the Radicals—had reasons for reaching across the bloody chasm. Some Radicals wanted a party that was not sectional. One of the most prominent northern Radicals who advocated reconciliation with former Confederates may be one of the least appreciated in this regard. Salmon P. Chase, former secretary of the treasury under Lincoln and chief justice of the Supreme Court in Reconstruction, had been an influential reformer and antislavery advocate from the antebellum period. He had pushed Lincoln for emancipation and counseled President Johnson to support black suffrage. After the war, Chase favored universal suffrage and amnesty, meaning that both black people and former Confederates should exercise the vote. While it was appropriate to deny suffrage to a small slaveocracy who had been responsible for the war—especially if they might interfere with Reconstruction—it was important for the South to function as a democracy. Continued military oppression contradicted the belief in self-determination. Like many, Chase hoped for restoration of political rights for former Confederates and regretted that the Fourteenth Amendment had disfranchised rebels who might be "serviceable candidates and efficient helpers." His leniency toward white southerners had conditions. They needed to accept the end of slavery, allow for universal education, grant suffrage to black people, and operate an impartial judicial system. They could not work against the government, discriminate against black people because of race, or use violence. Anyone who worked against peace and prosperity, according to Chase, should lose the rights of citizenship. To Chase, giving black men the vote armed them with a weapon against injustice and mitigated the need for extensive military presence.[7]

This brand of lenience by no means appealed to a host of former Confederates. The *Southern Opinion*, a Richmond newspaper that considered itself one of the disseminators of the Confederate tradition, certainly did not rank the chief justice among its friends. In 1868 the editor ran mock toasts in honor of the Fourth of July, an occasion that ex-Confederates refused to celebrate. Toast number ten began, "Eternal hatred to Chief Justice Chase." The positions that Chase advocated smacked of a revolution that could lead to social as well as political equality.[8]

The chief justice was not alone in seeing no contradiction between advancing black rights while promoting leniency with the right kind of white southerner. These people combined the emancipationist / reconciliationist memories of the war defined by historian David Blight. Or perhaps they could not be defined precisely by either. Horace Greeley and Gerrit Smith had been prominent abolitionists. Editor of the *New York Tribune*, Greeley had been famous for castigating Lincoln during the war for moving too slowly on emancipation. Like Chase, Greeley placed enormous faith in impartial suffrage as a means of protecting black people in the South. He also considered that white southerners would accept their situation more easily if they understood that black voting was a condition for the restoration of their own political rights. Greeley advocated good relations between African Americans and white people, stressing that both needed to be on board if Reconstruction were to succeed.[9]

Gerrit Smith saw little purpose in punishing the powerless. He wrote Chase in May 1866 to ask for leniency for Jefferson Davis in proceedings that the chief justice was about to administer. Seven years earlier Smith had funded John Brown's raid on Harpers Ferry; now he pressed for reconciliation. The South, he told Chase, had suffered enough in the war. Because the Confederacy was treated like a nation during the conflict— with prisoners returned and the belligerent status of the blockade in effect—he considered it wrong to try men in other than civil courts or to hold them accountable for treason. Plus, there were repercussions to consider. If the government hanged one man for treason, then it had to hang them all, which could lead to an awful purge of blood that might reawaken the rebellion. Instead, Smith urged peace and reconciliation.[10] Chase was sympathetic although not in agreement with Smith's legal interpretations. He also had additional reasons for suggesting peaceful relations with agreeable white southerners. He considered a run for the presidency—on the Democratic ticket. He did not press for a trial for Jefferson Davis. Greeley eventually posted bail for the ex-president, while Smith was one of the signatories for the bail bond.

The point is not to argue that these men represented the Republicans or the Radicals, but to demonstrate that reconciliation could be a goal even among those holding an emancipationist view of the Civil War. The same motivations that drew men to antislavery could push them toward advocating a peaceful reunion with their enemies. They might hold humanitarian sympathies for the oppressed or defeated, political aspirations to break the backs of the slave power by raising up white common folk or to have the nation live up to its professed ideals of freedom, or economic visions for a free-labor society and profitable enterprises in the South. A predominant ideal was restoration of the Union, which meant reaching out to southern white people as well as African Americans. Black people were to help themselves through hard work and good citizenship, including serving as an informed electorate. Although Radicals like Thaddeus Stevens envisioned the war as a means for bringing about greater change in society, most northern whites wanted restoration of the Union, an end to slavery, and peace between the sections. Even the most diligent supporters of emancipation and suffrage for African Americans believed that ex-Confederates should have political rights—provided they did not disrupt the other goals for Reconstruction.

Others, of course, did not feel so sympathetic to the men who had tried to kill them. Greeley provoked criticism for his benevolence toward Jefferson Davis and his calls for leniency. Additionally, many veterans held mixed feelings about their former enemies. They were pleased with reunion of the country, especially their sacrifice to save the Great Experiment in republicanism, and might even have respect for the men in gray who had survived the same ordeal by fire. This did not mean they sought reconciliation. These men happily waved the bloody shirt in elections for the next three decades. Many were sympathetic to the white men who blocked the decoration of graves by southern women at Arlington in 1869.

For obvious political reasons, Democrats were the most avid about building bridges with former Confederates. They needed southerners to defeat the Republican Party. In the 1868 presidential election, William S. Rosecrans, who had been a major general for the Union in the western theater of war, made overtures to military and political leaders of the former Confederacy. Even though Grant—the Union's greatest hero of the war—ran as the Republican candidate, northern Democrats believed they could defeat him with southern help. During the summer before the election, Rosecrans visited White Sulphur Springs in Virginia to canvass the ex-Confederates at the resort. Among the military and civil officers of the fallen government was Robert E. Lee, who cosigned with thirty or so former Confederates a document that presented their prescription for reunion. The document stressed that the best course for restoring southern peace and prosperity lay with restoration of the white leaders who had prevailed before the war. The North could leave southern affairs safely in the hands of the old guard because they accepted the end of slavery and it was in their best interests to promote peace. The group admitted it opposed political power for African Americans but attributed this to the belief that black people were not ready to exercise the franchise. Lee and his comrades claimed that they only wanted a "restoration of their rights under the Constitution," "relief from oppressive misrule," and the "right of self-government."[11]

Although it failed to affect the election, the White Sulphur Springs letter contained the precursor to the position of white southern moderates who appeared the most congenial toward reunion. Many of these men joined a movement that created the Conservative Party from former Whigs, moderate Democrats, and even disaffected Republicans—virtually anyone who opposed Radical policies or was upset with southern affairs. The party did not appeal to the most reactionary people; its adherents were fairly progressive in advocating the rebuilding of the South with the tools of northern capitalism. Although they were white supremacists, they preached peaceful reunion. The most recalcitrant rebels were traditionalists such as former lieutenant general Jubal Anderson Early who wanted to restore the antebellum order and tended to be less sanguine about cooperating with the North. The Conservative leadership accepted the terms of the government for reconstruction, with the proviso that former Confederate leaders avoided disfranchisement under new state constitutions. Unlike the signers of the White Sulphur Springs letter, they promised to cooperate with black suffrage and to restore peace in the South by having the "best men" maintain order between the white and black masses. They adopted a conciliatory posture with the North less from a wholehearted love of Union than as a political strategy to hold off greater social and political revolution.[12]

Similar movements occurred in other southern states beyond the

Old Dominion. In what was referred to as the New Departure, anti-Republicans throughout the region shared the opinion that the best course was to acquiesce in black civil and political equality to prevent disfranchisement of white people. Tennessee and Virginia were the first to capitalize on the strategy. In the case of the Old Dominion, Grant was receptive to these men as he struggled with an increasingly violent South. If the Conservatives fulfilled their end of the bargain, then the federal government would allow franchisement of the white electorate. Unrestricted suffrage for white people virtually guaranteed a Conservative victory in the elections for state offices. Through this means, Virginia avoided a Republican administration as the Conservatives came to power in the elections of 1869, winning the governorship, a majority of seats in the general assembly, and other key state offices.[13]

True to their word, Conservatives asked black people to join their movement. It was the smart thing to do. If it succeeded, the "best men" benefited from a divided black electorate and from containing the opposition. If it failed, they could claim they had tried to fulfill their pledge of responsible, civic stewardship while blaming African Americans for rejecting the olive branch. Conservative leaders encouraged black members throughout the party's ten-year existence. Hunnicutt, the former Radical Republican, changed parties in 1869 and counseled black people to vote for the Conservative candidate and against the disfranchisement of white people. Organizers in Richmond staged biracial barbecues to prove their good intentions, and the state organization openly endorsed Daniel M. Norton, a black leader on the peninsula, for a congressional seat.[14]

This is not to say that black people and Conservative leaders laid their differences aside. The new coalition recognized the dominance of white men, and its leaders easily resorted to racial baiting. Black people also faced violent repression in the Old Dominion. Historian Jack Maddex has identified this coalition quite correctly as "a paternalistic white supremacist party that presented itself to white voters as embodying the 'expressed will' of this race and welcomed black voters on the basis of their 'true interest.'"[15] Paternalistic notions did not stop at racial borders. White supremacy also meant supremacy over undeserving white people. Overall, the position of these men paralleled northerners who—like Chase, Greeley, and Grant—advocated universal suffrage as long as peace, stability, and justice were preserved.

Why African Americans supported such a party can be hard to fathom. Although a majority did not, some aligned with the Conservative movement because white Republicans were equally paternalistic or they were disgusted by the political corruption and lack of voice in setting organizational policies. In Richmond during the summer of 1873, black Republicans gathered to express their anger with the direction of the party. They had grown impatient for full equality and peace. The participants at the conference claimed that Republicans maintained antipathy between the races to benefit themselves by preventing black people from joining the Democrats. They disliked the control of the white leadership who did not consult African Americans on decisions affecting candidates and platforms. The black men at this convention asked for harmony between the races and equality before the law.[16]

The issue at hand, though, is not to offer a detailed examination of southern politics but to show how these complicated, shifting positions were part of public commemorations of the Civil War. Even though hardly dominant, the themes of reconciliation were found even during the height of sectional enmity in the immediate aftermath of the war. Former Confederates sometimes decorated the graves of the Union soldiers.[17] Similarly, orators or newspaper editors once in a while mentioned the respect that existed between former enemies who had suffered the common hardships of combat, as well as the common suffering by civilians who lost loved ones. As mentioned earlier, the ceremonies of freedom and memorialization had begun with reunion, but not necessarily reconciliation, in mind. A couple of things had to happen before greater sympathy between the sections became more apparent. First, the South had to appear to be a stable part of the United States, with state governments that upheld the demise of slavery, the primacy of the national government, and the suffrage of black men. In other words, the South had to accept enough of the North's terms for defeat so that every public gesture was not viewed as subversion. Second, the Confederate veteran had to be rehabilitated from a rebel who had killed good northern boys to an example of courageous duty, or at least no longer a reminder of painful loss.

■ ■ ■

THE LOYAL CONFEDERATE

Confederate traditions flexed more military muscle once federal controls eased. With the new regimes, northern confidence had grown that the political situation had stabilized enough that former Confederates were not going to start another rebellion. The ceremonies of the 1870s no longer presented the same threat that they had in the immediate postwar years. The processions that once had been restricted during Confederate Memorial Days now filled the streets in an assertive celebration of the heroes of the war. Women did not disappear from the proceedings, but leadership slowly and steadily gravitated toward males. Men cooperated with the ladies memorial associations and remembered to single out the women for their preservation of the past, but the veteran was on his way to gaining the limelight in the ceremonies for the Cities of the Dead.

Organizers of Confederate Memorial Days nevertheless tiptoed through sensitive areas as their commemorations underwent transformations linked to political currents of the 1870s and early 1880s. The strategy to trade reconciliation for political advantages was part of the Confederate ceremonial mentality. The reassertion of pride in the Confederate past had to coexist with assimilation into the nation. The prudent among the leadership of the Conservative South counseled against excessive displays of Confederate paraphernalia to prevent giving Republicans additional reasons to wave the bloody shirt at elections. Until the end of Reconstruction, the ceremonies had to lionize the Confederate soldier while leaving the door open for reunification, or at least to present why the infatuation with rebels did not jeopardize better sectional relations. In the process, orators and newspaper columnists stripped the veteran of politics, linking him neither to a war for slavery nor to a desire to establish a different government.

Virginia provides a good place for a glimpse into the grassroots beginning of the evolution of the Confederate tradition, especially how it asserted new military pride by creating the patriotic Confederate while carefully negotiating the waters of reunion. Although many scholars have featured the more hostile sentiments of die-hard rebels such as Early, the residents of the Old Dominion actually enjoyed a rather moderate reputation in the North because of the Conservative Party. Augusta County contained leaders who were important to the origins of the party. Alexander H. H. Stuart had served as president of the party's first convention; John B. Baldwin wrote the blueprint for the organizational framework. Stuart had been one of the people who approached Grant to allow ex-Confederates to protect the franchise and prevent the Republican Party from taking power. Moderate men lived not only in the Valley but elsewhere in the state, and they often wanted to get on with life and rebuild the South. They included veterans who had held high command and who opposed the stubbornness of their more reactionary fellow officers.

Although the most striking change in the 1870s was the way soldiers came to dominate the proceedings, this transition was not always abrupt. Early in the decade women still directed the memorial events in partnership with civic societies. In 1871 the Knights Templar, a fraternal organization involved with temperance, led the procession to Thornrose Cemetery. The Stonewall Band came next, but Confederate veterans filled the middle of the parade behind the local fire company and benevolent and fraternal organizations. Even students from the School for the Deaf, Dumb, and Blind were in line ahead of veterans. Soldiers marched as a collective rather than in their former, discrete military units. The pattern was remarkably similar around the state, with a mix of female and male organizations.[18] One consequence of the participation of these groups in Decoration Days was the virtual guarantee that the speeches of orators addressed an audience from a broad spectrum of classes, making them the perfect forum for politicians and community leaders. The organizations in processions included fire companies, Sunday schools, upper-class businessmen's associations, women's schools, and recipients of public charity. In Lynchburg members of the mechanics association and the typographical society had a place in memorial processions. Decoration Days drew spectators from a wide range of town residents, including the white working class.

The rising prominence of veterans was encouraged by legislation. Once the Conservative Party gained control of the general assembly in Virginia, legislators passed laws to allow the kind of celebrations that had been prohibited under Reconstruction. It would be only a matter of time before the Confederate veteran made a bolder showing. The editor of the *Richmond Enquirer* noted, "Many a long and weary year has passed since we saw 'our bold soldier boys' marching through the streets of this good old city. But they are coming, a portion of the things of old times is coming again, and we shall soon see in uniform many of those gallant boys and men who stood in the front of battle for old Virginia." The columnist added that it was a welcome sight to see the reorganization of the volunteers in their uniforms. "Let us encourage them in every way," he declared, then added so that all would know of the changed circumstances, "they are being organized under the laws of the State, and there is no hindrance whatever to their doing so."[19]

The veterans did come. By 1877 the procession in Staunton had assumed a military form organized by three divisions. Soldiers from the Civil War had moved from behind most of the civic organizations to the front of the procession, with the Stonewall Brigade Band, Staunton military companies, visiting units, and ex-Confederate soldiers in general con-stituting the First Division. Civic associations and the fire companies had moved to the Second Division, while the women and schools fell into the Third Division. Once at the cemetery, the infantry and artillery conducted salutes. By the end of the decade the new pattern was well established, with the band, military companies, and veterans leading the parade. The soldiers had covered a great distance since the 1860s, going from near invisibility to becoming the focus of the Confederate traditions.[20]

The message of reconciliation in Confederate ceremonies was de-signed, in part, to answer criticism that these events prevented sectional fusion. Even late in the decade, some northerners saw the Confederate Memorial Days as fostering ill will against the Republican Party. The Decoration Day events through the 1870s tried to honor the Confederate soldier while showing why that soldier now served as an asset to the nation. Answering the call of duty, a number of speakers stressed, was an American virtue and a gauge by which one might measure the trust-worthiness of a person. A speech in Staunton at the 1878 Confederate Memorial Day ceremony made the point especially well. The orator, Captain H. L. Hoover, tried to allay northern concerns that the cere-monies signified a challenge to the "dominant" party, meaning the Re-publicans. On the contrary, the speaker argued, loyalty to the Confederate past did not mean disloyalty to the Union. "No, sir," said Hoover, "there is nothing in the warmest devotion to home, country, or State, or section, at all inconsistent with the utmost loyalty to this Union. Our pride, then, in the soldierly conduct of our own boys is not only pardonable indulgence, but an honest and natural expression of our own patriotism." Acknowl-edging the presence of veterans on the other side of the chasm, Hoover indicated that critics of these celebrations suggested that the messages offended the Republican Party. "But be it ever remembered," he argued, "that he who is not loyal to his own friend, dead or living, to his own people and his own section, whether defeated or victorious, is not and can not be loyal to anything else in this world." In other words, if a person had been untrue to his own section in the war, he likely would be so again. But because the Confederate soldier had fought for a principle, he would remain faithful once he gave his word to support a different government.[21]

The unveiling of the John H. Foley statue to Stonewall Jackson in Richmond gives further insight into the passive-aggressive nature of the reconciliation movement among ex-Confederates. The governor granted permission to African Americans to march in the procession in order to undercut Republican reasons for waving the bloody shirt. The man making this decision was James Kemper, who had served as a general officer in the Army of Northern Virginia. He worked hard to stage a ceremony that represented the Conservative position of friendliness toward black people and peaceful rule by moderate white men within the South. Yet behind the scenes one Confederate general fought another over the symbolism of this celebration, in the process revealing how many in the South viewed the political ramifications of public rituals.

Nearly 50,000 people gathered for the unveiling of the monument in Capitol Square in Richmond on October 26, 1875. Coming ten years after the war and taking place in the former capital of the Confederacy, the ceremony was rife with political significance, especially because it fell near the end of Reconstruction when much of the white South tried to redeem the region from Republican governments.[22] Black militia companies and ministers had petitioned Kemper for a place in the ceremonies because Jackson, a fervent Presbyterian, had sponsored a Sunday school for black children. He taught them to read the Bible despite Virginia's having outlawed education for the enslaved. Early castigated the governor, calling him a Judas for allowing black people to participate. Early and Kemper shared similar military experiences, yet they reveal the divided mind within the Conservative Party. Early was suspicious of reconciliation. Kemper represented the mainstream of the party, aware that northern eyes scanned the celebration for what it revealed about political relations in the South. Of the two, Kemper represented the electoral majority of the state.

Both men demonstrated different approaches to African Americans: exclusion on the part of Early versus containment by Kemper. Early charged that African Americans wanted to exploit the event for their own purposes. He feared they would carry pictures of Lincoln or placards in honor of the Fifteenth Amendment and was worried that granting them permission to march would indicate that the men who organized the affair supported racial mixing. Kemper rejected such logic. He maintained that if Early was concerned with racial mixing, he would do better to let African Americans join the procession, where they would have a place assigned—near the end of the march, following the various fraternal and civic associations. Otherwise, Kemper warned, black people could enter the square near the front and provide a more racially mixed crowd. "By forming them as they request," Kemper added, the "audience will have very far fewer Negroes in it than would be there in case of no such formation." He added that every other Confederate soldier he had consulted about this had had no objection. Neither did the press.[23]

What was really on Kemper's mind, however, was his hope that the ceremony not give Republicans something to use against him during the elections. On October 11 the governor told Early point-blank, "Our Democratic friends North express great anxiety that nothing shall happen on the 26th to hurt the party. They say [Oliver P.] Morton & Co. [a Republican senator from Indiana] would pay half million to get some of our boys to tear down and trample on the U.S. Flag on that day." Kemper hoped to stifle attempts by former Confederates to wear their old uniforms. He had heard that Rooney Lee, son of Robert E. Lee, had planned to have people dressed in their Confederate gray and carrying battle flags. Kemper wanted none of this. "I beseech you," he wrote Early, "to write me a letter advising against all that sort of thing." He added, "I somewhat fear trouble." In a different letter on October 26, the governor showed he was quite aware that northern Republicans intently observed the proceedings for signs that Confederate sentiment remained stronger than that for Union. An event of this kind "is not only pleasing and appropriate honor to Jackson's memory" but was "best calculated to vindicate our White people against Radical lies that are told and used to our hurt and will have a good effect upon our own political relations as well as the general political relations of the country."[24] Once African Americans learned of the discord, most of the groups, except some black men who had been slaves of soldiers in the Stonewall Brigade during the war, backed out of the event.

In Kemper's exchange with Early we can see that those who orchestrated public events in the nineteenth century assessed their impact and symbolism. The content of parades mattered. It was not the quibbling of small minds to debate who should march in a procession and in what position. These affairs transmitted multiple messages to a variety of audiences, even if individuals in the crowd had no such intentions. National political affairs—especially the attempt to reconstruct a Democratic Party that had a chance to defeat Republicans—caused former Confederates to adopt a conciliatory posture that, as often as not, was not yet heartfelt but intended to aid their quest for home rule.

This strategy played a role in another, more widespread celebration of national life that at first appeared to be an effort at sectional reconciliation. The same year that Virginia dedicated the first statue of a public figure from the Confederacy, the nation was in the midst of celebrating its 100th birthday by commemorating the adoption of the Declaration of Independence. Even British observers noticed the new mood in the United States. The American correspondent for the *Times* of London felt obliged to comment in 1875 at what he saw at Decoration Days in the United States. "A very good feature of the celebration this year was the intermingling of the Federal and Confederate soldiers in the Southern cities. Both united in many places in decorating graves indiscriminately, and the services were calculated to smooth the asperities left by the war." Some speakers tried to make the case that Decoration Day itself belonged to neither section, but to the nation. In the midst of the problems of Reconstruction, depression, and rising unrest in general, northerners particularly could see the benefits of reunion to the country and the role of the Civil War in fusing a new spirit. "It is not only a Union of States, but a union of hearts that is wanted to make us great and strong as a nation," noted the *Philadelphia Inquirer*, "and there is no surer path to reach a perfect Union than over the ashes of the soldiers of the rebellion."[25]

The passing of time allowed some good feelings to surface. Ten years had passed since the war, and a number of people had tired of the sectional baiting that had gone on for decades. Some people obviously wanted to lay the past to rest and forge a new nation that could prosper domestically and internationally. Soldiers who had fought in the conflict looked upon their old days more fondly, with the first inklings of nostalgia that became more prevalent in the 1880s. Additionally, the idea was growing that many in the South had paid for their transgressions. Northerners who toured the region returned with sympathetic reports of a populace still bearing the burden of the conflict. In New Orleans, Edward King saw a people characterized by discouragement. "These are not of the loud-mouthed and bitter opponents of everything tending to reconsolidate the Union . . . but they are the payers of the price." He did not expect that discouragement to lift soon, "because the wearers know that the great evils of disorganized labor, impoverished society, scattered families, race legislation, retributive tyranny and terrorism, with the power . . . to wither and blast, leave no hope for this generation. Heaven have mercy on them!"[26]

The 1875 commemorations of the outbreak of hostilities between Americans and the British seemed to forecast the end of bitterness. Virginians and South Carolinians attended the ceremonies in Massachusetts. Fitzhugh Lee, a cavalry commander and the nephew of Robert E. Lee, was accompanied by the Norfolk Light Artillery Blues and some South Carolinians. Walter Taylor, who had served on the staff of Robert E. Lee, made the trip as well. The presence of these men was significant. Not only were prominent members of the rebellion appearing on a northern stage with their former enemies, but the composition of the group represented key regions of the colonial alliance: Virginia, South Carolina, and Massachusetts. Northerners treated their southern visitors respectfully. Southerners returned the favor by stressing the common heritage of the two sections. At night Lee and the South Carolinians went to a reception held by the mayor, at which the governor of Massachusetts extended the welcome. After a representative from the South Carolina contingent spoke, the listeners applauded and rose to their feet as the band played "Dixie."

When Lee went to the podium, he sounded the themes that were becoming popular among ex-Confederates most inclined toward reconciliation. He observed that "when I reflect that I am an American citizen, and that I, too, am a descendent of those men who fought on Bunker Hill, I feel that I, too, have a right to be here to celebrate their splendid deeds." A portion of the address touched on the symbolism of Memorial Days and the practice of decorating graves. The former general claimed that he and his fellow southerners demonstrated by their presence "that we are fully in sympathy with the sentiment which found expression upon recent decoration days, when loving hands entwined beautiful flowers about the graves of soldiers of both armies, without distinction." Were an enemy either foreign or domestic to threaten the United States, Lee believed that "Massachusetts and Virginia, California and Florida, would shout with one voice, 'if they desire to fight let them have enough.' "[27]

Not everyone in the South appreciated Lee's journey to Massachusetts. Traditionalists like Early believed that the visit was ill timed and smacked of fraternizing with the enemy. Opponents worried that Lee would accept any overtures from northerners without discrimination, possibly putting the Confederate South at a political disadvantage. Lee himself noted that he had received a great deal of criticism in southern newspapers. Some called him a turncoat and alleged that he was trying to gain visibility that he could translate into political support for a run for the U.S. Senate. He wrote Early that "the majority of our people condemn my course—every state paper I have seen save two (Gordonsville Gazette and Loudoun Enterprise) certainly don't do it & the articles appearing in those papers 'au contraire' I am told were written by men who don't know to this day & cant distinguish gun powder from turnip seed."[28] He strongly denied that personal political ambitions formed the underlying reason for the trip, but it seems likely that he was testing the political waters. While he held no public office at the time, in another ten years he would be elected governor of Virginia.

Lee's other comments to Early revealed that the former cavalry officer considered reconciliation a part of the strategy for beating Republicans. Lee indicated that the presidential election of 1876 would be critical for the South, and that building bridges with the right men in the North would result in a Democratic victory. Beyond the usual politicians, he mentioned a number of former Union generals who were worth cultivating because of their sympathies. On his list appeared Winfield Scott Hancock and John M. Schofield. The first was a prominent Democrat who ran for president in 1880, and the latter had shown leniency during his administration of Virginia during Reconstruction. By meeting halfway with such men, Lee reasoned, "I can aid them in placing the said Government in their hands once more—one that will do . . . justice to our section of the country." He chided Early that "by your holding back, you don't help these people to rid this country of the horrors of Radical misrule." He claimed, however, not to be a wholesale reconciliationist similar to John Brown Gordon, another former general turned politician in Georgia. Unlike Gordon, Lee said he did not accept "with eagerness all that comes from the other side." While he did not demarcate the line he would not cross, he left the impression that he would not accept anything that hurt the Conservative position.[29]

Others at the time saw through the overtures by southerners and considered them a political ploy. A Republican in Virginia recognized the danger for his party in the South. Writing as the centennial of 1876 neared, S. M. Yost, editor of the *Valley Virginian* in the Shenandoah Valley, declared that the calls for peaceful reunion and reminiscences of the Revolution were somewhat disingenuous. He indicated that former Confederates had met the first reports of the centennial with derision, saying that their participation betrayed southern manhood. Then a change came over the Conservative press as the editors realized the potential of the coming presidential campaign. Yost mentioned that the *Richmond Dispatch* had at first stated that the celebration would be inimical to ex-Confederates but now came out in support of the event. He claimed that the reason behind the change of heart had nothing to do with love of Constitution, government, or country but occurred because Republicans gained political fodder if the Democratic South refused recognition of the 100th anniversary of the Declaration of Independence.[30]

Regardless of the true spirit behind the gestures for sectional peace, some northerners were not ready to forgive. In Rockford, Illinois, the GAR post thwarted an effort to pay Jefferson Davis to appear at the county fair. The managers of the fair had invited the former president of the Confederacy to speak and promote "sectional peace." The local GAR cast aspersions against having an "arch-traitor to address the relatives and surviving friends of thirteen thousand men murdered at Andersonville alone by his orders." The *Chicago Tribune*, which had been a strong Radical organ during the war, considered the affair a mercenary gesture by the managers who asked Davis "to seal the era of reconciliation for $400." Eventually the arrangement fell through, and Davis did not appear.[31] Another person who would remain openly hostile to reconciliation through the late 1870s was James G. Blaine, Republican senator from Maine. In 1877 he spoke out against the idea that southern whites had softened in their acceptance of the Union. "North and South are still antagonistic forces," he told an audience in Connecticut. "The South holds views at war with the *prestige* and perpetuity of the Union." He made no bones about who formed the trustworthy element for voter support—and it was not former Confederates. "The nation should prepare for danger in season and avert it if possible. The remedy lies in the hands of the loyal majority of those who saved and should govern the country."[32]

As the centennial arrived, it appeared that the nation enjoyed good relations between former enemies. Congress had approved of a Centennial Exposition to showcase not only the birth of a republican government but also America's industrial might. While many cities and towns marked the occasion with their own events, Philadelphia served as the site of the official observance as the birthplace of the Declaration of Independence. The ceremonies opened on May 10, 1876, with more than 75,000 people attending. The largest display was planned for July 2 through 4. In a grand display of sectional harmony, the centennial committee had chosen Richard Henry Lee to read the Declaration of Independence from one of the earliest copies of the document. He was the grandson of the Virginia delegate who had introduced the resolution for independence. Held in Independence Square, the reading provided one of the centerpieces of the celebration and contained tremendous symbolism that South and North could use the vision of the old Union to overcome the more recent conflict.

Veterans joined in the centennial love feast. A special campground was reserved for the former soldiers who made their way to the commemoration. Although primarily northern units attended, a few Virginians had come, too, in the form of veterans of the 1st Virginia Infantry and the West

Augusta Guards. Also making the trip—to great fanfare by newspaper editors—were the Washington Light Infantry from Charleston and the Clinch Guards from Georgia. They conducted joint activities with the Old Guard from New York and a veteran's group from Boston. Former enemies camped within the same grounds, sharing coffee and food. They played a peacetime game of rounding up prisoners, with northern units overwhelming their southern counterparts and refusing to let them go until all drank to the health of Virginia.[33]

In the South, white people who had forsaken the July Fourth festivities staged processions that they had not supported since the antebellum era. In Augusta, Georgia, the occasion was "celebrated by the white military to-day for the first time since the war." The celebrations themselves contained elements that would have comforted northerners looking for a reunion of the heart. Two of the military companies in the Augusta procession carried the Stars and Stripes, while the band from the U.S. army stationed at Charleston led the column. Richmond had white and black military companies parading in the streets. Numerous excursions and picnics were reported there as well, and no violence marred the day. In Norfolk, black societies marched without incident, and U.S. flags were noticeably on display. Savannah, Georgia, residents turned out to observe the day with more spirit than they had in the preceding sixteen years. As in other places, the U.S. troops in the region joined the local people. American flags draped public and private buildings, and townspeople planted a centennial tree.[34]

That white southerners had made the same connection as Fitz Lee about the political use of this occasion became clear during the ceremonies in Charleston, South Carolina. Residents there used U.S. flags to prove the loyalty of the white citizenry during a local milestone, the centennial of Fort Moultrie. The anniversary of this Revolutionary War fort that guarded the harbor fell just days before the July Fourth holiday. The event featured—according to one newspaper estimate—nearly 22,000 flags, most of which were U.S. ensigns. Only one Confederate flag was reported to have been flown. To the editor who had hired reporters to conduct this census of banners, the results allayed concerns of southern loyalties. "Now, gentlemen," the item addressed northerners, "you must leave us alone and not call us rebels any more."[35]

Despite the overtures for sectional harmony, the centennial demonstrated that much of the South, whether black or white, held mixed feelings about the nation. The editor of the *Atlanta Constitution* indicated that "it is quite natural that we should not feel very enthusiastic either over the Fourth or the Centennial . . . so long as we are politically pro-scribed and a great political party constantly seeks to deny us the equality of citizenship." No deep interest in national holidays could occur, he added, "till the selection of a national democratic administration by the people assures us of a full and free share in the rights, privileges and glories purchased by common forefathers." The great hope for him was the election of a Democrat, Samuel J. Tilden, as president.[36] A Charleston newspaper also spoke of oppression, but instead of the federal govern-ment it was domination by black people that concerned the writer. When the holiday came, the editor proclaimed that the black population had claimed the day "as especially their own. Their colored military com-panies, their Union Leagues with Bible and candle, and their other secret societies march through the streets in the broiling sun, followed by a train of perspiring and palpitating friends." The columnist compared the par-ticipants with the Revolutionary founders who contested British oppres-sion. "The Colonists who threw off the yoke of Great Britain and main-tained, by force of arms, their rights as freemen had no such wrongs, grievous as they were, as those of which their Carolina descendants com-plain in this Centennial year. The Colonists were subject to pure and intelligent rulers of their own race. They were not the slaves of their own slaves."[37]

Another state under Republican rule found Democrats voicing similar complaints of degradation. People refused to support sending representa-tives to the centennial celebration in Philadelphia. The *New Orleans Demo-crat* asked its readers, "What has the hundredth anniversary of American independence given us but degradation for our State and these bitter and shameful things? If Louisiana is at the Centennial of American Indepen-dence, she is there in the person of those who are a disgrace to her and who reflect dishonour upon her; she is there, if there at all, in rags and chains, and because she has been driven there by the whips and kicks of those who rule over and disgrace her. Louisiana at the Centennial is indeed a bitter, burning, infamous lie."[38] Southerners in general provided poor support for the Centennial Exposition in Philadelphia. Of the states of the former Confederacy, only Arkansas contributed toward the financ-ing of the exhibition, appropriating $15,000 for the purpose. Some states from the former Confederacy erected buildings in Philadelphia, but typ-ically these were designed for visitors from their borders to have a place to refresh themselves.[39]

Reconciliation by former Confederates was predicated on home rule by Democrats or Conservatives. The range of opinions in the newspapers of former Confederates mirrored the differing perceptions about how best to win power back from Republicans. Traditionalists took the hardest approach and voiced the most ardent sentiments about degradation and oppression by the government and the black population. Moderates advocated peace and were optimistic about the gestures on both sides of the bloody chasm. The public could see these concerns expressed and debated in the ceremonies of the nation and region, especially in the example of veterans of the conflict.

■ ■ ■

THE CRIPPLED VETERAN

After Reconstruction—as the South faced independent party movements that included biracial coalitions—orators at Confederate Memorial Days focused more and more on the private soldier. They stressed how he had remained devoted to the cause of southern independence despite facing desperate times and privations. In his study of the Lost Cause, historian Gaines Foster unearthed the shift from celebrating top commanders and political leaders to commemorating the common veteran, but most have failed to see this change as coming, in part, from an urgent need for leaders to maintain the political loyalty of followers. To accomplish this, orators invoked the memory not just of the dead but of the surviving, crippled veteran. They sometimes employed the metaphor of the empty sleeve or the empty pant leg—a reference to soldiers who had lost limbs during their service to the Confederacy. Factionalism over political issues, speakers reminded their audiences, dishonored the soldiers who had died. Discord threatened to undo the sacrifice of the survivors, especially if it elevated the black man. While perhaps not quite as consistent or loud as the northerners who waved the bloody shirt, speakers used the image of the crippled veteran to prevent disgruntled white men from breaking party ranks and to build a new Democratic Party that was once again national. Race was fused with the Confederate experience to drive a wedge between white and black people who were finding common political ground.

A number of social, economic, and political forces were changing life as southerners knew it. Greater industrialization advocated by the adherents to the New South brought with it labor problems. Also, as redeemer governments assumed power—or Conservative regimes consolidated their hold on political offices—they invariably created discord among both black and nonelite white people by attempting to control productive resources while enacting policies that added to their own pocketbooks. Once in power, Democratic and Conservative legislatures in the post-Reconstruction South curtailed hunting, gathering oysters, and other means of subsistence by working men and woman by requiring new licenses for such activities. Using their influence with legislatures, planters eased the financial burden of fencing laws that had existed before the war. Legislation before the 1860s had forced farmers to enclose crops while leaving unfenced land open for anyone to graze livestock. This customary freedom was invariably restricted after the war, and poorer people were denied access to grazing lands for their animals. Country folk worried that political offices had become dominated by town folk who had increasingly little desire to protect the agricultural success of small farmers.[40]

Debt weighed on many farmers who saw themselves as giving up much of their own livelihood to protect the interests of rich people. Throughout the latter part of the nineteenth century, bad financial times hit the country with cycles of what we today call depressions and recessions. The economic downturns fell particularly hard on agrarian areas, awakening suspicion among rural residents that control of their lives was slipping toward cities and people who did not think like them. Stay laws or homestead exemptions protected people from losing their homes by placing a certain amount of shelter, furniture, and other chattel property beyond seizure from debt. These laws, however, proved to be too irresistible for the New South elite to ignore. They whittled away at these protections, overturning homestead exemptions, foreclosing on property, and forcing many white southerners into sharecropping. To protect their political positions, Conservative Virginians enacted a head tax that a person had to pay before voting; this prevented poor people in general from exercising the suffrage, even though the principal targets were African Americans. Just like the disfranchisement provisions later in the century, the tax did not discriminate solely by race.

In Virginia the Conservative government was surprisingly frank about feathering the nest of its supporters. The Old Dominion in the late 1870s featured two political factions: Funders and Readjusters. The former represented the men in the Conservative Party; the latter denoted people who feared the consolidation of power and corruption in government that seemed at the disposal of the railroad interests. The issue forcing the Readjusters together was whether to honor the prewar bonds that the state had floated for stimulating the construction of railroads and canals. Other former Confederate states had encountered this debt as well but had forgiven portions of it, recognizing that there was little chance to recover the full amount because of the economic disruption from the war. Virginia's Conservatives, however, did not lack boldness. The Funders pressed for the debt to be honored fully, with all investors receiving their stake. Not to do so, they claimed, risked discrediting Virginia's financial reputation, with the possibility of alienating potential investors. It was, they argued, a moral obligation that contained great perils if ignored. Funders declared that repudiation of the public debt represented the first step toward renouncing all private debts. One newspaper editor proclaimed that agrarianism—the belief that God gave the earth to humankind and that no one had the right to appropriate more than he could cultivate—lay at the root of the repudiation movement. "Property holders beware! The wolf is abroad! You know not how soon you may find him at your own door!"[41]

The Readjusters focused their attack on two targets: the men who benefited from the policy and the means by which the legislature paid the debt. Concerning the first, it did not take a genius to see that many of the investors who stood to benefit from paying the railroad debt were the Conservative Party members who voted on the legislation. Because of the party structure in nineteenth-century America, the broader electorate did not have control over who stood for elections—that power remained in the hands of the leaders. The same elites who decided on funding the debt picked the candidates for office. Worse yet was how the Funders secured the money for repaying the debt. Facing difficult financial times, they naturally robbed Peter to pay Paul, shifting funds from social programs. This meant taking money from the free school system that benefited both white and black people. Raiding school budgets to pay the prewar debts for railroad and canal investors was the final straw for many Virginians. Under the banner of the Readjusters—led by ex-Confederate general William Mahone—black and white voters staged nothing less than a revolution in the Old Dominion.[42]

Although African Americans made up the majority of this movement, the Readjusters were the most successful biracial coalition in the South. Beginning with its victories in 1879, the party dominated the state until violence and other measures broke its back beginning in 1883. While it thrived, the party controlled the governor's office, sent two members to the U.S. Senate, and represented six of Virginia's ten congressional districts.[43] Under their rule, Readjusters conducted a broader campaign than simply reducing the debt. Once in power, they repealed the poll tax, lowered property taxes, attempted to redistribute the burden of taxes toward corporations, shifted more resources to social welfare programs, increased funding for schools, and eliminated whipping as a punishment for crime.[44] Black and white people operated together, and they were led by a former Confederate general, which enhanced the movement's power for disenchanted white people. Throughout the South, "Mahonism" became synonymous with revolution and mongrelization of the races. W. H. Payne, one of the few Conservatives to win election to the legislature in 1879, expressed the sentiments of many of his colleagues when he wrote, "My fear, & the fear is very great, is that we are on the verge of a revolution social & political."[45] Payne and his colleagues had a clear mission: find a way to court Confederate voters back into the fold and to reconstitute a national Democratic Party for white men.

The impact of this movement on Confederate Memorial Days came through the emphasis on private soldiers. To a certain extent, enlisted men always had been part of commemorations. Ladies memorial societies even during Reconstruction had featured tombs to unknown soldiers, and the women of the Hollywood Memorial Association had erected a stone pyramid in memory of the Confederate soldier, not just officers. But the initial thrust of Confederate traditions dealt more prominently with military officers and civic leaders rather than with the man in the ranks. Beginning in the mid-1870s and accelerating in the early 1880s, orators increasingly mentioned the valor of the volunteer. To some extent the change was natural, as veterans' groups formed and spawned greater interest in the common soldier. Praising the common soldier had a number of merits, but it also was intended to keep white voters faithful to the Democratic Party.

Mahone was among the first in Virginia to demonstrate the power of capitalizing on the enlisted man and the memorial movement. Participating in Confederate Memorial Day was a must for anyone harboring political aspirations in the New South. The event provided a place to be seen and to promulgate a message heard by a cross section of society. Mahone dutifully appeared at these commemorations, but he also had the ability to go further. He could conduct reunions of his old brigade in Petersburg. One such meeting in 1875 attracted between 500 and 600 comrades in arms. A newspaper reporter at one of these affairs noticed that a colonel in the brigade delivered an "eloquent" speech that specifically praised the private soldier.[46] Mahone also made overtures to the Ladies Memorial Society of Petersburg, which had struggled to sustain membership and gain volunteers for cemetery upkeep. The organization turned over to Mahone the responsibilities for serving as its agent for improving the grounds, transferring the dead, and selling lots. While Mahone's motivation may have been to care for comrades with whom he had fought, it did not hurt that this gesture increased the chances that veterans might look kindly upon his political aspirations or view a man who himself was a railroad magnate as a friend of the common soldier.[47]

Mahone was not the only one to deploy Confederate service toward a political end. Conservatives used Memorial Days in a similar fashion. After the election of 1879 that witnessed the transfer of power in the legislature to the Readjusters, an editor in Virginia sounded themes that became part of commemorative ceremonies. Responding to initiatives passed by the new legislature, he raised the image of the crippled veteran to prevent white people from joining black people. "Make way there, you crippled Confederate soldiers of the Stonewall Brigade, and give your place to that able-bodied 'colored man and brother.' You fought and bled in defence of Virginia; you served her faithfully in war and peace; you are crippled for life, and performed the duties of your office well and faithfully, but you must now limp out on your remaining limb and give your place to an able-bodied colored man. The day of the crippled soldier is past, and that of the 'colored man and brother' has arrived."[48]

At the first Confederate Memorial Day after the election, participants in Staunton, Virginia, heard how diverging from the Funder position dishonored the memory of veterans. Opie, who delivered the oration, alluded to the bad economic times: "Now it is said by a great many that we honor the dead, but neglect the living." The statement referred to complaints in some quarters that Conservatives, many of whom were former leaders of the Lost Cause, had spent more money on Confederate Cities of the Dead than on aid for the debt-ridden. Opie added, "The embarrassment of her finances has prevented Virginians from making any organized effort in this direction; but I assert that no true soldier nor good citizen ever refused assistance to a soldier's widow or a soldier's orphan." Opie deliberately linked care of survivors from the war to current problems with debt. In his view, if the government did not support stay laws, communities at least were helping the most deserving members: those who had been part of the Confederate war effort.[49]

Opie played on the experiences of veterans during the conflict in the way that some Americans looked upon the struggles of Revolutionary forefathers. He mentioned that the Confederate Army of Northern Virginia never mutinied, despite the extreme hardships soldiers faced. Many had been half-clothed and half-fed; "though without pay, they never murmured." He did not make the connection to current affairs explicit or state that Virginians who balked at Conservative policies should sacrifice for the greater political good like the veterans and widows of the Civil War. This part of the message was left to participants to interpret. Other former Confederates, however, were not so understated. In 1889, after the height of the Readjuster threat had passed but with the memory still very much alive, Jubal Early was invited to give the Memorial Day address in Winchester, Virginia. After repeating the usual refrain about how the Confederacy was overwhelmed and not beaten, he concluded his remarks with a reminder of what the crowd had gathered to celebrate. The ceremonies, according to Early, reinforced the bonds that all shared because of the Confederate past. Then he pointedly told the crowd "that the Confederate who has deserted since the war is infinitely worse than one who deserted during the war, for the former has gone over to the enemy at no personal risk to himself, and simply from motives of gain, while the latter took his life in his hands, knowing that he would be shot if captured, and in a number of cases he was tempted to leave the service to go to the assistance of his family, which he was induced to believe was starving at home."[50]

Now and again, evidence surfaces that reveals how deliberate was the process by white Democratic leaders to divide the races to maintain political power. During 1889 an attorney from Lynchburg, Virginia, endorsed a friend's effort to seek the office of state attorney general. Charles Blackford told his friend point-blank, "I am glad that the issue is square upon the color line. It is the only one by which we can win. We must say to the white man 'You have got to rule Virginia', and we must say to the negroes you must take a back stand, and allow the white man to rule." He added, "The election must be carried peaceable if we can, but by force if necessary. We cannot turn our civilization over to an inferior race, and we had as well make the declaration clear and distinct, so that the northern people will understand that this is the issue upon which this campaign is to be fought." Then he expressed with remarkable clarity how to force the subordinate classes to toe the line. "You cannot keep the lower class of white men in line unless they distinctly understand that they are to make their selection between the negro on the one side and the white race on the other." This had to be the main message of any campaign, "otherwise the tariff and other matters which are perfectly immaterial in comparison, will beat us."[51]

It is difficult to determine the impact of these messages on the people who gathered at Confederate Memorial Days. Few people record their responses to such occasions. Contemplation of the symbolism of orations rarely appears in diaries. The evidence that exists suggests that most of the preaching by Conservatives probably occurred in front of members of the congregation who already shared the faith. People stayed away if they mistrusted or doubted the speaker's message. The participation for the 1881 Memorial Day in Staunton, for instance, fell off enough to elicit comment in the press. A correspondent blamed the smaller crowd on the weather, but it is equally plausible that it had something to do with the tense political times. The newspaper observed that many of the absentees were people from the country. The anger during these third-party efforts often pitted country against town, making it possible that people either boycotted the event or found little interest in a celebration that was dominated by the Conservative regime. In South Carolina the appeals failed. Voters there were more captivated by an antielite movement in which they rejected their old war hero Wade Hampton, regardless of requests to preserve the memory of the Civil War.[52]

It is more certain that ex-Confederate leaders considered Memorial Days as a forum for trying to reach the common person and create solidarity through the Civil War experience. Bradley Johnson, a former Confederate general living in Maryland, understood this fact as he and other traditionalists tried to figure out how to defeat Mahone. He counseled Early to join the national Democratic Party canvass but not to give up on the message of Confederates versus a combination of Yankees and the Negro. If pushed to choose between local and national parties, most Democrats would come on board—especially if Conservatives abandoned the debt issue and raised the color bar in a newly constituted Democratic Party. It was a smart plan. Lewis E. Horace was a member of the executive committee of the Readjusters, but he wrote Mahone in 1880 that he remained a die-hard Democrat. He saw nothing incompatible in the positions: "I expect to cooperate heartily in Federal politics, with the Democratic Party, in State politics with the Readjusters."[53] The strategy thus became a complicated one: play to the folks at home by using the Confederate past against a combination allegedly engineered by Yankees but reach out nationally to some of those same Yankees to defeat the Republican Party. Sectionalism and reconciliation worked together; race merged with partisanship in the Cities of the Dead.

The Readjusters were not the only biracial coalition in the postemancipation South. Between 1865 and the turn of the century, historian Jane Dailey has observed, "every state south of the Mason-Dixon line experimented with political alliances that spanned the color lines." The Republican Party itself represented a combination of black with white voters. These combinations occurred perhaps more frequently in the Upper South, but even in the 1880s the Lower South—supposedly the most solid part of the region—featured dissension within the Democratic ranks. According to Dailey, "In the 1880s independent coalition parties eclipsed the Republicans as the vehicle for interracial political cooperation in the South."[54] The focus on the private soldier and the crippled veteran in Memorial Day ceremonies thus contained a variety of appeals. On one hand, it was a natural turn of events as organizations such as the United Confederate Veterans began to form throughout the region. On the other hand, it provided an additional reason—not the only one but important nonetheless—for white solidarity.

■ ■ ■

MIXED FEELINGS IN FREEDOM CELEBRATIONS

Throughout this period, Emancipation Days and Union Memorial Days revealed mixed feelings on the part of African Americans. Some ambivalence existed over the slave past. There was embarrassment over enslavement and the feeling that its continued remembrance only perpetuated stereotypes. Others, such as Frederick Douglass, worked hard to keep alive these memories in order to heighten vigilance against the decline of their liberties. Whatever a person's position on this issue, even advocates for remembering slavery sometimes questioned the propriety of freedom celebrations because black elites worried that rowdy behavior reinforced racist beliefs that African Americans could not shoulder the burdens of citizens. The speakers at these events demonstrated the increased frustration with the Republican Party and the struggles to create unity for celebrating the holiday. There were, however, a few areas of agreement in the messages of black civic rituals. African Americans wanted equal rights and protection from violence; they used the black soldiers as a reminder of the race's contribution to the nation and as justification for those rights; and they found in the venues offered by freedom celebrations a place to debate, construct, and disseminate partisan political positions. In the process, the tone within freedom's rituals grew more aggressive as orators who once conceded that the freedpeople needed to prove themselves worthy of citizenship now argued that black people had demonstrated they could care for themselves.[55]

Throughout the 1870s, Memorial Day was an occasion that awakened both pride and resentment within African Americans. It was a useful holiday for advocating black rights. It automatically highlighted their connection to the nation as a people who had fallen in service to the government. It placed black and white people at the same commemorative event in an apparently common cause. It kept alive the role of the black veteran in helping to save the Union, serving as a source of black pride and affirming the race's abilities. And it declared their loyalty to the government.

Yet the day was not without problems for African Americans. White paternalism and prejudice often marred Memorial Days in the South. At the Hampton Normal School in Virginia, the black community participated in the Memorial Day exercises, but in a way that unsettled black observers. One correspondent titled his report, "Another Day With Prejudice" as he noted how the stores in the region seemed to be "kept by men and women, and the streets filled with a people whose chief business appeared to be hatred for the negro." The writer added, "Two of three companies of black soldiers passed me early in the morning, I heard the taunts and jeers, the laugh and angry words their presence drew from the lookers on." He was equally disappointed when he visited the school. A student barred him from entering the facility. Asked why, the student replied, " 'Well, General Armstrong [the school's head, who was white] don't want colored people to visit the school.' " White people, according to the student, did have the right to visit. Hearing the exchange, passing students stopped to educate their black visitor on the paternalistic nature of the school's white administration. The listener concluded that occasions such as Decoration Day were being used to trot out the students for white benefactors: "A show for the *gentry* to sing negro ditties." Students did not take part in the federal decorations at noon but were encouraged to join, ironically enough, a tribute to Confederate dead at 4:00 P.M. Because of this, a minister remarked "that while our children are learning letters, they are also learning to accept degradation." Months later the author of this report, George Teamoh, still churned over the event. He chafed at how the program insulted black people. He concluded, "The above is the unhappy result of the Confederate and Federal alliance in doing honors to our dead."[56]

Black people did not shun Decoration Days, but their support depended on the nature of the celebrations, who organized them, and what they commemorated. Late in the century, Richmond's black community still turned out for the day but made it a celebration of civic pride, with benevolent societies assuming prominent positions in the march. Black and white spectators lined the streets, and about 2,500 people went to the cemetery to listen to an address by a local minister.[57] What was becoming evident, however, was the waning participation of white people. On Federal Decoration Day in Staunton in 1883, the only white person was the driver of one of the hacks. A local pastor who gave the oration commented on the fact that white Republicans were absent, adding that officeholders and leaders seemed the most gracious only when they wanted black votes. By 1891 the ceremonies in Alexandria, Virginia, were similarly devoid of white people.[58]

If any day truly belonged to African Americans, it was Emancipation Day. Changes in the physical format of freedom celebrations were not as dramatic as in Confederate Memorial Days. The ceremonies had settled into a familiar pattern from the 1860s. Vastly diminished was the presence of the secret societies that had proliferated in the first years after the surrender. Processions now featured black soldiers, local police, community officials, and the usual concentration of fraternal and benevolent societies, including the Masons, Knights of Pythias, and Odd Fellows. Other groups appeared that were unique to the civic rituals of African Americans in the South. The GAR, with black veterans as part of the membership, marched at both memorial and freedom celebrations. Female auxiliaries to the GAR also paraded, as did women's militia units that drilled especially for such occasions.[59]

Labor organizations made a more pronounced showing in the period of mixed feelings. Black organizations included unskilled workers who, unlike white groups, used the occasions to assert the ability of the race to care for itself. The black street processions of the late nineteenth century featured such workingmen's societies as the Oysterman's Association on the coast at Hampton, Virginia. The marchers wore red shirts and carried a silken banner that read, "To proclaim to the world that the Negro free is a better laborer than the Negro in bondage." Hampton was not the only town to include such groups. The emancipation celebration in Washington, D.C., in 1883 made room for the Hod Carriers and Brick Makers unions. A newspaper item specifically recruited labor organizations by announcing that the chief marshal was looking to add more representatives "from the trades." Eventually, the Knights of Labor joined the procession.[60]

By including labor or workingmen's organizations, the commemorations of African Americans reinforced their independence while suggesting how to raise the race to the next level of achievement. "Suffrage and the exercise of it is valuable to us," said Isaiah Wears, a black orator, "and we should cling to it with unflinching tenacity; so also is education a valuable auxiliary in our advancement; but neither the one nor the other, nor both, can supply the place of industry and labor in the process and potency of our elevation." Sounding like Booker T. Washington, Wears said that his listeners should look to the industrial areas "as the portal through which we must pass to elevation and success. Work, work, is what we want. Let us besiege every department of industry, whether in private or public hands, and importune for employment."[61]

One part of freedom celebrations resisted uniformity: the day on which to mark emancipation. Some communities celebrated the surrender of the Confederate army, with the date differing even within a state. Richmond observed April 3 in memory of the Confederate evacuation of the capital, but Southside Virginia near Appomattox held festivities on April 9, the day that Lee asked Grant for peace. The surrender was commemorated well into the 1890s—and for good reason. "We do it," reported one account about celebrating the day of Confederate defeat, "because we held that our real deliverance was accomplished by the 'surrender.' If Lee had never been beaten and the Confederacy never crushed, the proclamation would have been of no avail."[62] African Americans also marked anniversaries of when slaves heard of their freedom. The most recognized celebration that is still being observed is Juneteenth, which commemorates the order read by Union major general Gordon Granger in Galveston, Texas, on June 19, 1865. People in east Texas, western Louisiana, southwest Arkansas, and southeastern Oklahoma held events on this day.[63]

By the 1880s, black people were observing an incredible array of commemorative events of freedom. Emancipation Days were held variously on September 22 and January 1. Black people in Washington, D.C., continued to honor April 16, the anniversary of freedom in the district in 1862. Texas and other parts of the Southwest threw Juneteenth into the mix. Surrender days were favored in Richmond and Southside Virginia and undoubtedly in other parts of the South. African Americans honored July Fourth and marched in Fifteenth Amendment parades to commemorate the Constitutional protection of suffrage. The use of public space in this fashion, no matter how segregated, bothered ex-Confederates. One man described in a novel his feelings concerning these scenes in South Carolina: "The negroes pour into the city for every chance of excitement or pleasure, and then all work is suspended in the country. Upon the Fourth of July, Emancipation Day, and other especial days they take possession of the streets and all of the parks, and litter the public places with their dirty scraps." He concluded, "The effects of the war we may outgrow, but the effects of Reconstruction are apparently irreparable."[64]

The centennial years of 1875–76 raised mixed feelings among black Americans concerning the national government run by Republicans. In both years, violence greeted black commemorations of the nation's birth. Black people in Vicksburg, Mississippi, gathered at the courthouse in 1875 to observe what they hoped would be a time of peace and amicable feelings on the part of northerners and southerners. A white mob entered the courthouse, demanding that the celebration end and the people disperse. They began beating members of the audience who rushed from the building. In a short time, more white people gathered, shots rang out, and two African Americans fell dead, with several others mortally wounded.[65] More violence came in Hamburg, South Carolina, in 1876. A July Fourth celebration triggered a rampage by white people. Two white men in a buggy had come upon a black militia company drilling in the streets on Independence Day. They became outraged that the black company blocked their passage, even though marchers claimed that there was room for the buggy to go around the group. On July 8, white men marched to a meeting place of African Americans to try to bring one of the leaders to a hearing over the incident. They were led by a former Confederate general, M. C. Butler. Shots were fired; a white man was the first to fall. The crowd grew and kept up a fire on the building in a siege that lasted more than four hours. Before the night ended, six African Americans were shot down and another three were wounded. No federal reaction came, which angered black people who believed they were owed better support from their government.[66]

Black people had designs on using the Centennial Exposition to demonstrate the progress of the race, but again they faced disappointment. In August 1875 a convention of black newspapermen meeting in Cincinnati formed a committee to pressure the centennial commissioner to allow exhibitions by African Americans. They wanted to ensure that the "religious, literary, educational, and mechanical interests of the Negro would be fully represented." The effort failed; African Americans were excluded from much of the festivities. A visitor noticed only one exhibit pertinent to black people: a statue of a freed slave with arms outstretched and clutching a crumpled sheet signifying the Emancipation Proclamation. Few black people were employed at the exhibition except as waiters in the restaurants, barbers in hotels, and messengers and janitors. The centennial organizers did invite Frederick Douglass to attend the opening ceremonies on May 10, but prejudice almost prevented him from making it to his assigned seat. Police momentarily barred his way onto the platform reserved for dignitaries because they refused to believe that a black man would be allowed on the stage.[67]

The violence, the snubbing, and the conciliatory policy of a Republican president with the South created rising displeasure with the Republican Party. As mentioned above, black Republicans in Richmond held a conference in 1873 to express their impatience. The centennial and the end of Reconstruction only exacerbated their anxieties. Yet African Americans faced difficult choices. They scarcely could abandon the organization, even if they were unhappy. One historian has noted, "While virtually all blacks involved in politics remained loyal to the Republican Party—the Party of Lincoln—in 1876, it was becoming increasingly clear that the Party no longer considered African Americans' civil and political rights an important component in its platform."[68] The best of a bad bargain in the early 1880s was to create whatever coalitions they could at the local and state levels, while retaining allegiance to the GOP in national affairs.

The impact can be seen in the use of Emancipation Days and other public rituals to promote greater independence among black people. Orators, as historian David Blight has shown, adopted a different posture in public celebrations from the mid-1870s. They retained the themes that black people were true patriots of the nation and deserved rights as citizens. After 1876 they more urgently pressed the idea that the race needed to be self-reliant. John Mercer Langston, a black abolitionist who later represented Virginia in the U.S. Congress, said, "If we have colored banks, we must have colored bankers; if we have colored schools, let us have our own teachers."[69] The strategy among some leaders became not quite a reverse color bar—it did not exclude white people or advocate separation—but promoted economic and social independence among African Americans.

After 1877, as white people in the South began to reclaim Independence Day—no matter how mixed their feelings about it—and as white Republicans complicated the observances of Decoration Day in the Cities of the Dead, freedom celebrations assumed a distinctive position. African American leaders asserted that freedom day should be recognized as a national holiday, and some talked in 1882 of petitioning Congress for this objective. If enacted, "we would have such a celebration that would forever honor the names of our brave colored soldiers and those great abolitionists who did so much in giving us a day to celebrate."[70] African American periodicals acknowledged the importance of the day for black people, even as they recognized the discriminatory nature of the nation. The Emancipation Proclamation "which to Lincoln and his associates in the Government, was but a necessary measure for the subjugation of the rebellious states, was to the Negro the paper that made him a man." In 1885 another columnist suggested, "The celebration of this day should grow more and more into importance with us." He added, "A national monument ought to be erected by the Negro in memory of the glorious day for which he had just cause to celebrate. Every Negro should know the sentiments of the Emancipation Proclamation as well as he does the Lord's prayer."[71] Representatives of the National Colored Convention that met in Louisville stated in their first resolution, "The shock of embattled arms, was the lullaby of a nation born in a day. We cannot forget the heroic men who made possible the struggle in which treason and slavery were consigned to a common sepulcher, nor would we be unmindful of the measure of devotion and patriotism that the white and colored soldiers rendered the nation."[72] Finding a place for this day on the nation's calendar would keep this fact before the public.

Political instruction, always a part of these events, became even more important in the 1880s. The message in black ceremonies no longer stressed cooperation with poor white people but focused on the need for greater self-reliance among all African Americans.[73] Unlike immediately after the war, black speakers instead of white Republicans dispensed the advice. During Emancipation Day celebration on January 1, 1880, in Portsmouth, Virginia, the celebrants used a political meeting at a precinct house to hear local notables read the Emancipation Proclamation. The orators spoke of the Readjuster movement and the need to reduce the state debt. At least one of the speakers urged consolidated action among all Republicans, "especially the poor white and poorer colored people."[74]

This collaborative spirit soured with the collapse of the Readjuster movement. By 1885 black people in Norfolk had begun to look upon cooperation as an attempt by local, white Republicans to "control not only the Negro's vote, his church, societies and household, but his celebration of the Emancipation Proclamation." For a few years, some members of the black community even boycotted the event.[75] There were many reasons for the decision, including the quandary over whether the memory of the slave past only reminded people of degradation. Sometimes black people faced financial loss if they attended festivities on a day that was not recognized by the government as a holiday. In 1883 black employees of the federal government were allowed to attend the emancipation festivities in Washington, but it came at a price. Leaving work for the day resulted in the deduction of either a day's leave or a day's pay.[76] But it was also clear that many of the people who stayed away from emancipation observances had grown disenchanted with the changing political climate, detested being co-opted by white people who did not have their best interests at heart, or feared reprisals from a white backlash ever more prone to open violence.

When African Americans in Norfolk held the commemoration in 1885, the ceremonies contained a new stridency that included black people arguing for collaboration with white people, but only if it served black interests. African Americans did not wish to prevent white-black cooperation but urged caution to ensure that they first concentrated on building African American solidarity. One speaker at an Emancipation Day observance in Norfolk, Thomas Norris Jr., stressed the combat service of black men in the Civil War, adding that "no white soldier, who marched to the music of the Union, possessed a more lofty conception of the sacredness of the war for the Union than the Negro."[77] Using logic that would become more prevalent later, Norris marshaled statistics to prove the progress of the race since slavery. The illiteracy rate by 1885, he proclaimed, was 52 percent—a decrease from nearly 90 percent in 1865. He also stressed the amount of landownership and the number of students in schools as measures of real gain. A second speaker, Colonel J. T. Wilson, indicated that the freedman had grown to a freeman, an improvement stimulated by race pride. Echoing John Mercer Langston's emphasis nearly a decade earlier on the need for self-reliance, he pointed out that black people were poor because they were not united and were especially unwilling to support one another in business pursuits.[78]

The Republican Party itself came under fire for failing to protect the lives of African Americans. Norris reminded his audience of the violence that had taken place in 1883 in Danville, Virginia, that had resulted in the deaths of African Americans. The Republican Party conducted a meaningless investigation into the incident. He noted that many now advocated that black people emigrate from the South to the West or the North. Still others suggested that they "divide," meaning that they consider independent political action. "Free will is an endowment of God," he said, adding, "independency in speech and actions are the dictates and impulses of a true man. Curb yourself to a single party, like it is forced by inherent inclination, and you soon lose sight of the fact that you are free and independent men." He advocated division for a number of reasons: the Republican Party had done nothing to remedy the injustices that were flagrant in the South, alignment with the party caused violent reaction by the Bourbon South, independent action demanded recognition, and "we will cease to be the 'bone of contention.'" He added that the party had risen to power largely because of the people in the audience, "and meager positions have been the compensation."[79]

The 1884 presidential election was an important milestone on the road to reunion. With the victory of Grover Cleveland, the Democratic Party had defeated the Republicans for the first time since 1856. To former Confederates, this election signaled the possibility of a renewed partnership with the North and the success of their strategy to realign with national Democrats. Reunion was being achieved partly by race, but also as a conscious political strategy. It was an alarming turn of events for African Americans who, after the failure of independent movements, found themselves bound to a party that did not seem to want them, except on election days.

Yet one may have overlooked these underlying problems in this self-described era of good feelings because of evidence that Blue and Gray clasped hands across the bloody chasm without eliminating black people. For the moment, there seemed to be room for all people in the nation's parade. The inaugural procession of President Cleveland featured a sight that created in at least one observer some mixed feelings. Clover Adams, spouse of Henry Adams, who had been part of the Liberal Republican movement, saw what she called a "strange sight." The parade featured Rooney Lee, a son of Robert E. Lee and a former classmate of Henry's at Harvard, riding on a black horse in front of a regiment of veterans wearing the Rebel gray. This symbolized the distance the country had traveled in the twenty years after Appomattox: the son of the man who had tried to split the Union rode at the head of the comrades who had done their level best to accomplish the task. What followed, however, was even more striking. Behind these former rebels marched a regiment of African American veterans in their Union blue with weapons topped by gleaming bayonets. One band accompanying the marchers played "Dixie." The next band played "The Union Forever, Hurrah, Boys, Hurrah" and "Marching through Georgia," the latter a celebration of Sherman's famous devastating march through the Confederacy. Clover Adams could not help but be struck by the juxtaposition of these images, and especially that "every one looked gay and happy—& as if they thought it was a big country & they owned it." On one hand, the ceremony signaled rapprochement between the sections, with black and white people given their place in the nation's parade. On the other hand, this same Grover Cleveland before whom these men marched refused to review the Emancipation Day parade in Washington in 1886. The signals were mixed; however, they were becoming ever clearer to African Americans. What to do about them was a different and far more complex problem.[80]

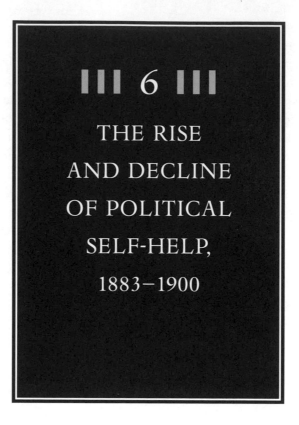

III 6 III

THE RISE
AND DECLINE
OF POLITICAL
SELF-HELP,
1883–1900

On May 29, 1890, Richmond residents unveiled the statue of Robert E. Lee that still sits on Monument Avenue. With first light the city bustled with activity, accompanied by martial music. The crowd was estimated at 100,000, with the procession of veterans, according to one observer, taking two hours to pass. Important generals from the former Confederacy had come, including James Longstreet, Joseph Johnston, and Jubal Early, as well as less prominent figures such as M. C. Butler of South Carolina—the man who had been instrumental in the Hamburg massacre of 1876. Confederate flags were everywhere. Some of the veterans marched in the gray uniforms worn during the war. Not many black people participated, but some could not help but watch. An old man, possibly a former slave, intently took in the events until he finally blurted out what the display meant to him: "The Southern white folks is on top." He was not the only person making such a connection. The black press in Richmond condemned the event as an indication that the white public clung "to theories which were presumed to be buried for all eternity." Among these were the notions that a state could secede from the Union, "and that dealing in human beings, selling children from their parents, wives from husbands, sisters from brothers were right and the South in contending for these things by force of arms was right." Some northerners, especially staunch Republicans, joined in the criticism. A New York regiment declined to participate because its older members refused to walk under a Confederate flag.[1]

Not quite four months later, a very different commemorative event took place in the same city, this time to promote a national celebration of emancipation. The movement had been sparked by the unveiling of the Lee monument. Thousands of African Americans jammed the Exposition Grounds on October 16 to cheer the arrival of the procession, which took thirty-five minutes to pass a particular point. Although delegates had come from around the country to see if they could agree on a national holiday for freedom, most of the marchers were from within the Petersburg-Richmond region, with the usual forty or fifty civic societies in line. The contrast in the symbolism with the Lee monument unveiling could not have been more striking. Instead of Confederate banners, the marchers displayed U.S. flags and pictures of Abraham Lincoln. Members of civic societies carried framed pieces of cloth bearing inscriptions such as "In 1860 slaves, in 1890 bankers" and "The Solution to the Negro Problem is Finance." John Mercer Langston, the black congressman from the 4th District of Virginia, addressed the audience, offering himself as a living example of how a person born in the slave quarters had walked into the halls of Congress.[2]

Black orators used such occasions during the 1880s and 1890s to advocate self-reliance so the race could become, among other things, a greater political force. Self-help, or the ideology of uplift equated with the accommodationist approach of Booker T. Washington, was considered by scholars to include a rejection of the partisan approach in favor of uplift of the race primarily through building economic strength. Economic uplift, so the interpretation has gone, presented a safer path than party politics to advance the race. Historians recently have discovered a more complex use of self-help as a form of resistance underneath a public stance of accommodation. Few, however, have recognized that this thought still advocated a political solution—one that fell short of black separatism while striving for an independent, black electorate.[3] In the speeches delivered at freedom celebrations of the last decades of the nineteenth century, political self-reliance and economic improvement often appeared as twin, interrelated goals. The creation of economic interdependence within the black community to enhance its electoral strength was frequently sounded in the public ceremonies of the black South. Without economic freedom, so the reasoning went, black people remained vulnerable. A united community with financial independence was necessary for independent action that might include breaking ranks with the Republican Party. At the 1890 emancipation celebration in Richmond, one person put it this way: "Our position is independent. We must vote for the party that will recognize our manhood and protect our lives. We have discharged our obligations to the Republicans and we never owed the Democrats anything. In eight or ten States in the South we have enough votes to defeat either party. Independence in politics is our only salvation. We number 10,000,000 and yet we are the weakest people here. It is because we are not united. Our safety is in union."[4]

Even in an era that featured the coming of disfranchisement and segregation, African Americans had legitimate reasons for believing that political action offered the possibility of maintaining and expanding their rights. They had achieved material gains that allowed speakers to boast of the number of property owners, bankers, and educated persons among them. The fraternal and civic associations in their parades reinforced the existence of a black professional class—as did the speakers on the podiums. Additionally, black people believed their patriotism for the nation would be rewarded. They had fought as soldiers in the Civil War and proudly displayed the U.S. flag and other symbols of nationhood. Finally, they had the franchise. The federal government may have proven less than adequate as an ally, but African Americans believed that the Republican Party needed black votes if organizers hoped to defeat a surging Democratic opposition. The black man who watched the unveiling of the Lee monument showed that even nonelites had internalized this faith in the party of Lincoln. After concluding that white people were on top, he relaxed and smiled while taking comfort in another thought: "But we's got the government!" he proudly exclaimed, "We's got the government!"[5]

With the decline of biracial partisan coalitions such as the Readjusters, freedom celebrations exposed at least three main strains among black political, social, and business leaders concerning relations between the races. The most accommodationist faction publicly acknowledged the white perception that the race had to bide its time and work its way up through more menial jobs until it proved that black people deserved equality. At the other end of the spectrum were strident voices arguing for an independent black electorate that did not automatically cast its vote with the Republican Party. This militant wing found its greatest voice in T. Thomas Fortune, editor of the *New York Age*; George T. Downing of Rhode Island, an entrepreneur and activist dating back to prewar abolition; and eventually John Mercer Langston. In the middle fell a larger number of people who found certain aspects of the polar positions attractive but did not embrace either of them fully. Many moderates did not like the obsequious tone of the most accommodating wing, yet they were concerned that stressing a separate race activism could hurt them by maintaining the color barrier and encouraging further discrimination through a white backlash.[6]

In the final decades of the nineteenth century, Emancipation Day commemorations became more popular venues for disseminating political messages, even as they created increasing debates among black people. Members of a new generation of younger black men and women who rejected black nationalism nonetheless might share the sentiments of Alexander Crummel that the slave past was an embarrassment hardly worth celebrating. Although Emancipation Day honored the race's struggle for freedom, it commemorated a time when African Americans had been enslaved, resurrecting emotions of inferiority, shame, or hatred.[7] Others, particularly prosperous members of the black upper class, believed that commemorating emancipation was important and should be encouraged to educate the public on history, reinforce certain moral values, and convince white people that the race had progressed to the point of deserving political and economic equality. Still others wanted to use the occasions to urge independent political action, which incited a reaction from Douglass and other leaders who considered this strategy as only dividing the black vote and handing power to the Democrats. Although discontent with the GOP was apparent, many were not ready to abandon it altogether.

■ ■ ■

TO DIVIDE OR NOT TO DIVIDE

Economic uplift that resulted in a strong, independent electorate provided one answer to the dilemma facing African Americans with the collapse of independent party movements. Widespread criticism of the Republican Party became particularly acute with the twentieth anniversary of the Emancipation Proclamation in 1883, yet there existed an almost fatalistic acceptance that the party was the principal organization to which

African Americans must belong. The southern Democratic Party had emerged from the independent movements with a renewed commitment to white supremacy and restrictions on black voting. The Readjuster movement was losing momentum, broken by violence and a call for raising the color bar. Some African Americans gave up entirely and went over to the Democratic Party, but this did not appeal to most. Others used self-help as a last-ditch effort to force the Republican Party to pay attention to its black constituency.

Uneasiness with the Republican Party can be found as early as Reconstruction. Even though they found some of the policies hypocritical or paternalistic, African Americans viewed Republicans as having the best alternative. With Redemption—or the restoration of Democratic rule in the South—the party at times lost credibility with black people, as it seemed mired in corruption or failed to protect its most faithful supporters. The recollections of a black officeholder provide rare insight into the contention that existed within the southern wing of the party and into how commemorations of the war were invariably intertwined with contemporary events. Born a slave in Virginia, George Teamoh had served in the general assembly of the state after the war. In his autobiography written in 1874, Teamoh boasted that he belonged to the party, "but only so long as it keeps the faith."[8]

Like many people in America at this time, Teamoh was concerned with corruption, especially by patronage hacks who feathered their own nests instead of leading like statesmen. In Teamoh's view the party consisted of two organizations: the GAR and the Union League. The former, primarily but not exclusively white, was the veterans' group that had formed for Union soldiers. The latter, primarily but not exclusively black, contained political clubs organized in the South before black people had won the franchise. What bothered Teamoh was that veterans who were part of the GAR had gained political appointments based on their war records; consequently they were installed for their loyalty rather than their ability or morality. Too often, they lived down to the credentials.

Teamoh believed that the GAR should disband because it had outlived its time. He considered it a patronage machine born in opposition to the Ku Klux Klan, with its officeholders installed by force rather than consensus. This meant the organization contradicted the principles of republicanism that it espoused. He added, " 'Lo the poor sailor and soldier' have been jointly made the convenient vehicle in which to drive a corrupt trade in politics, as in election times they are generally appealed to from the ascertained fact of their oneness in sentiment." According to him, a better way to memorialize those who had fallen in the Civil War "would be, admitting such organizations as the G.A.R. are to be disbanded, (and they should be)—to organize a great national party for freedom and equal rights, to be made up of all who fought and all who did not fight in the war which gave freedom to our country."[9] It is difficult to say how many shared his view; however, it is clear that different opinions existed among black people about what to do about the party.

By the twentieth anniversary of emancipation in 1883, black people were openly questioning their habitual support of the Republicans. The most oft-cited advocates were the editors of the *Savannah Echo* in Georgia, the *New York Age*, and George T. Downing of Rhode Island. They opposed corruption within the party and wanted to break the hold of bosses who ignored participatory governance and failed to award patronage to African Americans. In early 1884 the editor of the *Weekly Echo* proclaimed that the Republican Party needed the united support of "the Negro American" in the presidential campaign or it "will go to the dogs. It is, therefore, proper for the colored leaders to make the bosses toe the mark, as to an equal division of the spoils according to our voting strength." He added, "Make the demagogues come to time."[10]

Opposing independent political movements that threatened support for Republicans was the leading black figure of his time, Frederick Douglass. Time and again throughout the 1880s and 1890s, Douglass argued that the GOP offered the only choice for African Americans.[11] Critics of independent political action referred to the option as "dividing." Voting "independently" to them meant dividing the black vote and handing power to the Democrats. A supporter of Douglass, the editor of the *Washington Bee*, articulated the position. "The Democratic party has been in power, and what was the condition of our people?" he asked, adding, "servitude after the meanest character and forced amalgamation of the races thus causing a great faction of the colored people to be born bastards." The editor continued that it was not the party that was the problem, but its leaders. "It is not the party. The principles of the Republican Party are liberal. Those of the Democratic party are narrow and are only confined to the individual members of that party. There is liberty on one side and slavery on the other, justice and equality are the mottoes of the party we support, and tyranny, blood shed and the meanest acts that can be perpetrated are the principles of the Democratic party, which we condemn."[12]

Discontent with the party did not disappear because of these arguments. African Americans periodically held national conventions to discuss issues. One such convention scheduled to be held in Washington, D.C., in the tempestuous year of 1883 revealed the contending factions. Organizers for the national convention had placed on the agenda issues of fair pay for labor, equal public schools, protection of civil rights, enforcement of political rights, and equitable distribution of patronage. While most black people supported such a meeting, many were angry with Douglass's Washington-based cronies for trying to keep the convention in the District of Columbia. Southern blacks lambasted the district's "political wire-pullers" for their dictatorial ways. Douglass was caught off guard. He noticed that the proposal met with little favor among Republican newspapers, and he admitted being "surprised that the editors of colored newspapers have generally opposed the convention." Republican whites feared the convention would pass resolutions against the GOP, while African Americans suspected that the meeting would be controlled by the current administration, because Douglass seemed to be the mouthpiece for the national party. In the end, the convention was held, but in Kentucky—far from Washington.[13]

When the meeting convened in late September 1883, the delegates reflected the fissures within black leadership. They refused to endorse the sitting president, Chester A. Arthur, or the Republican Party. They were unhappy that Arthur reached out to white independents in the South who were openly anti–African American. Resolutions decried the erosion of the Fourteenth Amendment and stressed the need to have greater enforcement by the government to protect civil and political rights.[14]

The convention even featured a battle over Douglass serving as president of the proceedings. Detractors depicted him as blindly adhering to the Republican Party and feared that he sided with the men in power at the expense of his race. He was opposed for leadership of the convention by D. A. Straker of South Carolina, who according to the Washington-based *People's Advocate*, "was sent by a state convention, which condemned the national republican party in unmeasured terms." The opposition found Douglass unacceptable for the presidency because "his inflexible devotion to republicanism and republican organization were called in question." Douglass won the appointment handily with 201 votes, but 50 of the delegates voted for Straker. This was not an insignificant minority. The next evening, Straker answered repeated calls to take the platform by issuing an address that featured public criticism of Douglass. While acknowledging the progress made by the race, he pointed out the obstacles in the way—among them Douglass, whom he charged with failing to raise his voice in the "dark hours of 1877, when Louisiana, South Carolina, and Florida were sacrificed by President Hayes." This brought Douglass to his feet to defend himself. He told the audience that he had protested the conciliatory policy in an interview with Hayes but felt himself largely alone without "representative men of the race." Douglass said he opposed the Hayes policy and added that he was a Republican, "but an uneasy Republican." A majority of the participants clearly still honored the famous black leader, but disgruntlement with political affairs existed in sufficient strength that they rejected the resolutions to endorse the administration.[15]

Discord continued the next year when the party announced its choice of James G. Blaine for the presidential candidate. Black people, of course, were not the only ones unhappy with Blaine. Reformers in general considered that Blaine represented elite politics that promised to restrict decision making to a small group of insiders. They also believed the candidate was a pet of monopolists. Free traders despised his support of the tariff, which was one of the reasons the *New York Times* and the *New York Evening Post* failed to endorse him. Southern Democrats hated him because they considered Blaine an unreconstructed Yankee who was not interested in reconciliation. To them, Blaine was one of the originators of the campaign policy of waving the bloody shirt, tarring the Democratic Party as the organization of secessionists who would cause more mischief if they returned to power.[16]

African Americans had additional reasons to be unhappy with Blaine. What appeared to white people as authoritarian rule via a closed caucus was interpreted by African Americans as a deliberate snubbing of them because of racism. Opinions of the party ranged widely. The most militant black newspapers, like the *New York Age*, believed "the Republican Party has very evidently struck a very large rock." The paper added, "The grand old ship, around which so many and furious storms have spent their fury in vain, appears to have sprung a leak, not unlike the one which carried down the parties out of which it was carved in 1856." Others were more moderate. The *People's Advocate* in Washington accepted Blaine halfheartedly while indicating that he had been nominated without black support. The editor added that "he cannot be elected without their aid, that is certain," especially if the party hoped to carry the electoral-rich state of New York. In the South the *Virginia Star* remained hopeful of victory, if not enthusiastic about the choice of candidate. The editor there did not think that Democrats could defeat the Republican Party, which had held power for more than two decades.[17]

The Virginia editor, of course, was wrong, but the resulting election provided one more reason for black leaders to seek greater independence in political affairs. They saw the black electorate drifting from the party and hoped that independent voting might at least preserve African Americans as a solid voting bloc. The work of historian J. Morgan Kousser confirms the basis for these fears. He showed that black support for Democrats threatened to become a significant minority during this period. More than one-third of black adult males in North Carolina, Georgia, and Alabama voted Democratic in select gubernatorial elections in the early to mid-1880s. Five other states recorded more than 20 percent black support for the Democratic candidate. The meaning behind the figures is clouded somewhat because of the intimidation, coercion, and fraud that accompanied these elections, but the bolting of black voters was great enough, and real enough, to concern black leaders.[18]

At a variety of public events, speakers claimed that African Americans had the potential to make a difference politically. Captain R. A. Paul, a black Virginia politician, addressed the Acme Literary Association in the African Methodist Episcopal church in Richmond to convince the audience that "the American Negro has been and is now a political factor of far greater importance in the governmental affairs of our State and country than has been considered by many." He claimed that African Americans had "controlled the political complexion of this great nation for at least eight years." In the disputed election of 1876, Republicans needed nineteen electoral votes from the South to win. This could not have been accomplished, Paul noted, without the black vote. In 1880 black Republicans continued to have an impact, with the Democrats falling twenty-nine electoral votes short of victory. What would have happened, Paul asked his audience, if New York had voted Democratic, helped along by a swing in black voting? The state went Republican by 20,842 votes and had a black voting population of 20,059. If 9,000 had stayed away from the polls, Democratic candidate Winfield Scott Hancock, not James A. Garfield, would have been elected. Paul asserted that African Americans composed important constituencies in other northern states. Ohio had 21,706 black voters; Garfield won there with a majority of 26,105. In Indiana the black vote was at 10,739; Republicans carried the day by 5,000 votes.[19]

Paul concluded with statements that captured the function of political uplift. Only nineteen years had passed since freedom had come with the Thirteenth Amendment. In that time, black people had entered both houses of Congress and the legislatures of all the southern states and were represented by a minister to the courts of foreign countries, a marshal of the Supreme Court, and a register of the U.S. Treasury who signed the currency of the country. Paul also pointed out the existence of black judges, jurors, and lawyers in courts. "The question may be asked, Can the Negro, with this immense power, be kept in his present abject condition? To this enquiry I answer, 'No,'; for if the signs of the times indicate anything, they tell a glorious future for the American black man." The speaker encouraged his audience to follow the tenets of uplift—to acquire intelligence and wealth, to cooperate, and to encourage one another in the trades, professions, and business—as a means of eradicating prejudice on the part of white people, but not as a substitute for political action.[20]

A majority of African Americans continued to support the party, but even Frederick Douglass expressed disappointment with the organization. In 1885 Douglass offered his opinions about a recent campaign to an acquaintance in Butte, Montana, which ran under the headline, "Criticizes Republicans, but Has More Faith in Them Than in Democrats." Douglass wrote, "I cannot say I am much elated by the victory by the Republican party, though I am glad that the Democratic party has met with defeat." He added, "I have my fears that the victory of the Republicans may make them even a little more indifferent about protecting human rights under the constitution than they were when they were in power before. It is the shame of the Republican party that it could protect the rights of American citizens everywhere but at home."[21]

In the 1880s, Emancipation Day orators were not unanimous in arguing for independent political action, but a healthy strain of this belief ran through many speeches. Emmanuel K. Love, a prominent Baptist cleric in Georgia, told an Emancipation Day audience, "We should not allow any party to hood-wink us and lead us at will. We should be more independent and act for ourselves." This statement came after Love had reaffirmed his support of the GOP and argued against division of the black vote as pure folly. Yet like many African Americans at the time, he searched for reasons to remain with the party, beyond gratitude for its having been the organization that supported freedom during the war. The minister delivered to his audience the message that became increasingly important through the 1890s:

I repeat it that the Negro must look away from any and every political party for personal worth and greatness. He must look to himself. I urge that our people get an education, save their money, live within their income, buy homes, be honest and virtuous, unite together in doing a business, form real estate and mercantile associations, have confidence in each other[,] be true to the race, have faith in our great possibilities, have undying love for race pride, scorn legal or illegal amalgamation, be sober, stop being millionaires on the streets, and paupers at home, pay your debts, contract no more than you can pay and protect to the extent of the last drop of blood in your veins the virtue of our women and we will get all the respect, rights and recognition we want.[22]

Love encouraged uplift of black people through economic and social improvement, but to help create a coherent force that could make a political impact.

African Americans entered the 1890s with various meanings surrounding the notion of uplift, and these spilled over into the content of Emancipation Day observances. Most black leaders used freedom celebrations to highlight financial independence and race pride as an integral part of the struggle for rights. A significant minority hoped to go further and have black voters function almost like a party within a party to persuade the Republicans to pay attention to African American interests, leaving the possibility open for fusion if the proper circumstances arose. Still others, like the editor of the *Washington Bee*, grew cynical about all politics. This line of thought fit the approach noticed by historian August Meier that advocates of self-help shunned politics in favor of economic and social improvement. An editorial professed that black people in the United States needed first and foremost "co-operation in all branches of business. There is nothing to be made out of politics, but broken bones and empty pockets."[23] Opponents of division had been winning the fight in the latter 1880s. But Confederate celebrations created a shock that gave political self-help one last boost in the 1890s, intertwined with an effort to create a national Emancipation Day.

■ ■ ■

THE PROBLEM OF THE LEE MONUMENT

The unveiling of the Lee monument in Richmond signified a benchmark on the road to reunion. The Lost Cause had become celebratory, no longer an occasion for mourning, and ex-Confederates more often espoused reconciliation with the North. Interpretations of the war based on the Lost Cause were becoming more acceptable to northern white people. These trends did not go unchallenged. African Americans refused to go quietly from the nation's commemorative scene. Many pushed harder for a national Emancipation Day as they pointed out the contradictions of celebrating as heroes the Confederate military figures who just as easily could have been convicted as traitors. Some white northerners also had problems with the adulation over Lee and other Confederate heroes, but this position was fading with the passing of the wartime generation. Only a half-dozen years remained before waving the bloody shirt reached its climax, but it was losing vibrancy as a new generation of young men—people who had not fought in the war—began dictating the ceremonial and political directions in both sections.[24]

The unveiling of the Lee monument incorporated unabashed worship of the Confederate past, but in a way that did not threaten national allegiance in the present. Gathering for the festivities were some of the surviving top general officers of the rebellion, such as Jubal Early, John Brown Gordon, and Fitzhugh Lee. Also in the crowd was the Pickett-Buchanan Camp of Confederate Veterans of Norfolk, whose members wore their old gray clothes from the war. The procession that began at noon contained more than 20,000 people and continued until 4:00 P.M., when everyone reached the final destination. Speeches at the unveiling and commentary in newspapers indicated that the war had come because of states' rights and not slavery. With the peculiar institution eliminated as a factor in causing the conflict, seceding southerners became Americans who upheld the example of the Revolutionary generation in defending principles of self-determination. Additionally, they had begun to raise the refrain that elimination of slavery had been a positive outcome of the conflict, with the nation better off in the bargain.

Even the proliferation of Confederate flags did not create as much controversy as one might have thought. It is likely that a majority of white Americans believed, like a *New York Times* correspondent covering the event, that there was nothing to be concerned about. Even though he admitted seeing widespread display of the rebel flag, the writer added, "but everywhere they were entwined with the Stars and Stripes, and on no occasion has there been more of genuine loyalty and devotion to the Union displayed than to-day." Similarly, a columnist for the *Cincinnati Commercial Gazette*, a leading Republican organ in Ohio, saw no danger in the display of the "conquered rebel flag." The writer believed it would be "ungenerous to protest" against southerners making this display. "It is their funeral."[25]

White criticism came primarily from Republican newspapers. A little after the unveiling of the Lee statue, the *Detroit Plaindealer* editorialized about the commemorative event and other holidays in the South: "The exhibition of rebel flags on all holiday occasions in the South, is not the only way the people of that section show that they have not accepted the results of the war. They have openly and wantonly murdered Republicans for years. It could not be expected that these people would revere the American flag when they have no regard for the Nation and the Constitution." In a similar fashion, a newspaper in Springfield, Illinois—the home of Lincoln—indicated, "This shameful disregard for the flag of the Union and of higher respect for the flag of treason, was disgracefully demonstrated at the unveiling of the monument to the late Gen. R. E. Lee at Richmond, Va., May 29th." The columnist added that many could appreciate the sentiment for honoring Lee, who admittedly had some admirable traits, "but when they put up that ensign of treason—the stars and bars—and make it a god to display, and to worship, we, as an American citizen, offer our solemn protest and demand in the name of our fathers, in the name of the constitution and in the name of every patriotic impulse that such things shall not be tolerated." It was not unusual to hear similar themes in portions of the South. The *Louisville Champion* declared, "They hold their lives by the mercy of the nation they attempted to destroy," and the rehabilitation of the "infamous" ensign of the Confederacy "is rank treason."[26]

Republicans also castigated organizers of the unveiling for holding it just one day before Union Memorial Day, the holiday reserved for commemoration of the dead who had fallen in service to the United States. It seemed as if the event had been timed, in fact, to dishonor a very significant Memorial Day, the twenty-fifth anniversary of the conflict's end. Most communities were enjoying an increase in enthusiasm over the day, especially to honor the old veterans. A U.S. congressman who served as the orator for the observance in New York City told his audience on this occasion, "The statue at Richmond seems like a weak and clumsy protest against the flood of years." He added that he hoped that those who carried the flags of the rebellion "will some day be able to distinguish between the flag of their country and the common curiosities of history."[27]

A Decoration Day gathering at Gettysburg featured a prominent senator taking to task the main figure of the celebration in Richmond. The speaker pro tempore of the U.S. Senate, John J. Ingalls, a Republican from Kansas, reminded his listeners that twenty-five years had passed since the last shot of the war, which he referred to as the birthday "of a redeemed and regenerated republic." At one point in the oration, the senator—obviously very much aware of the activities in Richmond a day earlier—considered the nature of R. E. Lee. Like many men of his time, he did not deal with Lee the soldier; it was a given that the leader of the most successful army in the rebellion had considerable gifts as a military commander. Lee's character, however, was fair game for Ingalls. While calling the Confederate general a man of "lofty character," the senator tried to show why Lee did not deserve adulation as an American hero. Ingalls mentioned that Lee was reputed to have loved the Union, claiming it to be perpetual. "Had Robert E. Lee adhered to those lofty and ennobling sentiments," said Ingalls, "he would to-day have been the foremost citizen of this Republic in the estimations of all its citizens." The senator reminded his listeners that Lee had been educated at West Point at the expense of the government. For twenty-five years he had drawn his sword under a flag and a Constitution that he had sworn to protect. Yet two days after he resigned, his love of Union was so strong that "he laid aside his support" for that Union. According to Ingalls, Lee violated his oath "and took leadership of the most causeless rebellion that ever occurred since the devil rebelled against heaven."

Warming to his subject, Ingalls added his voice to the accusation that organizers of the Lee unveiling held their ceremony to dishonor Union Memorial Day. Those who claimed to "have furled the flag of treason and rebellion forever, who professed that they have come back under the Constitution of the United States," were the same ones clasping Confederate flags in their hands. They did so around a day that had been "for a quarter of a century almost made sacred by the common concurrence of the loyal and patriotic people of the Republic for the consecration of the graves of the Union dead." He pulled no punches in suggesting that former Confederates had given "a great abject lesson in treason, in disloyalty, in perjury, in violation of faith, of public and private honor." In the span of a few paragraphs, a leading senator in the U.S. Congress branded former Confederates as liars who had no honor and included Lee with people who were traitors and whose word could not be trusted.[28]

Anyone with a discerning eye could see that a preponderance of the orators who attacked the ceremony were Republicans of a certain kind: die-hard party supporters, including a majority of African Americans, and particularly older members of the party. Ingalls himself faced reelection that year. Supporters of Confederate traditions turned the attack around by claiming that mean-spirited men of the North, not them, wanted to keep the memory of the war alive for political reasons and were blocking attempts to have a truly united country.[29] It was clear from major organs of the nation, such as the *New York Times*, that significant portions of the northern public also did not see Confederate ceremonies as an expression of disloyalty. To northerners, it could appear that ungrateful African Americans were either behind this effort or being misled by party organizers who hoped to keep them around for elections.

There were hints, however, that more than partisanship lay behind at least some opposition to the flag. Current and former military figures may have been willing to forgive their former enemies, but they would not forget the sacrifice that had been necessary to preserve the Union. While happily participating in reunions of veterans of both sides, former soldiers perceived the resurgence of the flag at the Richmond event as a sign of disrespect for the nation. Flags of the Confederacy were nothing new at events featuring soldiers, but the Lee monument seemed to be an affair much different from the traditional reunion of veterans. It was a commemoration that affirmed a particular civic identity for the white people of a region. And it raised questions for some Union veterans of whether the defeated foe truly did embrace the nation.

One enlightening controversy involved the 7th New York Regiment, which revealed the impact of a changing of the generations. The members of this unit refused an invitation to attend the Richmond event, in the process revealing divisions within the organization. The rejection caught southern organizers off guard because the unit had a history of seeming to reconcile with southern regiments. During the centennial a regiment from Richmond visited New York and was treated hospitably by the 7th, also known as the Old Guard. The northerners had turned over space in their armory to house the southern visitors during their stay. It was believed that both regiments had developed a cordial relationship, and it appears that some of the men within the northern unit had voiced their desire to march in the Lee ceremonies. Once it became public, however, the invitation created outcry among the partisan press in the metropolis. All waited for word on the final decision as members of the unit deliberated the invitation.[30]

When the Old Guard issued a statement about why it refused to go to Richmond, it appeared that waving the Confederate flag still mattered to some people after all. The polite answer for the rejection was that a scheduling conflict had arisen. If the group attended the Lee unveiling on May 29, it jeopardized its attendance at the Memorial Day parade in New York on May 30. Other reasons, however, lay underneath the decision. A spirited meeting of the Old Guard held on April 12 revealed that older veterans were less inclined to make the journey than some of the younger ones. A reporter identified the supporters as "younger officers and the immature soldiers." A later report indicated that some of the young men had been born in the South, had moved to the North, and were enthusiastic about returning to their native region with the unit. "The older men, however," continued the report, "were alert to perceive that much more was involved in the undertaking than a mere pleasure excursion."[31]

A source identified as a "prominent officer in close sympathy with regimental headquarters" revealed what truly bothered the older veterans. He and his comrades appreciated Lee's character and accomplishments as a soldier, "but we cannot afford, as Northern men, to lose sight of the fact that those achievements were obtained while Gen. Lee was in rebellion against the National Government, through whose liberality and fostering care he had obtained his professional education." Those who argued against going did so because they could not be assured that the orators at the event "will not be diametrically opposed to the genius of the union of States. We cannot afford to give even moral support or countenance to any sentiment which shall seem to uphold the 'lost cause.'" If the Confederate flag flew over Richmond, "the Seventh Regiment would be false to its traditions and its record if it consented to march under it without expressing dissent."[32]

This concern over the symbolism of a flag assumes greater meaning if we reflect on what was happening during this decade in parts of the South. Even more than thirty years after the Civil War, some people only warily raised the flag of the United States. It took seven years for leaders of an African American school in Calhoun, Alabama, to muster the courage to fly the U.S. flag outside the building. When they did so in 1899—or nearly a decade after the Lee monument was unveiled—it was an event worth celebrating. People came on a Saturday in the spring; some traveled on foot, and many arrived on the backs of mules. A few reportedly walked fourteen miles to take part. One man had started out the day before the event to ensure that he arrived on time. The inevitable procession was held. Once at their destination, the participants formed in concentric circles around the flagpole: boys who had been in the procession were the closest, teachers were in the next circle, and relatives and visitors were behind. The assembly sang patriotic songs. A reporter noted, "We were glad to hear our national hymn sounding and resounding around our flag, raised for the first time on this old Southern cotton field, where slavery, the whipping posts, and the blood hounds *had been* in their worst form, but where then we were all singing the blessings of liberty." Even in this ceremony came the message of uplift heard elsewhere. A speaker who said that America meant having the chance to work one's way up by effort was greeted with a shout: "Dat's all we want. Just give us a chance." After the Pledge of Allegiance, the correspondent noticed an old woman who had come to the ceremony despite struggling to walk. She reportedly took in the celebration and said, "Nevah did I see dis t'ing befo'. My ears done hyeah strange t'ings dis day."[33]

Black people had reason enough for being angry with the unveiling of the Lee monument, but some were outraged at learning that members of their race had been in the crowd. White people by far formed the majority at the ceremonies for the monument. A northern correspondent, in fact, made a point of noting the lack of participation by African Americans: "With the exception of the colored military organizations, the colored people have manifested but little interest in the coming event." Here and there, however, African American faces appeared in the crowd, a situation that former Confederates tried to exploit as proof that harmony existed between the races. A handful of old men showed up who had traveled with the Army of Northern Virginia as slaves of officers. One of them, "Uncle" Tarleton Alexander of Charlottesville, apparently said he had "always voted the Democratic ticket." Like other African Americans there, he wore badges that represented various camps of the Confederate veterans. Two former slaves accompanied Jubal Early to the festivities. Early introduced them to a Virginia politician, adding, "These are respectable darkies; none of your scalawag niggers."[34]

Reactions to this report among African American editors ranged from disbelief to outrage. The story appears to have originated in the *Virginia Star*, a black newspaper in Richmond, and spread to the North via the *New York Times* and the *New York Mail and Express*. The *New York Age*, one of the nation's most prominent African American newspapers, dismissed the significance. "Of course Afro-Americans took no part in the ceremonies," a columnist observed. "They were, in the main, silent spectators." The item proposed that the only hope for the races was for "relics of the dead past" such as Early and the former slaves to pass away. The writer also shook his head over the celebration itself, adding, "In no other country in the world could the celebration, symbolizing disloyalty and disunion, have taken place."[35] Taking a stronger approach, the editor of the *Washington Bee* was outraged that African Americans even went to the dedication. He minced no words: "Every Negro that participated in those ceremonies ought to have a rope around his neck and swung to the tail of the horse upon which the dead ex Confederate is mounted." This sentiment contained special vehemence in a time when African Americans repeatedly faced lynch mobs. He added, "We have Negroes in the District of Columbia that will not participate in the Emancipation of the freedom and it is ridiculous to see Negroes leaving the city to participate in an arch traitor's ceremonies." The columnist concluded that the North should be on the alert because "the South is just as ready to secede today as it was in '61."[36]

African Americans remained hopeful that their military service in saving the Union carried weight and would nudge white Republicans toward them and away from former Confederates. They were partly correct, but they could not know, as one historian has shown, that Republicans in the 1890s were undergoing a change that had disastrous consequences. The party was turning from its base in the South for numerous reasons. First, the older idealists and humanitarians who believed in black rights were dying or were being defeated in elections. These included Blaine, John Sherman, Benjamin Harrison, and the same Ingalls who had attacked Lee in his 1890 address. Economic issues dominated northern attentions, and people cared less about atrocities in the South. After 1894 the GOP did not need to carry a single southern congressional district to control the government. According to Kousser, "To increase its majority by seeking Southern Negro votes risked alienating Northern racists."[37] Black people did not see this coming at the time. In 1890 it still seemed as if they "had the government." They emerged from the Lee monument unveiling with vestiges of political self-help intact and tried to protect their place in history and the nation with an effort to establish an Emancipation Day holiday.

■ ■ ■

STRIVING FOR A NATIONAL EMANCIPATION DAY

The idea to establish a single day on which to celebrate freedom apparently originated in Richmond with George W. Williams. A Union veteran and outspoken black leader, he had become well connected with financial, religious, and political leaders. More to the point, he was in synch with John Mitchell Jr., the editor of the *Richmond Planet* who became a force behind a national freedom celebration. Mitchell was born in 1863. He had taken over the newspaper in 1884 and quickly built it into one of the strongest voices for African American rights in the nation. The masthead of the newspaper captured his spirit: it featured an arm with a flexed bicep and what appeared to be lightening bolts emanating from a clenched fist. His contribution was recognized by peers who elected him to serve consecutive terms in the 1890s as president of the Afro American Press Association. Mitchell also served on Richmond's Common Council as a representative from the black-dominated Jackson Ward of the city. In that capacity he had voted against an appropriation of $7,500 to underwrite expenses for the ceremonies for the Lee monument. Two other black members from the same ward opposed the resolution, but the measure passed overwhelmingly.[38]

Using the enthusiasm generated by the silver anniversary of the end of the war—and the specter of rising Confederate traditions—the Richmond organizers pressed for a national gathering in the autumn of 1890. A couple of weeks after the unveiling of the Lee monument, bold type in the *Planet* promoted a Grand National Celebration for the twenty-seventh anniversary of emancipation. First scheduled for September, the event was shifted for unexplained reasons to the middle of October. Williams, Mitchell, and others argued that the time had come to show African American unity, raise consciousness over political action, and remind white people that black military service proved not only their manhood but also their importance to the nation. While acknowledging that Lincoln had a hand in emancipation, black speakers professed that God had been the one guiding him. This position left room for the interpretation that black people also served as God's agents in winning their own liberation, paid for by the shedding of their blood. As the event neared, Mitchell summed up: "It is preposterous to think that a race of people oppressed for more than two hundred years by the most galling bondage the world has ever seen should not have a national day for the observance of the same, one during which they can express their thanks to Him who rules the Universe for an emancipation, solemn, awe inspiring, terrible in the sacrifice of bringing it about and yet glorious in its accomplishment."[39]

Even though many agreed that such a day belonged on the nation's calendar, the problem was when to celebrate it. Mitchell performed a service for historians by polling members of the community and running a sampling of public sentiment on the topic. Opinions varied widely on the subject, which was more complicated than it might at first appear. Part of the fault belonged to Lincoln, who had issued both a preliminary and a final version of the proclamation. This created the dilemma about whether to recognize September 22 or January 1. The latter enjoyed a slight edge among African Americans because it was when the proclamation had become official. Yet practical considerations—many of which were mundane but important nonetheless—mattered in the choice of a holiday. Weather had to be considered. January proved more fickle than September for holding processions. But autumn, according to representatives from the Deep South, did not work for people in that region because the holiday interfered with the cotton harvest, complicating the possibility of taking a day off from work. Another person suggested that January 1 was the best day because most people had a holiday anyway, and thus more could participate. Shopkeepers lost no business, and workers already had the day free.

Further muddying the waters was the variety of means through which freedom had come. While Lincoln remained a respected figure, a number of people declared that the proclamation had no real effect, and that other events were more representative of the coming of freedom to black people. For enslaved African Americans in Washington, freedom arrived earlier than in many places, on April 16, 1862. Richmond residents had a different experience, favoring an annual commemoration on April 3, when the Confederate army evacuated the city. As one man put it, that was when he "shook hands with the Yankees."[40] Others suggested that freedom came only with the surrender of Lee's army at Appomattox on April 9, which one respondent suggested was the day "the dog was killed."[41] That date did not suit parts of the Lower South that considered the surrender of Joseph E. Johnston's army in North Carolina on April 26 as the end of the war. In the deeper South, June 19 was important in Texas. A minority of people advocated ignoring emancipation in favor of commemorating passage of the Thirteenth Amendment, which officially ended slavery. A man told the *Planet*, "In the first place I think that Mr. Lincoln's Proclamation didn't amount to any thing from a legal standpoint. It freed nobody. Understand me that it had a very marked moral effect, but the 13th Amendment really gave freedom to the slaves. I believe that we should celebrate the passage of that Amendment, if we desire to celebrate the act by which we became free."[42]

The discussion revealed common attitudes that the organizers themselves may not have noticed. Members of the upper levels of the black community dominated the discussion. Many of the people Mitchell consulted were leading preachers, bankers, business owners, and officers of fraternal societies. Some held positions concurrently in all of the secular, religious, and fraternal worlds. The Reverend W. W. Browne, for example, not only led a congregation but also served as president of a savings bank connected with the True Reformers. One of the ministers from the 5th Street Baptist Church hoped to capitalize on the religious connections by trying to mobilize African Americans to the Emancipation Day cause via the pulpits, which he viewed as "the greatest revolutionizing force." Consequently, strong religious and moral impulses merged with political motivations to instill certain values in the black community. Emancipation Day served as one instructional vehicle for teaching the young about the sacrifices under slavery, the achievements of the race since those days, the proper comportment for conducting their lives, and the means of achieving greater rights.[43]

The opening ceremonies occurred on October 15, with political symbolism and discussion noticeably present. Not all participants favored using the convention for partisan ends, because fear of reprisals was always a concern. Similar to the way African Americans in 1866 claimed that the first freedom celebrations had no significance beyond a day of thanks, the Reverend J. A. Taylor—who served as chair of the proceedings— denied that the meeting had "been called for political purposes, but in order to give thanks for their freedom." Everything about the meeting said otherwise, and one historian of the proceedings noticed the "political assertiveness" of the participants. Organizers extended an invitation to the Farmer's Alliance to send delegates. It is unclear how many answered this call, but the gesture clearly signaled that the political side of uplift was still strongly under consideration. The decorations on the rostrum at the end of the main exposition building featured the colors of the United States, with banners of red, white, and blue. Behind the speaker hung the flag of Virginia, but it was draped among the Stars and Bars. Under this colorful display hung an engraving of Abraham Lincoln. Even though Taylor said the group had assembled not to stir up embers of the past, he added, "What we want is race pride. Don't love everybody better than you do yourselves." He continued: "Nobody is going to respect you when you don't respect yourself. I want to see the time when we will rise in our manhood, our virtue, and in every other department." He underscored the need for unity. "All the white people will think more of us for being united. We are not working for Virginia, but what we want is to select a day that will suit for all the people in the country."[44]

After Taylor spoke, the discussion increasingly turned to how to achieve greater rights. George T. Downing reinforced the need to lift up the race, which on occasion required leaving the Republican Party. He mentioned to the audience that he had supported Grover Cleveland, a Democrat, for president "because he thought he had the ear of the South and would help them."[45] Various other strategies were suggested by members of the convention. African nationalism was raised but explicitly rejected. The assembled proudly called themselves Americans, and one man added, "When the white people pick up horse, foot and dragoon and go back to Europe, then we will pick up horse, foot and dragoon and go back to Africa and until then let us not consider the things of the past but look to the future."[46] Others reaffirmed support for the Republican Party. This may, in fact, have been the most popular sentiment around the country; however, the need for independent partisan activity was urged strongly by members of the convention, suggesting the possibility that the most militant voices were attracted to the movement for national Emancipation Day. One speaker flatly stated, "I am for home rule." He added, "Our position is independent. We must vote for the party that will recognize our manhood and protect our lives. We have discharged our obligations to the Republicans and we never owed the Democrats anything. In eight or ten States in the South we have enough votes to defeat either party. Independence in politics is our only salvation. We number 10,000,000 and yet we are the weakest people here. It is because we are not united. Our safety is in union."[47] No agreement was forthcoming on this position. Nor was there much talk of what form this independent activity should take. Despite the invitation extended to farmers' alliances no one issued strong appeals for uniting with them or revealed specific plans to associate with any third party.

The next day, October 16, featured a parade and other festivities that reinforced the call for uplift, the importance of respectability, and the military ability of African Americans. White observers believed the procession was the largest ever staged by African Americans in the city. The marchers stretched for two miles and took thirty-five minutes to pass. First in line came the police, followed by the chief marshal and several hundred people. Next came military units, followed by the civic and fraternal societies that formed a majority of the parade and represented the black middle class. Banners declared the prescription of this group for racial uplift and revealed the divided mind among black leaders over the benefits of political versus financial uplift. One of the banners read, "In 1860 slaves; in 1890 bankers." Another proclaimed, "The solution of the Negro problem is finance." Still another observed, "The dollar ballot is always counted—stick to finance." A number of African Americans obviously felt stung by past political action and had little hope that partisanship would help. There was more agreement on what they celebrated. At one point the procession stopped in front of City Hall while participants loudly cheered the dates of April 9 and September 22. It was an electric day, with spectators catching the thrill of the display. A reporter from the *Richmond Dispatch* noted that a black women over fifty "was dancing vivaciously and singing at the top of her voice from gladness of heart."[48]

On October 17 the convention settled down to the business of establishing a national day for commemorating freedom and fostering race pride. Approximately 200 delegates from throughout the South attended, although one report placed the number at 300 to 400. Delegates floated the familiar candidates for consideration. September 22 had support as the origination of emancipation but also because it presented a better time for outdoor celebration than January 1. A brief movement to recognize April 3 died quickly. A delegate from Norfolk spoke against commemorating the ratification of the Fourteenth or Fifteenth Amendment, which had not done "a pinch of snuff" for Virginia's black people. A number of people spoke out in favor of January 1. George Williams, the originator of the convention, led the list of those calling for a vote on that day, which eventually became endorsed by convention. The results showed an overwhelming majority favored tying a national commemoration to the date that Lincoln's proclamation took effect in 1863.[49]

It is difficult to determine the impact of this convention. Despite the wishes of the delegates, January 1 became neither a national holiday nor the only freedom celebration in many communities. Local traditions continued. But some evidence indicates a momentary surge in these commemorations and the initiation of new festivities. Whenever a region established a holiday, whether a new practice or an expansion of local custom, January 1 was often chosen. For example, the area around Tuskegee held its first emancipation celebration on January 1, 1894. Similarly, Indianapolis added the date to its ceremonial calendar around 1890; in 1895 the *Freeman* noted that the January 1 celebration was only the fifth or sixth occurrence. As the century came to a close, a newspaper published in Hampton, Virginia, commented, "We are glad to see the increasing and worthy observance of this important anniversary."[50] Yet it is unclear whether the Richmond convention influenced these choices, or if January 1 simply had become the logical date to adopt for the occasion.

The Richmond event, however, demonstrated that strong support existed for freedom celebrations; with political activism remaining a vibrant element. Most African Americans believed the events were useful in showing that they took seriously the responsibilities of citizenship. There was a general sense that demonstrating how the race had elevated itself would lessen discrimination, or at least blunt the arguments that denied equality. Emancipation Day could prove their unity, their political readiness, and their independence—especially by highlighting a black bourgeoisie.

Although the form of Emancipation Day ceremonies did not change much after its inception, the political assertiveness of the late nineteenth century did have an impact. Celebrations still featured a parade with local militia companies, both male and female. As with Confederate traditions, African American rituals incorporated a more formal place for veterans. Augmenting the militia units in the later nineteenth century were newly formed black posts of the GAR. Richmond's African Americans, for instance, founded one post in 1883 and promptly put it to ceremonial work in the community's Decoration Day parade. Organizers wanted to capitalize on this military role because it reinforced a number of key ideals: independence, manhood, and faithfulness to the government, to name a few.[51] Important associations continued to hold key places in the processions, highlighting the black middle class. The parades ended at cemeteries or other symbolic public places, where orators inspired the celebrants and reaffirmed positions on the problems of the day. A local person deserving special recognition was often honored with the task of reading the Emancipation Proclamation to the assembly. Banquets and picnics usually concluded the proceedings, accompanied by music from the many bands.

Besides the more formal representation of veterans through GAR posts, black Memorial Day and Emancipation Day activities in the South contained other elements intended to help the cause. Orations usually wove in several themes. It became a commonplace to praise the black soldier, for reasons that should be apparent. Uplift of some kind formed another thrust of these speeches, which argued for education, moral training, and work as the means for achieving progress.[52] Speakers made almost a fetish of quoting numbers to cite the accomplishments of the race. To prove intellectual advancement, they marshaled statistics on the number of black schools that existed in the country, the number of students enrolled, and the number of teachers. Others pointed out the extent of black professionals or listed as many public officeholders as they could. To show the financial progress of black Americans, speakers indicated that they paid taxes on hundreds of millions of dollars worth of property. Like one speaker in Eastville, Virginia, they might even recite the net worth of well-known men and women, revealing from the podium that black attorney J. W. E. Thomas had between $50,000 and $60,000 worth of assets.[53]

Time and again, too, the addresses focused on the need to educate the next generation, not only to create the next wave of professionals but also to promote race pride among young boys and girls. In tying civic responsibility to education, African Americans differed little from white Americans in the late nineteenth century who increasingly looked at schooling as the means of inculcating civic values in the young. This effort in the black community, however, also included Emancipation Day as one of the classrooms for teaching these lessons. The Negro Conference that met at Hampton University each year around the turn of the century filed reports on various aspects of African American life, which were compiled annually in the *Hampton Bulletin*. One of the areas that this body carefully monitored was education in public schools. A report in 1905 revealed that African Americans expected their schools to have an additional mission of teaching racial pride among the young. On his travels, the interviewer had posed the question, "What do the schools of your city do to foster race pride among colored boys and girls?" Thirteen respondents listed—along with teaching students about the lives of celebrated African Americans and to love their own color and hair—the celebration of Emancipation Day. Another report in 1909 paid particular attention to how the Calhoun Colored School in Alabama marked the day. "On emancipation Day old slavery songs are sung and stories of slavery are told by the old people. Usually an outside speaker makes an address."[54]

Speakers continued to harp on the need for unity among the black race, with self-reliance as a goal. Through the remainder of the 1800s, independent politics vied with financial uplift as contending strands of self-help. Both actually started from the same place—advocating a self-reliant black person. The 1898 celebration in Richmond featured Gregory W. Hayes, president of the Virginia Seminary in Lynchburg. He reiterated the need for independence, which included political party behavior as well as financial well-being. The crowd reportedly applauded when Hayes "enunciated the doctrine of true Negro independence, regardless of all political parties." He added that he longed to see the day when all parties would ask, "How will the Negro vote!" A poem titled "America in 1898" that was published to commemorate the event also spoke of political action, rooting the heroes of black people in the Republican Party. The spirit of this anniversary, went some of the language, called back to earth the great men who had passed and who stood up for human freedom.

Speak, ye heroes! Brave, and immortal all,
Speak! Lincoln, Seward, Blaine, aye, as of yore.
Garfield, Stanton, Thaddeus Stevens, Grant.
Speak out! And teach us, for we shall heed.
Tell us of manhood, freedom dearly bought,
That liberty may be with us as a creed.[55]

With the turn of the century, political uplift was on a downward spiral as a theme in Emancipation Days. African American leaders labored under incredibly difficult situations in which they saw rights eroded one by one. Lynching showed little signs of abating, and the slaughter of black people occurred in places such as Wilmington, North Carolina, in 1898. Increasing oppression caused greater consternation about how to press forward and, not surprisingly, created rifts within the black community, with positions ranging from black nationalism to accommodation. In 1892 an editor of a black newspaper in Florida encouraged African Americans to divide their vote by joining with the Farmer's Alliance and the People's Party. The item claimed that this would obliterate "'the color line' in politics." Virtually in the same breath a Richmond newspaper opposed the position as only helping the Democratic Party. Politics with the white man was business, the *Southern News* item concluded, but with the negro, "it's religion."[56]

As the twentieth century arrived, the quest for unity and self-help continued. In 1902 one of the contributors to the proceedings of the Hampton Negro Conference indicated that many were frustrated by the inability to gain a consensus for a variety of issues. In an item titled "Cooperation Essential to Race Unity," W. S. Scarborough saw a complicated battle ahead: "We have foes to fight. They are within; they are without." Within African American ranks, he noted, there was too much falsehood and jealousy. Some of this sentiment betrays a class sensibility in which a successful man did not want to feel apologetic to his less fortunate colleagues. Scarborough even lamented that the race did not appreciate its members who had succeeded. "We are not true to self, we evade and we try to deceive self." Instead of blaming the masses, he was convinced that it was the preacher, the teacher, and the editor who had created this problem. He was searching for answers, as were many of his comrades, for the continual erosion of equality that required more than an ideology of uplift when facing the violent efforts of white supremacists encouraged by a tacit government. Among the casualties littering black America of the late nineteenth and early twentieth centuries was the efficacy of political self-help. Left standing in the debris were a narrowing range of options, with accommodation growing more apparent.[57]

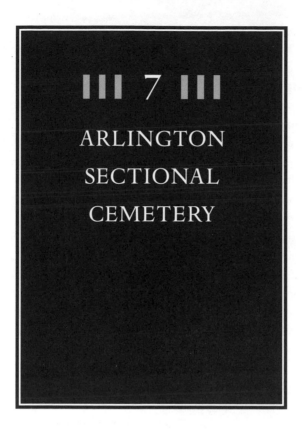

||| 7 |||

ARLINGTON
SECTIONAL
CEMETERY

In 1914 Woodrow Wilson committed a political blunder over commemorating the dead. The southern-born president declined an invitation by the GAR to speak at Union Memorial Day in Arlington Cemetery. Although a disappointment to the veterans, Wilson's decision came as no great surprise. He had refused a similar request the preceding year, and few people expected anything different this time. What perplexed the veterans, and then increasingly angered them, was Wilson's promise to the Daughters of the Confederacy to address the throngs expected for the dedication of the monument in the Confederate section in Arlington on June 4—same cemetery, different crowd, much different meaning. The sitting president of the United States was ignoring the celebration of the men who had saved the Union while honoring the men who had tried to reject that same government. Irony turned to comedy when Champ Clark, Speaker of the House and a Democratic political rival, happily chimed in that *he* would be delighted to address the Union veterans on the nation's Memorial Day. After a visit from a representative of the Democratic congressional committee, Wilson had a change of heart and agreed to speak at both celebrations, even as he denied that Clark's appearance had anything to do with his decision. Not surprisingly, the Speaker of the House received a louder ovation than his president when both were introduced on Union Memorial Day.[1]

Wilson survived a minor bump along the campaign road, but he had received a reminder that some northerners still took the Civil War very seriously. Although Americans had put to rest sectional conflict, a president could not snub Union veterans in favor of their Confederate counterparts. Fifty years after the war the northern press still employed the adjective "loyal" to describe the men who had sacrificed themselves to save the Union. Republicans still relished the opportunity to pounce on gaffes by an opposition president. Senator Joseph Bristow, a Republican from Kansas, typified the responses of Republicans when he said, "The members of the Grand Army of the Republic doubtless never expected to see the day when a President of the United States would refuse to speak a few words in commendation of their heroic services to the country until driven to do so by public indignation."[2]

The president recovered five days later in an address before a large assembly that included Confederate and Union veterans as well as the grand commander of the GAR. In his speech, a president more concerned with the Mexican border declared that the dedication at Arlington symbolized the end of sectional discord. "This chapter in the history of the United States is now closed," he said, "and I can bid you turn with me with your faces to the future quickened by the memories of the past, but with nothing to do with the contests of the past, knowing as we have shed our blood on opposite sides, we now face and admire one another."[3] The commander in chief of the United Confederate Veterans agreed. Bennett Young fully appreciated the special nature of the scene before him: a commemorative event of the Confederacy that attracted the president of the United States and the principal organization for Union veterans. The Stars and Bars were intertwined with Old Glory. Small wonder that Young remarked, "Nothing more strange and unwonted has ever happened in national life than the exercises of this afternoon. It's happening marks another step in the complete elimination of sectional passions, suspicions, or prejudice." He added that the event "gives assurance that North and South have clasped hands across a fratricidal grave."[4]

More had changed than Young or the people assembled at Arlington realized. Memorial Days and freedom celebrations remained useful occasions for making a political point, but they no longer held the same relevance for partisan behavior. The organization of the Confederate section in Arlington took place during a transition in the American political landscape, a period defined by one historian as the decline of popular politics. For a variety of reasons that included disfranchisement of black people, participation in elections dropped as the twentieth century arrived. The style of American campaigns also changed; street activity diminished as a party ritual. Political issues still wormed their way into Civil War memorialization, as Wilson learned the hard way at Arlington, yet the ceremonies no longer contained their intimate connection with mass mobilization and party instruction. Confederate traditions put forth a classless, apolitical view of the conflict that promoted harmony between rich and poor white people based on racism and a shared past defined by the Lost Cause. This interpretation of why the Confederacy had formed rooted itself in the right of self-determination, or good American values. Slavery was not mentioned as a factor. Partisanship still made use of these occasions, but it was harder to play one party against another because of the mixed background of participants, and because the ceremonies embraced northern and southern white people.[5]

Emancipation Days, meanwhile, had arrived at their own crossroads. They remained important occasions in black neighborhoods, but with disfranchisement they no longer contained the strident demand for independent politics. The fiftieth anniversary celebrations of freedom more often than not featured controversy as white and black organizers increasingly adopted the accommodationist themes stressed by Booker T. Washington. In the case of the fiftieth anniversary of emancipation commemorated in Richmond, the majority of African Americans failed to support the event. Organizers of Emancipation Days in Washington debated whether outdoor processions should be held at all, with many of the best men and women arguing against the rituals in favor of indoor, controlled exhibitions that featured the industrial abilities of the race. The observance of freedom, according to one scholar, shared the trajectory of national political campaigns: "By century's end, both had gravitated toward a more subdued presentation that focused on practical goals with less concern for catering to the tastes of the masses." With the entrance of Jim Crow around the turn of the century, they lost their utility as an agent for political rights.[6]

If commemorations of the Civil War were no longer a part of partisan activities, they never lost their role as validation of a group's privilege within the national polity. The graves at Arlington and the freedom celebrations in southern towns spoke volumes about the relative positions of power of white rebels and African Americans. Reconciliation had been achieved around the turn of the century. While some of this was affected by racism and comradeship, there was also a political rationale at work. The details of this story can be followed through the evolution of Arlington Cemetery as it changed from a place of sectional rancor to a site of sectional healing.

■ ■ ■

A PLACE OF SECTIONAL DISCORD

With rare exception, a person transported magically from the North of the 1860s to the dedication of the Confederate monument in Arlington would have found the occasion difficult to comprehend. The cemetery was founded upon the presumption of sectionalism, not fraternity. It had been the home of R. E. Lee, who oversaw the estate as the executor for his deceased father-in-law, a descendant of George Washington. As is well known, the federal government seized the property during the conflict for default of taxes—a mere $92 and some odd change, which the Lee family could have covered easily. It is inconvenient, to say the least, to pay one's taxes when at war with the collector. So the estate of Mary Custis passed into federal hands, with $26,800 paid by the government at an auction in January 1864 for the pretense of clearing the title to prevent the Lee family from reclaiming the property. People at the time understood that Arlington Cemetery emerged as the antithesis of the spirit of reconciliation.

The grounds were first used officially by the government as a home for African American refugees. Washington, D.C., had become a magnet for escaping slaves, creating the usual dilemma for federal authorities about how to handle the influx of people. An enterprising officer in the Quartermaster's Department suggested to his superiors that they move the freedpeople to the south side of the Potomac onto land that had been abandoned by departing rebels. In May 1863, Lieutenant Colonel Elias M. Greene estimated that the existing quarters could handle from 500 to 750 field hands. "The force of contrabands, males and females, now idle in this City, and a dead weight on the Government," he observed, "can be employed to very great advantage in cultivating the above lands, raising corn and millet, and cutting Hay (of which it is estimated more than one thousand tons may be cured) for this Department." In short, Greene wrote, "the arrangement I propose will not only in my opinion conduce to the sanitary and moral improvement of the contrabands, but will save the Govt an immense amount of money." His superiors agreed but ordered him to locate the settlement where it did not expose the residents to battle or recapture.[7] Within months Greene had established a village whose industry received praise. Observers also noticed that the inhabitants consisted of, among others, former slaves of the Lee family and survivors of the colonization experiment in Haiti.[8]

Many of the residents who passed away were buried on the grounds, creating a situation that became significant a few years later. White Union soldiers lay intermingled with civilians of both races. African American soldiers also were interred, as were hundreds of Confederate soldiers who had died in Union hospitals as prisoners of war. Burials had occurred on the estate without plan or any thought to create discrete sections of different populations. This condition gained some attention late in the war, but became even more important later in the century.

Official use of the cemetery as a burying ground for the nation's heroes began roughly a year after the freedpeople had settled there. The change came at the instigation of Quartermaster General Montgomery C. Meigs, who was trying to solve a space shortage. Because the government had purchased the estate in January 1864, the grounds were a godsend as bodies poured into Washington during Ulysses S. Grant's campaign to Richmond. A cemetery at the Soldiers' Home had reached capacity. In a letter to the secretary of war on June 15, 1864, Meigs asked that the estate be used as a national military cemetery. At the same time, he requested that interments of the general population cease and that the bodies of soldiers be placed on the heights near the Lee mansion, with all graves marked and with the proper enclosure. Before the next spring arrived, the government had buried several thousand men in the new cemetery.[9]

The creation of a soldiers' cemetery resulted in segregation, which was apparently unintended by the cemetery's founders. From the time that the grounds became a national cemetery devoted primarily to soldiers, interments of white people occurred on the heights, while black teamsters, laborers, and soldiers remained in the northeast corner of the estate. Also in this section lay many of the Confederate dead. An unidentified report to the secretary of war sometime after the war, probably from either Meigs or Daniel Rucker, who supervised the Washington area burials at the time, gave the details: "Had my intentions been distinctly understood and carried out no interments would have been made in this quarter of the cem'y[;] all would have been buried on the Hill and nearer to and encircling the mansion."[10] Subordinates apparently believed otherwise and naturally created the separate burial grounds by race.

Among the first to capitalize politically on the segregated nature of the graves was a columnist for the *Washington Daily National Intelligencer*, a Democratic newspaper. The writer appreciated that the section for African Americans was located in the northeast corner, "the farthest possible from the white, a circumstance which, fortunately escaping the notice of the Radical Congress, doubtless saved the infliction of any amount of empty ethnological discourse in the last session." The writer was comfortable with a separation of the races but used this case as an example of the duplicitous nature of the Republican support of African Americans. With the effort "to enforce negro equality upon this District and the country at large by the intemperate politicians in high places, it is pertinent to inquire why this distinction by the head of the war office is so conspicuously made in the habitations of the dead. If the negro soldier, while living, is entitled to an equality with the white soldier, it may well strike thoughtful men with wonder that it is not deemed fit for them to sleep together in the chambers of death." He concluded, "The authorities which would put the negro side by side with the white man at the ballot-box would have taken care to mingle these dead bodies in like manner if there were any *voting* to be done on this solemn camping ground."[11]

Black editorialists offered a similar critique. In 1871 the *Washington Chronicle* reported on the black disenchantment with Arlington on Decoration Day. A number of African Americans broke off from the main event on the heights near the mansion to visit the colored section below. When they arrived, they found no stand erected, no orator, no flags, and no flowers for decoration. Black leaders in Washington requested "the removal of the remains of all loyal soldiers now interred in the north end of the Arlington cemetery, among paupers and rebels, to the main body of the grounds at the earliest possible moment." The black editor of a New Orleans newspaper declared that the situation proved the hypocrisy of white Unionists and called for African Americans to boycott Decoration Day. "If the assistance of our race in the late war was of any account, we ought to secure a recognition from our white friends who, however strong and determined, could not have won the victory without us. And even if it were of no account, the pretensions of equality made by the white Republicans toward living negro voters, ought to leave no room for evidences of contempt towards the negro dead in these cemeteries, which are visited with such enthusiasm when white graves are to be decorated."[12]

The comments again illustrated that Americans on both sides of the bloody chasm interpreted national cemeteries not as apolitical cultural artifacts but as texts that announced the loyalty of the interred and the living. Conditions of graves and signs of respect spoke volumes about how the government—especially the white Republicans who controlled the mechanisms of the state—considered the contributions of African Americans and the status of former Confederates. Black people were angered to know that their soldiers who had fought and died for the liberation of the race lay next to "paupers and rebels" and not with white comrades. On the other side of the divide, former Confederates chafed at the lack of respect shown to their graves and at the efforts to bar them from decorating them on the GAR's holiday.

Many northerners, of course, did not mind keeping the sectional flames burning. Future president James A. Garfield of Ohio received the honor to serve as the orator of Decoration Day in 1868, the first year the GAR observed the occasion. Garfield had served in the Union army and risen to major general before he was elected to the U.S. Congress. Before the war he was an ardent free-soiler, which drew him to the Republican Party. While most of the speech was innocuous and was not designed to provoke former Confederates, at one point he came close to calling Lee a traitor. He reminded the assembled about who had lived on the estate and what Lee had done to help the rebellion. "Seven years ago," Garfield said, "this was the home of one who lifted his sword against the life of his country, and who became the great imperator of the rebellion." He added, "The soil beneath our feet was watered by the tears of slaves. The beauty of yonder proud Capitol awakened in their hearts no pride, and brought them no hope." Fortunately, there was a happy ending. "But, thanks be to God, this arena of rebellion and slavery is a scene of violence and crime no longer. This will be forever the sacred mountain of our capital. Here is our temple."[13]

The hard line against rebels in the cemetery softened in the mid-1870s, corresponding with the changing mood among certain northerners. In the case of Arlington, the shift toward greater respect for former Confederates can be traced to 1874. In 1873 Secretary of War William Belknap had turned the cemetery over to the GAR on Decoration Day. Because the event honored the soldiers who fell in defense of the Union, the decoration of Confederate graves was restricted by an order on May 24, 1873. The policy was challenged in 1874 by Senator John J. Patterson of South Carolina. The senator's background was not typical of political figures from the Palmetto State. A carpetbagger from Pennsylvania, he had been part owner of the *Harrisburg Telegraph*. He had served as a captain in the Union army. After the war he moved to South Carolina, where he belonged to the Republican Party. He did not reveal his motives for protesting a renewal of the order from 1873, but it probably originated in a desire to placate constituents and show that the government was not entirely unsympathetic to former rebels.

Belknap reported to the senator that the order had been misunderstood; it only restricted groups from decorating on the GAR's special occasion. Anyone wishing to decorate graves other than those of Union soldiers could do so on another day. Belknap confirmed that no restrictive order would be issued in 1874. "The grounds of that Cemetery will on that day be opened to all orderly persons who desire to decorate any of the graves within that enclosure." The GAR decided to leave well enough alone and stopped interdicting attempts to decorate Confederate graves on Union Decoration Day. Yet here was another case of a Republican official, this time holding office in the South, arguing for courtesies for former Confederates.[14]

The following year another southern representative pushed the commemorative boundaries further at Arlington. Eppa Hunton, U.S. congressman from Virginia, worked on behalf of Mrs. C. P. Culver to gain permission to improve the graves of former Confederates. The secretary of war granted the petition to allow civilians to "fit up, in the manner proposed, the portion of the grounds in the southwest corner of the cemetery where the Confederate soldiers are buried by themselves, and also to erect suitable headstones at those graves, and also at the graves of the other Confederate soldiers buried elsewhere in the grounds, among Union soldiers, should you desire to do so." The petitioners intended to build walks, to landscape, and to replace the wooden headboards that were rapidly decaying.[15] Hunton's participation again underscores the ironies behind reunion. Ten years earlier he had been a brigadier general in the Army of Northern Virginia and was captured on Lee's retreat toward Appomattox. Now he sat in the halls of Congress trying to further the interests of former Confederates.

This was still, however, the era of mixed feelings. On one hand, observers noticed the reconciliation trend signified by the tending of graves in cemeteries throughout the country. In 1877 a columnist for the *New York*

Tribune felt obliged to note that "this year for the celebration of Decoration Day the principal question has been the honor due not to the graves of Union but Confederate soldiers." The item also observed, "Ten years dulls even personal sorrow for the dead; in a good many places Decoration Day is already observed not as an anniversary of tender sorrow, but of general jollification." On the other hand, a northern correspondent noted the bitterness that Arlington conjured. Touring the grounds in 1874, the reporter observed, "The place is sad beyond description." The graves created a somber mood that promoted reflection. Yet, he added, "it is quite impossible not to imagine that a spirit of true revengefulness had much to do with the selection of this place for the holy purpose to which it is put. He was a blind man who chose this spot for the last resting-place of our soldiers, thinking that retaliation upon the Lees would always be an object to be desired, and he was barren of honor to cause the revered dead to play so ignoble a part in the scheme of procuring pain for a foe."[16]

Such were the mixed moods that Arlington evoked. It took a different time, a different president, and a different war to bridge the bloody chasm and lay this ambivalence to rest.

■ ■ ■

MCKINLEY AND THE CONFEDERATE SECTION

The origins of the Confederate section in Arlington date to the Spanish-American War and a president's desire for three things: reconciliation of the sectional heart, consolidation of southern support for overseas expansion, and reclamation of his reputation in racial affairs. President William McKinley found the perfect forum for blending conciliation with his political agenda in the peace jubilee scheduled for Atlanta in mid-December 1898. He electrified former Confederates as he pronounced it time for the federal government to tend the graves of *all* the fallen from the Civil War. The address has been viewed as a triumph for reconciliation, but historians rarely have included all three reasons behind the trip. In a second address in Atlanta, McKinley clearly announced his intentions to win southern support for expansionism. He needed to lobby the southern power structure, which held lukewarm sentiments toward the war with Spain and now had reservations about maintaining the territorial gains from the conflict. But the president had another audience in mind as well. He covered more than 2,000 miles by railcar within a week, visiting not only the former capital of the Confederacy at Montgomery, Alabama, but also the new center of black educational activity at

Tuskegee. While there, the president endorsed Booker T. Washington as white America's favorite black leader, in the process trying to appease black voters who were unhappy with him over the government's failure to do anything about a massacre in Wilmington, North Carolina.

From our vantage point, the Spanish-American War and its immediate aftermath provide the exclamation point to sectional reconciliation. Fighting a foreign enemy drew Yankee and Rebel together into a common cause. Former Confederate generals led men into combat once again, but this time under the Stars and Stripes of the United States. Southern whites worshiped the Confederate past and waved the flags of the rebellion, but their service in the Spanish-American War proved that, when needed, they would follow the flag of the United States into battle. Fate helped by selecting a man from North Carolina for the grim honor of being the first soldier slain in the conflict. Military authorities also deliberately chose as major generals Fitzhugh Lee and Joseph Wheeler, both of whom had been Confederate general officers. The crowning touch to national reunification came with McKinley's gesture to care for the graves of southern dead, which symbolized that former Confederates had achieved acceptance by the nation in which they lived.[17]

Yet reconciliation appeared less certain at the time and had to be won by actions on the part of the McKinley administration. Support by southern white people for the war was mixed at first. White men of the South did enlist and fight and were led in some cases by former Confederate officers. White southerners in general, however, took longer to warm to the cause than black people. African Americans viewed the Cuban people with some sympathy—as colleagues in the battle against oppression. Because Afro-Cuban leaders attempted to set up a republic, black Americans thought that a successful example of self-government would reaffirm the logic of their own fight at home. They also saw the coming conflict as a chance to prove once again their loyalty to the country, their manliness as protectors, and their worthiness for equality. White southerners, on the other hand, supported the war partly out of economic motivations for finding increased markets for cotton. They also had humanitarian and political sympathies for a people who appeared to struggle under a restrictive government reminiscent of the military occupation of the South in Reconstruction. Some did not want to assume the role of overseas carpetbaggers. Southern congressmen were overwhelmingly against annexation of the islands even after the war, and a majority of senators from the former Confederate states refused to ratify the treaty with Spain or support retaining the Philippines.[18]

The struggle that made Cubans appealing to African Americans made some white southerners cautious about helping in the war. J. Bryan of Virginia wrote a friend that the death and wounding of men in Cuba "does not make me any more patient in this war for humanity." For him, the situation raised echoes of the Civil War. He continued: "I have heard it said that there was a white man killed or wounded for every adult negro in slavery, and whether the revolutionary change in the negro's condition was worth the awful sacrifice is hardly a question that you or I would determine in the affirmative; and I believe that the Cuban cause is very much in the same degree." As one historian has pointed out, there were companion fears that annexation would "bring millions of dark-skinned people under the government of and possibly into the United States." This same historian also observed that partisanship was a factor. Southern white Democrats did not mind complicating the lives of Republicans, and some worried about the expansion of centralized power, especially if it benefited the GOP's hold on the presidency.[19]

For McKinley, touring the South had greater ramifications than simply reunion. Historians have characterized him as a sentimentalist who had only reconciliation at heart, or as a president who had made internal peace one aim of the Spanish-American War. While true, the interpretation ignores him as a sitting president trying to secure the gains of that war and convince the American public of the necessity of expansionism. Writing in the 1990s, Edward L. Ayers was one of the first scholars to notice the additional goals that motivated the president: to secure ratification of the treaty with Spain and to keep the Philippines as a possession of the United States. The intentions were clear to the people who witnessed McKinley's tour, especially when the president followed up his comments in a second address to a different crowd in Atlanta. When reporting about the speech delivered on December 15, the *Washington Post* featured the headline, "Expansion His Theme: The President Faces New Destiny of the Republic."[20] At the same time, McKinley did appear to hold honest sentiments for reconciliation. Reports suggested that before he had been elected, he had been moved when he saw the untended graves of Confederates at Fredericksburg. More importantly, he was smart enough to know how symbolic those graves remained in the psyches of white southerners, and what it meant to have the government care for them.

On December 14, 1898, McKinley delivered his address to the Atlanta Peace Jubilee from within the hall of the Georgia state legislature. The president opened by declaring that the war had proven that sectional ties no longer existed. The nation stood as one. He was also pleased to attend a celebration that marked the signing of the treaty with Spain (even if the agreement still required ratifying). He then led into the section of the speech that received so much acclaim throughout the former Confederate states. "Every soldier's grave made during our unfortunate civil war is a tribute to American valor," said the president. He acknowledged that when those graves were dug, wide differences existed between the sections. But he added that "the time has now come in the evolution of sentiment and feeling under the providence of God, when in the spirit of fraternity we should share with you in the care of the graves of the Confederate soldiers."[21] A couple of days later, the president's remarks at Savannah, Georgia, reaffirmed the overall motivations of his tour. He wanted the nation to move forward to greatness, which was impossible without unity. "There is cause for congratulation," he told the crowd, "that with the grave problem before us growing out of the war with Spain we are free from any divisions at home." He added, "There are, happily, now no domestic differences to check the progress and prosperity of the country which our peaceful relations with the whole world will encourage and strengthen."[22]

The president's pledge to have the government care for Confederate graves aroused a burst of enthusiasm that spread from the chambers of the Georgia legislature throughout the country. Almost immediately southerners understood the importance of what the president had said. The legislature passed a resolution praising the president: "These be words that might fitly be written with letters of gold in pictures of silver. They do credit to the heart and head of the distinguished citizen who uttered them—a man who has proved himself to be the Chief Executive of the entire Union, capable on great occasions of rising above party and sectional lines."[23] Murray F. Smith, a state senator from Mississippi, commented, "I do not believe that any speech has been delivered in thirty years that has had such a wide spread beneficial effect in the South as President McKinley's speech at Atlanta. It absolutely thrilled me to such an extent that it brought tears to my eyes." A judge from Tennessee immediately sent a note to the president: "As a son of an Ex Confederate, as a kinsman of Confederate dead, as the father of two boys who proudly wore the blue under your call, I want to add my personal thanks for the noble, wise and generous sentiments uttered by you at Atlanta." A correspondent for the *Washington Post* captured the heart of the issue. "They felt that the Chief Magistrate of this reunited nation realized their patriotism and drew no line of demarcation in his appraisement of American citizenship."[24] Some in the North joined the chorus for the president. A resident of Toledo, Ohio, considered the remarks of McKinley "patriotic and magnanimous," and the U.S. Grant Post of the GAR in Brooklyn passed public resolutions calling the gesture "the best statesmanship and the broadest patriotism that seeks to unite more completely the North and the South by calling to remembrance rather the valor of the men who bravely died than by keeping prominent the issues and penalties of a lost cause."[25]

This response may seem overzealous and resemble the romantic hyperbole of the late nineteenth century, yet Confederate veterans and their descendants attached enormous significance to the president's gesture. The return of the battle flags to the south failed to stir reactions of a similar magnitude. Perhaps it was the powerful combination of symbols that stirred souls to this extent. The president of the United States had made a special journey into the South to make the announcement, instead of simply issuing a statement from the White House. His offer meant that the government took the lead on the project, assuming the costs for refurbishing and maintaining the graves. And he used bodies, not an abstraction like the flag, as the medium of exchange for this unity.

Flags were an important symbol, but McKinley's offer touched something deeper and more personal in attempting to comfort families who had lost loved ones and who feared that the graves had gone untended. The unequal treatment of Confederate and Union dead had irritated white southerners since the war ended. In a column that sounded as if it had been written for 1898, a Richmond editor had observed twenty-nine years before McKinley's speech, "We would gladly bury the animosities of the past in the grave of our Lost Cause. We long to see the day when all the dead shall be the common care of all the living." The item concluded with remarks about Confederate Decoration Day: "The ceremonies which we perform to-day should be perpetuated, and never—no never, neglected, until that period arrives, if ever it do, when a common government and reunited people shall pay the same honors to the dead of both sides." When the president met those terms nearly thirty years later, there was small wonder that a woman from Georgia wrote, "We are all McKinleyites now. So often have I been in the national cemetery at Chattanooga and wished that our Confederate dead could have their graves so well kept by the government, and in my heart felt rebellious that it was not so. The speech of President McKinley went straight home to me, and in less than one hour after reading it, I had hoisted the Flag over our house."[26]

McKinley continued to win the hearts of southern white people while adroitly keeping Union veterans on his side. After Atlanta he journeyed to Alabama, where he addressed a crowd in Montgomery, the first capital of the Confederacy. The governor of the state accompanied him, as did Joseph Wheeler. The latter was a native son, former Confederate officer, and newly christened hero of the Spanish-American War. During this part of the trip, it became clear that no white southerner was going to concede that the Civil War had been wrong. At one point the governor said, "We of the South have nothing to regret except our dead." Although the governor followed the comment with an immediate pronouncement of loyalty to the United States, McKinley offered a shrewd quip that registered well with his northern constituency: "The Governor says he has nothing to take back. We have nothing to take back for having kept you in the Union. We are glad you did not go out, and you are glad you stayed in." A veteran from Toledo, Ohio, applauded the president for a remark that "was prompt, to the point, and most gratifying to the Boys who wore the Blue." Northerners forgave the South's lack of guilt for the war, as long as it was clear that former Confederates embraced the nation—and that the leader of that nation did not forget about the veterans who had saved the country.[27]

Not everyone was happy with McKinley's tour and the conciliatory gesture. Southern Democrats interpreted that the president was trying to capitalize politically by putting his opposition on the defensive. Some northerners were offended by the continued proliferation of rebel flags and symbols of the fallen Confederacy. A lumber company owner from Pittsburgh wrote McKinley, "Is the time not opportune, now that you have beyond all doubt won the lasting affection of the southern people, for you to suggest to them in some appropriate manner, that they in the interest of one Flag and one Country, should now lay aside their confederate badges and flags, and replace them for all public uses with the glorious Stars and Stripes?" McKinley himself received mild criticism from the editor of a Republican newspaper in the North when he allowed a Confederate veteran in Macon, Georgia, to pin a badge on his chest that contained "a rebel emblem." The columnist apparently wrote that it was poor form to have the president "displaying an emblem that certainly had no place on the breast of the president of the United States."[28]

A more serious concern emerged in the black press. In the *Richmond Planet* John Mitchell claimed he had suspected before the trip that the president cared more about atrocities overseas than those in his own country. After devouring the president's annual address to Congress, the editor found the document more remarkable for what it did not say: "There is absolutely no reference to the internal disorders at home, and the butcheries in the Carolinas find no place in the lengthy document." This was a direct reference to the president's lack of action against the so-called riot in Wilmington, North Carolina. This disturbance involved the unprovoked killing of black people in that city on November 10, 1898, by armed white supremacists who attempted to break the power of a black majority. White people had captured the election two days earlier but followed that victory with butchery. A former Confederate veteran named Alfred Moore Waddell said, "We will never surrender to a ragged raffle of negroes, even if we have to choke the current of the Cape Fear with carcasses." Deaths were officially set at seven, although Waddell estimated that his mob killed at least twenty. McKinley had done nothing about this disturbance, and he had not even issued so much as a comment on the situation. This disheartened and outraged African Americans, who believed the Republican administration had abrogated its responsibility to protect the lives of citizens.[29]

After the president extended his offer regarding the Confederate graves, black men like Mitchell reached the conclusion that McKinley was selling out to the white South to head off antiexpansionist efforts by Democrats. It took him awhile to make the connection explicit in his newspaper. At first he stewed about the tour, puzzled and upset that the mood in Washington favored compromise with former rebels. He indicated that black people could not fathom why so much consideration should be shown to one section "which when an analysis of the vote of the recent elections is made did not furnish a Republican majority in any of the states of the late Confederacy." He also noted that "some of the rankest Democrats" from the South were awarded with high positions in the military and that southern Democrats were becoming nearly as influential as northern Republicans. "What is the meaning of all this?" he asked. Mitchell answered the question himself as he observed northern Republicans' delight with the president's tour. It dawned on him that the president was trying to win support for the treaty with Spain and continued efforts to expand the

American empire. The president himself likely helped Mitchell reach this conclusion. McKinley made public his views on the Philippines while speaking in Savannah, Georgia, on December 17. "To-night he has burned his bridges behind him," reported the *Washington Post*. "He has taken a stand in favor of holding the Philippines, which is so emphatic that the most extravagant utterances of Senator Lodge in the same direction seem weak and feeble."[30]

Black Americans did more than write about their concerns; they also protested. A reporter noticed that the local committee in charge of the Atlanta Peace Jubilee tried to restrict participation of African Americans. The Atlanta Federation of Trades denounced the management of the event "because the negro members of the stone quarry men's association were not allowed to appear in the parade. The labor leaders in their resolutions say that as the color line was not drawn in the war there ought to have been no discrimination in the peace jubilee." Labor organizations boycotted the event and refused to march in the parade. No further mention was made of this incident.[31] Nor did McKinley make any statements about discrimination in the country or the need to end violence against black people. He was not about to broach a subject that upset the white South.[32]

Instead, McKinley went to Tuskegee to endorse Booker T. Washington's peaceful approach for uplifting the black race—a strategy that de-emphasized politics and agitation in favor of practical training for economic self-help. Washington explained in an autobiography that he had lobbied hard for the visit by the president. He was not alone. Many black southerners, such as the leaders of Spellman Seminary and a black industrial college in Savannah, Georgia, sent the president letters encouraging him to visit their institutions. After Washington made two trips to the White House to convince the president that his visit would be a comfort to the black race, the president agreed. But Washington had to make a few more calls on the capital. His last trip came after the killings at Wilmington. "When I told him that I thought a visit from the President of the United States at that time to a Negro institution would do more than almost anything else to encourage the race and show to the world in what esteem he held the race, he replied that he was determined to show his interest in us by acts rather than by mere words, and that if I thought his visit to Tuskegee would permanently help the race and the institution he would most gladly give up one day of his administration to visit Tuskegee."[33] McKinley picked for his symbolic stop a black institution perfectly suited for his mission. The president demonstrated his concern with the advancement of African Americans without commenting on the Wilmington violence, and he did so in the company of a person acceptable to many white people.

The big day came on December 16, although the visit to Tuskegee, Alabama, in the morning was balanced with an appearance in Montgomery in the afternoon. Washington treated the president to quite a display. McKinley reviewed more than 600 boys and 300 girls from the normal school. Then came a parade of what observers estimated to be between fifty and seventy floats, each representing an aspect of training at the school: "the tinner, making his cans, the blacksmith forging a shoe, the dairy maids making butter, the carpenter constructing furniture, the architect drawing plans." McKinley appreciated the effort as he endorsed the school and the course that Washington had laid for uplifting the race. "Patience, moderation, self-control, knowledge, character," the president told the crowd, "will surely win you victories and realize the best aspirations of your people." Shortly after the visit, a delighted Washington wrote the president with thanks: "Your visit to Tuskegee has resulted in bringing about a sympathy and union between the races of this section that is almost marvelous. We all feel that the impression is permanent. You have helped every black and white man in the South, and we are deeply grateful to you for your visit and unselfish help, and noble work."[34]

The results of the trip were mixed. There was no mistaking the triumph for sectional reconciliation. Public reports and private correspondence in the white South overwhelmingly ran in favor of the gesture. The Civil War finally seemed to be over, and the nation was now ready to get on with new business. It is unclear, however, if the president gained support for his expansionist agenda. The Senate ratified the treaty with Spain, and the United States held on to the Philippines; but more southern senators voted against the policy than for it. The trip to Tuskegee helped cement the position of Booker T. Washington as a preeminent leader of his race and showed McKinley as sensitive to the efforts of black Americans to improve themselves.[35] Ugly racial violence still remained, as did discontent with the government on the part of black people. But a sizable part of the country felt pretty good about itself and ready to flex its muscle internationally.

The most visible impact of the president's visit was the eventual creation of a Confederate section in Arlington, as well as legislation requiring the government to care for the bodies of all the soldiers who had died in the Civil War. Almost immediately, Dr. Samuel Lewis of Washington, D.C., seized upon the president's words at Atlanta as ammunition to lobby for improving the Confederate graves at Arlington. A physician who had served as an assistant surgeon at Chimborazo Hospital in Richmond during the war, he commanded the Charles Broadway Rouss Camp of the United Confederate Veterans in Washington. A few months before the president's tour, the doctor had inventoried the graves of Confederate dead as part of the chapter's historical committee. His findings stunned him. He wrote a friend that with the exception of "a very few of the older clerks in the Quartermaster's Department of the U.S. no one in Washington supposed there were more than ½ dozen Confederate Dead left within the District." Even the superintendent of the cemetery seemed in the dark about the actual numbers. Lewis's preliminary inventory identified 136 graves of former Confederates.[36] Lewis was especially bothered that the bodies were scattered across the cemetery, "intermingled with federal soldiers—white and black—and their graves undistinguished by any mark or characteristic from those of Q. M. Employees, Citizen refugees, or negro contrabands." Later in 1899 the group discovered another 128 bodies buried in the cemetery of the Soldiers' Home before it had reached capacity and Arlington had become a soldiers' cemetery.[37]

In a relatively short time, the Confederate section became a reality. Lewis and his comrades prepared a petition that went to the president on June 5, 1899, asking that the remains of the southern soldiers at Arlington be gathered in a section and marked appropriately. McKinley was sympathetic and gave executive endorsement, but funding required congressional approval. At the next session, Congress authorized an appropriation of $2,500 for reinterring in a Confederate section the 128 bodies from the Soldiers' Home and the 136 scattered throughout the estate. McKinley approved the act on June 6, 1900, but work was delayed until lists of the dead were published in case relatives wanted to remove the deceased. In May 1903 the first ceremonies were held to dedicate the section, which consisted of about three and a half acres and 264 graves laid out in a circular pattern. Each grave was marked with a white marble headstone inscribed with the number of the grave, the deceased's regiment and state, and "C.S.A." At the ceremonies, Lewis fittingly paid special tribute "to our lamented President William McKinley and the United States Congress."[38]

Oddly enough, the strongest opposition to the Confederate section of the cemetery came not from northerners but from southerners, and especially from certain women's organizations that served as guardians of the

Confederate past. The protests originated between June 1900 and May 1901 when the government delayed initiating work in case families wished to claim the bodies. Discontent emanated most from the ladies memorial associations. First to step forward were two organizations from Richmond, Virginia: the Daughters of the Confederacy and the Ladies of the Hollywood Memorial Association. Leading the charge was Janet H. W. Randolph of the Daughters of the Confederacy. The women wanted to bring their dead boys home, in this case to Hollywood Cemetery, instead of leaving them on northern soil. They claimed they did not want it to appear as if the South accepted charity from the Union government. They also referred to a rumor that the GAR planned to desecrate the graves. Even the many who likely dismissed this rumor as propaganda retained concerns about the care that northerners provided the graves. Ultimately, the women reasoned that it was better that the bodies were surrounded by comrades.[39]

Additional motivations lay behind their opposition. Some undoubtedly were concerned with maintaining the relevance of the ladies memorial associations, which had suffered through the 1870s and 1880s from a decline in volunteers as the recovery of bodies dwindled and men assumed greater direction of memorial activities. It was difficult for these societies to recruit new members without a mission that seemed as relevant as that of the heady days of the 1860s when women felt on the front line of important civic and political activity. The associations were enjoying a comeback in the late nineteenth century, helped by the surge in Confederate organizations that made preservation of the Civil War veteran and his helpmeets into nearly a fetish. It was becoming a sacred duty to pass on this heritage to the next generation, especially as the old soldiers passed away.

The Richmond women also still saw a political implication behind ceremonial activity. They believed that the leaders of the Confederate Veterans, and Lewis, had become too accommodationist with the Republican-led government. The women feared that the men cozied up to the administration to milk it for patronage. "Genl [Fitzhugh] Lee is making a living out of the U.S. Govt. [as a general] and Genl. Gordon would like to, and McKinley would like a few Southern votes." Janet Randolph stated firmly, "We want our dead and notwithstanding the extreme generosity of the Government in allowing Dr. Lewis out of *Our Taxes* the magnificent sum of $2500.00, we are going to have our dead." It was also important to the organization to make sure the cemetery and its accoutrements properly told the story of the Confederate soldier and served as an instructional medium for generations to come. Randolph stated that when the bodies were in their rightful place, the organization planned to put over the graves a "Monument to tell how & where & for what they died."[40]

Lewis conducted a full-scale lobbying effort to create the Confederate section and belittle the women's arguments. He first ensured that he had the endorsement of Confederate veterans, seeking out high-ranking former Confederate officers such as Wheeler and Stephen D. Lee for the project. His camp also polled other chapters of Confederate Veterans to marshal support for the reburials. H. A. Herbert, a Washington attorney and former secretary of the navy, furnished practical reasons why any veteran should welcome the Confederate section. "If we reject this appropriation, that will be an end to the whole matter; congress can never again be expected to do anything more in the direction of caring for the Confederate dead." Additionally, the government had the resources to provide permanent care for the gravesites, something the ladies memorial associations could not guarantee. He pointed out that the women of Richmond had to petition the state legislature for donations because they did not have the means to move the bodies. Perhaps most importantly, reasoned Herbert, leaving the bodies in their own section at Arlington would have a greater positive effect for the Confederate cause. Digging up and reinterring bodies in cemeteries throughout the South "would add but little, if anything, to the beauty, attractiveness, or a sacredness of these existing cemeteries." Removing bodies from the district "would be giving up the Capital of what is now our common country, entirely to the Union dead; the Confederate dead will have no interest and no memorial telling them of their deeds anywhere within the reach of the city that was named for GEORGE WASHINGTON, the greatest of American rebels!"[41]

Once Lewis and his colleagues won the approval of veterans, they easily persuaded their network of congressmen and bureaucrats that the opinions of the Richmond women represented a minority. A committee of five sent to Secretary of War Elihu Root the results of a meeting of the Confederate Veterans Association in March 1901 that unanimously adopted resolutions for the government to go ahead with the reburial plans. The committee reassured the cabinet officer that although the objections to the reburials came "from highly esteemed and most reputable sources, supported by apparently formidable protests, it is a fact that a comparatively small number is represented." The petition to the secretary indicated that Wheeler, Stephen D. Lee, and other former Confederate military leaders endorsed the reburial plan. The petitioners added to the list of supporters the Ladies Southern Relief Society of Washington.[42] Root eventually ordered the plan to be executed. He had waited to see the sentiments of the South before acting. He had considered asking Congress to rescind the act, had the endeavor been widely unpopular, but he received so many reports of enthusiasm that he concluded that the Richmond women alone objected to it.[43]

Root's assessment was not totally accurate. Another women's organization tried to stop the creation of the section, although not as resolutely as the Richmond women. The newly formed Confederated Southern Memorial Association also preferred to bring the bodies home from Arlington. The memorial associations were somewhat defensive at the time, fearing that they faced absorption by the newer women's organization, the United Daughters of the Confederacy. In 1900 at a meeting in Louisville, Kentucky, the Confederated Southern Memorial Association established itself as a clearinghouse to link the memorial societies still functioning throughout the South. It hoped to provide a united voice for greater lobbying power while allowing the autonomy of individual chapters. The founders courted support from the Confederate Veterans. One of the organizers explained to John B. Gordon, commander-in-chief of the United Confederate Veterans, that the memorial associations "bring to you more tangible demonstration of work done than any other organized body of Southern people, men or women." The writer continued: "We are not willing to lose our identity as memorial associations, nor to merge ourselves into the younger organization, 'The Daughters of the Confederacy.' We hope by this federation to commemorate our efforts and stamp our work upon the hearts of those who come after us, and thereby insure its continuance." She added that the founders would consider it an honor to meet with the annual reunion of the United Confederate Veterans, with whom they felt a kinship. "Many of us are veterans—veterans as much as the gray, battle-scarred old soldiers—tho' we bided at home."[44] What better way to help the cause and show their importance than by bringing home the bodies of their southern boys?

The organization also revealed that most southern whites had been as surprised as Lewis at the number of bodies in Arlington. As word spread, enthusiasm had built among some of the societies to work with the Confederate Veterans to raise funds to return the bodies not to Richmond but to their native states. Additionally, a congressional committee that McKinley had charged with determining the number of Confederate graves in the North—many of which contained the bodies of men who had died in prison camps—had come up with an estimate of roughly 30,000. It seemed logical to the legislators that they should coordinate efforts to address all of these veterans' organizations, rather than simply aiding some in the Washington area. The women sent word through sympathetic veterans' chapters and through their congressmen that they thanked the government for its offer but would rather not accept.

Located in Washington, the Rouss Camp had on its side the right connections and the momentum for reconciliation found in many areas of the country. A member, probably Lewis, wrote the superintendent of the cemetery about the genesis of the women's group, underscoring how young it was ("not yet a year old") and thus suggesting that it did not represent southern sentiments. This was true to a point. The umbrella organization was new, but its members had worked together since nearly the end of the war. He added that the government had been close to executing the plan for the section "when the patriotic women above mentioned appeared with their well-meant but ill-advised and ill-timed interference; going so far as to bring to their aid the influence of their local members of Congress and other influential persons to have our local work set at naught, and their disturbing, impracticable schemes laid before the government and brought to the attention of the country and made much of in the public press."[45] When dealing directly with the organization, however, Lewis tried to reason with its members and even to appease them. He understood that the women did not want to appear to be accepting charity from the government. But Lewis tried to assuage these feelings by saying that they were all part of the government now and "form a very important part as to our views and desires regarding the cause of these dead comrades. Not on the plea of charity or favor of any kind, but as a right—a just and equitable right."[46]

A couple of factors satisfied the women enough to drop their opposition. The men of the Confederate Veterans apparently reaffirmed the right of the women of the Confederated Southern Memorial Association to set the memorial calendar, one of their roles since the 1860s. Although New Orleans—the headquarters of the association—had staged Confederate Decoration Days on the anniversary of the battle of Shiloh in early April, the leadership decided that a more fitting date would be the anniversary of Jefferson Davis's birthday on June 3. Shortly afterward, the Charles Broadway Rouss Camp and the Ladies Southern Relief Society followed suit, recommending that services be held on that date. June 3 thus became recognized as the closest thing to day of a "national" observance by former Confederates, although many localities did not abandon their own peculiar dates of significance.[47]

Second, and more important, all of the organizations supported efforts to win from Congress legislation for the government to assume the obligation for improving and tending the graves of approximately 30,000 southern soldiers who had died in northern prison camps, hospitals, and other military installations. The legislation did not win immediate support, taking from the end of 1902 until March 9, 1906, to secure approval. When it passed, the law provided $200,000 for reburying the Confederate soldiers and sailors who had died in all of the former northern prisons and hospitals. The act was reauthorized in 1910 and 1914. The government dutifully began to tend the graves of all the Civil War dead. McKinley's offer to the South had become a reality.

■ ■ ■

THE PROBLEMS WITH FREEDOM CELEBRATIONS

By the late nineteenth century, opinions had become more divided about the message that Emancipation Days should send. Class sensibilities provided one bone of contention, with certain of the black elite arguing against outdoor celebrations because of the tendency of white people to use the mob's behavior as justification for discrimination. Other problems beset the celebrations. Depending on who controlled the events, Emancipation Days adopted the vision of Washington's Tuskegee—that of uplifting the race through economic independence gained by skill in the practical arts. Although the celebrations continued in most black communities, they no longer maintained a connection to partisan political engagement. Political self-help was barely evident as violent repression and a reticent national government caused black leaders to reconsider the practicality of pursuing rights through political parties and the ballot. Some African Americans wished to forget the slave past, which seemed to perpetuate unflattering images of black people. By the time the fiftieth anniversaries of freedom occurred, the ceremonies were beset by ambivalence on the part of black Americans.[48]

As with the decline of popular politics, there were fewer open attempts to court the masses. To some extent this had been a trend since the 1880s. Washington, D.C., in particular featured differing groups trying to seize the day for a particular meaning. Calvin P. Chase, editor of the *Bee*, and his supporters favored a more staid celebration and came out against parades, which were organized by a rival, Perry Carson. Chase estimated that each

Emancipation Day procession cost about $5,000. Consequently, he favored holding observances in church and donating the money that would have been spent on public processions to help destitute young women. In 1891 he told a group in the Metropolitan Baptist Church that he reasoned the anniversary was meant to show the distance the race had come from slavery. If so, he said, "if we continue to follow brass bands, and emancipation chariots, and spend $5,000 for one days frolic, or demonstrate which is the biggest man, and we do this for 29 years, there can't be much improvement in our condition." He added, "Our condition is improved, when we can convince our more fortunate white fellow citizens that we are not beholding to them; that we are manufacturers, producers, as well as consumers."[49]

Chase was not alone in thinking that the parades provided only an opportunity for black people to embarrass themselves with unwonted displays, violence, and waste. Considerable debate existed within the district over what should be done with Emancipation Day. P. H. Bethea, a member of the Federation of Men's Church Clubs wrote Washington activist Mary Church Terrell about the problem. He chaired the organization's committee on emancipation, which believed "much good would be derived from celebrations properly arranged and properly conducted." The group considered these activities a way to "make more race consciousness, stimulate confidence in many, and cause more harmony among us and respect from others." Unfortunately, Bethea had encountered much opposition to the celebration. "Some have said that we did no great deeds of heroism in connection with the Emancipation Proclamation to celebrate, and that we should celebrate, if anything, the things that show where the Negro fought bravely." His organization favored holding the event but wrestled with the efficacy of the remembrance and wondered if it should be abandoned. One of the consequences of neglecting the anniversary, according to Bethea, could be an erosion of racial identity. Yet he considered even this possibility may have merits, if it also meant an end to the color bar.[50]

The correspondence also reveals that Emancipation Days were not the only public activity for black women to pursue for social and political change. With the rise of a black middle class and their attendant associations, women found numerous outlets beyond commemorative displays for feeling part of a broader movement. Terrell is a case in point. As president of the Bethel Literary and Historical Association, she won accolades for an address delivered to veterans surrounding the district's

Emancipation Day observances in 1892. So her support of this day was apparent at least early in the decade. Yet her activism did not stop there. In 1896 she and other women organized the National Association of Colored Women. Part of their motivation arose from discrimination by white women's groups that claimed black women were morally unworthy. As evidence, they cited cases in children's court for improper guardianship that suggested a greater number of unmarried women and a higher incidence of childhood truancy for blacks than for other ethnic groups.[51] Terrell and her comrades in the National Association of Colored Women targeted kindergartens as the places to expend energy for moral uplift. By concentrating on the training of children, they thought they could improve conditions and whittle away at the reasons for white prejudice. This necessitated training mothers to do the most that they could with meager resources to maintain homes and protect the health of their children. They had to learn the proper way to sweep, dust, and sew, while gaining the ability to read so they could appreciate education and foster the thirst for it in their young. "By setting a high moral standard and by living up to it," Terrell wrote to a newspaper in late 1899, "we know that we are daily refuting slanders circulated against us in the press by malicious and irresponsible people."[52] The emphasis in Emancipation Days on teaching the next generation to remember the past and gain positive lessons from the struggles for freedom was part of a much broader effort within the black community, in which women took a meaningful role.

The semicentennial of emancipation revealed another dimension to the increasing ambivalence surrounding these occasions. The necessity of seeking financial support from Congress, state legislatures, or municipalities often proved frustrating, even for accommodationists. Booker T. Washington attempted to gain legislative and funding support for emancipation anniversaries well before the semicentennial in 1913. As early as 1909 he had tried to promote the idea among ministers in the District of Columbia. He was fairly optimistic that he could secure the $250,000 requested. Within a year, however, the Tuskegee leader doubted that the federal support would come. A bill to fund a celebration did make it through the Senate, but it never passed the House.[53]

Frustrated, Washington finally declared unilaterally that the week of October 19–26, 1913, would be the time to celebrate the fiftieth anniversary of freedom. He understood that various communities already had plans that conflicted with this date, but he hoped to create a semblance of uniformity. It was clear that he hoped the observances would feature his prescription for racial uplift. He asked that schools, churches, and other societies unite in "an exposition of the progress in commercial, professional, intellectual, moral and religious directions, made by members of the race in that community." He also encouraged organizers to work with existing county or state fair organizations, to seek local and state aid, and to secure the "most representative man obtainable" to serve as speaker. He leaned on the upper echelons of African Americans for disseminating the plan. Washington attempted to spread his outline for the celebrations throughout the county by having black community leaders read statements before churches, lodges, and other meetings.[54]

While the federal government at first failed to support these activities, the states of New York, New Jersey, Pennsylvania, and Illinois appropriated funds to stage semicentennials of emancipation. This was, however, a mixed blessing. On one hand, state legislatures provided the resources that often determined if celebrations were staged at all. Expositions required capital for constructing exhibit halls, paying staff, and advertising the affair. So it was essential that African Americans collaborate with white people. On the other hand, distributing the public's dole put government bureaucrats and party officers—most of whom were white—in the position of selecting the persons who administered these funds. Consequently, white bureaucrats enjoyed indirect control over the content of the celebrations because they tended to select for key positions the black people who most closely mirrored—at least on the surface—their assumptions about black men and women.

Of all the state-sponsored celebrations held in 1913, only New Jersey's seems to have passed without controversy. New York featured intense arguments over patronage, with African Americans divided by factions fighting for scarce resources. Washington was disgusted by the turn of events, telling a friend that "white people are not interested in this continual scrapping."[55] In Illinois, two rival commissions formed: one selected by the governor and another branded as "unofficial" by the administration. Looking over the state of affairs, John Mitchell commented from Richmond that "already, the tendency of our people to disagree and to disgrace themselves is now in evidence and the daily newspapers are being called into service to discredit the present management."[56]

As the next round of anniversaries neared in 1915, various states vied for the honor of holding the national exposition, with Virginia winning the honors. African Americans in Richmond won an appropriation from the U.S. Congress of $55,000 and the endorsement of Woodrow Wilson. Once again it was a mixed blessing because of the man selected by the governor of the state to lead the effort. Giles B. Jackson, a Richmond attorney, was head of the newly formed Negro Historical and Industrial Association, also headquartered in the former capital of the Confederacy. Like many of his colleagues, he was trying to combat discrimination by highlighting the accomplishments of the race. But he had several strikes against him: a history of careless accounting, of using funds as patronage for friends, and of being too accommodating to white Americans. He may have been part of the white-led Conservative coalition of the 1870s, for he claimed to have had the confidence of governors in the Old Dominion from Kemper to the present. Then again, he may have been a political opportunist who played both sides of the aisle, for he also claimed to have been a friend of every president from Grant to Wilson.[57] Jackson was what white folks called the good Negro. He stayed within prescribed boundaries and acknowledged that equality for blacks would come slowly through patient mastery of the industrial arts.

Jackson had experience coordinating expositions, as well as provoking scandal. In 1907 Virginia held the Ter-Centennial Exposition for the settling of Jamestown. Through an association he formed as the Negro Development and Exposition Company, Jackson had won from the U.S. Congress $100,000 to construct exhibits to highlight the achievements of black people. Other African Americans opposed the event, which placed the black exhibit in a building separate from the white displays. Critics alleged that, as one scholar has observed, "it would be a jim crow affair—a promoter of existing segregationist policies—and, at a period of time when most blacks were seeking integration into the mainstream of American society. They feared that participation in such an endeavor might be interpreted by white society as support of a segregated society." Jackson defended the exhibit as no more segregated than other institutions in the black community, such as churches and schools. Although the exposition took place, garnering praise from white politicians and Booker T. Washington, financial wrangling characterized the affair, as did charges of excessive patronage by Jackson.[58]

The selection of Richmond for the site of the fiftieth anniversary celebration came about through equal portions of persistent lobbying and happenstance. Thomas S. Martin, a U.S. senator from Virginia, introduced a bill to bring $55,000 to his state to allow black people to "celebrate their emancipation, their achievements, and the progress they have made in education, in industrial enterprise, and in the work of the world in all respects." Other states competed for the money. Illinois wanted an appropriation for a similar exposition, and the senator from there argued that it made sense to do something for the state that had given the country Abraham Lincoln. As Martin's bill worked its way through the Senate, a colleague from New Hampshire suggested that the words "in the South" be stricken so the Richmond event would be considered to have broader appeal, further justifying congressional funds.[59]

The mythological and sentimental ideal of the faithful slave provided a rallying point for those trying to win the appropriation. White southerners at this time loved to tout the supposedly faithful darkie who had loved his or her master. This included the figures of mammy and the male slave who had remained by his master's side during the Civil War. At least one person in the Senate, however, was not convinced. James K. Vardaman from Mississippi, a renowned white supremacist, did not fight the appropriation but said he did not believe it was a good idea. To him, it was not worth putting on a display of black achievements, because "the white man has done more for the negro than the negro had done for himself." The senator from Alabama, Frank White, took issue. He indicated that African Americans had contributed much to the white race through their toil. Moreover, southern whites were grateful to black people for what they did during the Civil War. "When all the colored man had to do to obtain his freedom was to cross the line and take up arms against our section, he stood by our side and fought our battles with us." He added that the "black men of the South carried their dead masters back to their wives." This, of course, was only partly true. The senator used some of the examples of black support of masters to extrapolate loyalty for the entire race, many members of which ran off when they could and fought against former masters as Union soldiers. Whether the logic had any effect, the Senate authorized the appropriation.[60]

The turn of events gave Jackson pause. What had begun as a regional observance had escalated into a national one. When President Wilson said he would attend, suddenly $55,000 did not seem like enough money. "Since President Wilson has consented to come and view our exhibit, it would be almost suicide to the race we represent for us to be compelled to curtail the plans we have in view. We want to present to the President of the Nation the evidence of the thrift and progress of the Negro, and to show how he has prospered in the South, and especially in Virginia under her institutions." Jackson pressed for an additional $25,000 from the state of Virginia. The governor declined, explaining that he did not want to call the legislature back for a special session. An additional $7,500, however, did come in from black organizations in New York. The president, however, did not visit the exhibit.[61]

The great exposition to the black race opened its doors at the fairgrounds in Richmond on July 5 to high acclaim from white newspapers, which relished the accommodationist nature of the event. Jackson's exposition symbolized to white people cooperation of the races and the niche that black people could occupy: the mechanical and industrial occupations. Several days before the event, Wilson issued a proclamation from the White House endorsing the celebration and applauded the funding for it as encouraging "the negro in his efforts to solve his industrial problem."[62] Similarly, Richmond's white people proclaimed that the celebration proved that harmonious race relations existed. The *Richmond Dispatch* showed an appropriate amount of municipal chauvinism. "It is a matter of pride with Richmond," espoused one columnist, "that her colored citizenship has inaugurated and assured the success of so ambitious an enterprise." The event underscored to this writer that white people were concerned with the well-being of African Americans because "negro health and negro happiness are related inevitably and inextricably to his [the white man's] own."[63]

From most black people the exposition in Richmond elicited either aversion or apathy. Some supported Jackson's exposition. All of the prominent black schools except one—Tuskegee—had sent exhibits; why Tuskegee abstained is unclear. African Americans in New York displayed perhaps the most enthusiasm for the event and were rewarded by the exposition's organizers with their own day. Yet as one neared Richmond, support from black people diminished. Within five days after opening the exposition, the board of directors expressed disappointment in the turnout. White people attended, but the participation of African Americans was not as strong as the directors had wanted. To rectify this situation, the board cut admission fees and opened the grounds free to all, with the exception of the main exhibition hall.[64]

In the meantime, black editors in Virginia vented their disgust with the exposition. The usual charges of mismanaging funds fell on Jackson, which led to an investigation by the state accountant. A newspaper from Newport News wrote on the last day of the fair, "Today ends the existence of one of the greatest farces that has ever been inflicted upon the people of this section of the country." What angered this particular writer was Jackson's distribution of patronage. Instead of giving advertising revenues to African American newspapers, Jackson had created his own periodical, the *Industrial Herald*, to advertise the exposition. The *Indianapolis Freeman*, one of the most influential black newspapers in the country, added about Jackson, "We are not sure that anything could have saved his show. We are sure, however, that he made no great effort to make it a go." The columnist suggested that Jackson was overconfident because he had support from the government and his state, so he did not feel obligated to seek the aid of his black friends.[65] The *Richmond Planet* joined the *Petersburg Colored Virginian* in calling the event a "miserable farce." The *Planet* had virtually ignored the celebration, while the Petersburg editor wrote, "This so-called exposition, however, served one purpose well—it made clearly apparent the fact that the negro race has now reached a point in intelligent discrimination where it refuses to be humbugged by every wild-cat project promoting scamp who seeks to further his own ends at its expense." The columnist addressed Jackson directly, saying, "As a leader you are a failure, a miserable and obnoxious one. You have never deceived the black folks and we believe that you have played upon the credulity of the white for the last time, that is to any harmful extent."[66]

Not everyone shared these sentiments. A spokesman for the New York Colored Commissioners, in a letter thanking the governor for hospitality while attending the exposition, added, "It is to be regretted that the Negroes of Richmond did not respond to the opportunity opened to them to display their talent and genius." He added, "I assume this is due to nothing more than petty jealousy, which, on an occasion of such magnitude, should have been set aside. To this extent Mr. Giles B. Jackson labored under a disadvantage, which should never have obtained, because race loyalty demanded that the citizens of Richmond lay such aside."[67]

The writer made an important point and mentioned one of the problems surrounding Emancipation Day. Not everyone jumped aboard the wagon of race pride if it meant riding with the likes of Giles B. Jackson. He was not evil incarnate; neither was the discord surrounding him any greater than that for organizers of white expositions. These events had voracious appetites for funds, and government authorities never fed them enough, expecting income to flow from investors and admissions. Overspending was the norm, not the exception. The state accountant eventually cleared Jackson of misdeeds; he seemed to be inattentive to accounting rather than a practitioner of outright fraud. For African Americans, however, the celebrations contained greater consequences. White celebrations did not have the burden of proving the worthiness of their subjects, whereas everything about the black celebrations contributed to prejudices against the race.

Locally, many communities continued their freedom observances well into the twentieth century, but the national effort never quite regained its balance. New generations of African Americans continued to harbor mixed sentiments about remembering slavery or questioned the utility of doing so when struggling with current oppression that was much more immediate. Wherever the anniversary required the authorization of white people, it became—like Giles Jackson—the purveyor of an accommodationist vision of an inferior people with great potential for elevating themselves, but with equality always remaining a hill yet to climb.

■ ■ ■

AND BACK TO ARLINGTON AGAIN

Before President Wilson stumbled into trouble for agreeing to dedicate a Confederate monument in Arlington, someone had to put such a monument in the cemetery. To achieve this, key heritage organizations collaborated with veterans' groups to produce an ostentatious bit of memorial statuary. The result of their efforts reaches thirty-two feet into the sky and is surrounded by ornamentation out of keeping with the solemn nature of most of the cemetery. The monument also contains vignettes that reinforce happy race relations in the Old South, with a slave following his master into war and an officer kissing his child held by a mammy. The memorial has left an ironic legacy that few visitors probably notice: the highest monument in the nation's cemetery towers over the graves of the soldiers who had tried to leave the Union.

Opposition to the Confederate section had decreased as the memorial and veterans' associations realized that the government also supported a wider effort to maintain graves of soldiers buried in northern locations beyond Arlington. Women's memorial associations also learned that they could supervise the memorial traditions—at least to the extent of establishing the day for the events and leading the fund-raising for monuments. The women and their male allies were on balance happy with the federal posture to tend all the graves of Confederates in the North, understanding that the government had greater resources for this purpose than individual states or cemetery organizations. They watched with more than keen interest as Senator J. B. Foraker of Ohio introduced legislation to underwrite this undertaking with $200,000 worth of federal monies. The most strident wanted statuary that validated the cause for which many white southerners had fought and remembered the site as the home of R. E. Lee. With the number of visitors who came to the grounds each year from all over the country and overseas, locating a monument in the nation's capital offered greater exposure and symbolism than any similar edifice in a southern cemetery.

The bill to fund caring for more than 30,000 Confederate graves took more than three years to pass, but the delay appears to have been caused by the usual difficulty of winning attention in a calendar filled with more urgent matters. Legislation was introduced in the Senate in late 1902 and passed that chamber in early 1903. It never went further, having been entered too late in the legislative calendar to win serious attention. The same thing happened the following year; the Senate approved the bill, but it languished in the House. Samuel Lewis fretted over the delays and especially resented the campaign by veterans' groups and women's organizations to build an overly ornate monument, for he feared that might awaken controversy that would derail the congressional effort. He had become alarmed when the GAR post in Philadelphia opposed a monument by the Daughters of the Confederacy for the Confederate graves in the cemetery at Germantown. "The re-burial at Arlington had been accomplished quietly and without friction," he told a member of the United Daughters of the Confederacy much later, "but the erection of a Monument there was held to be a matter which would likely create great objection among the Union people. And the Camp became apprehensive that objections which might be raised to the erection of the Monument would have reflex action upon the Bill pending in Congress, and militate against its becoming law."[68]

The statement made by the monument also caused some debate. Lewis's camp favored a modest presentation that did not awaken northern anger. Another Confederate Veterans camp, number 171, supported a bolder statement of the Lost Cause. Attorney H. A. Herbert, a leader of the rival organization, believed the situation demanded audacity. "This monument will be more conspicuous—that is to say, it will be seen by more people—and will attract wider attention than even the Davis Monument at Richmond," he wrote, adding, "and for this reason all the daughters and sons to whom I have talked have entered heartily into the idea that the local organizations here ought to be assisted as widely as possible in erecting it."[69] The two veterans' groups made several attempts to reconcile their differences, including an effort to form a joint committee, but to no avail. When Lewis complained about the rival camp to Stephen D. Lee, one of the national officers of the association, the response revealed that squabbling over these issues often beset the supposedly united Confederate Veterans. A frustrated Lee finally wrote back, "I beg you for my sake— cooperate cordially in raising funds for the monument. It seems to me we 'old fellows' ought to stop fighting . . . , as there are no Yankees to fight, they [former Confederates] must differ & quarrel among themselves. This is not peculiar to one locality, but it occurs else where."[70] Eventually the tide of opinion was too great against Lewis. Members of his own camp began to drift away from him. He looked too nervous and out of touch. Sectionalism by now had become an old shoe in the nation's closet— comfortable, familiar, and without threat.

On March 9, 1906, Congress passed legislation for tending the graves of all Confederates who had died in prisons or hospitals in the North. The legislation set aside the $200,000 for the project, along with $2,500 per year for administrative expenses of locating bodies. The law used the Confederate section in Arlington as a pattern for what was to be done with the graves: white marble headstones with uniform inscriptions and proper fencing. Approximately one month earlier, President Theodore Roosevelt had endorsed the monument for the site, viewing the statue as a chance to promote unity of the nation. The president commented that the memorial would sit within proximity of the graves of the Union soldiers who had died in the Civil War and the monument to the soldiers of his regiment who had died at Santiago in the Spanish-American War.[71]

Lewis shared the lament of the ladies memorial societies, which had felt increasingly irrelevant to a new generation of Confederate celebrants. The memorial societies did not want to lose their role as leaders for setting the memorial agenda for the region, but it was happening. Lewis was experiencing a similar change in generational leadership. He believed that the Confederate Veterans should serve as the main group directing the commemorations of the war, but he recognized that the United Daughters of the Confederacy and the Sons of Confederate Veterans were competing strongly for the honor—and winning. Those two groups "by the independence of their organizations however unintended, in effect thrust the veterans to one side, and absorb for themselves the interests of the younger generations." He admitted that the women were unaware of the effect on the Confederate Veteran Associations. "Time will bring them to a better appreciation of the worth of the Confederate soldier and his cause, but alas, also, before that time shall dawn the last Confederate veteran will have passed to his reward in heaven."[72] Lewis exaggerated the extent to which veterans were being pushed aside, yet he embodied a subtle but significant change concerning the commemoration of the Civil War. A new generation was taking over, and it consisted of people who had grown up with few restrictions on celebrating the war and fewer concerns about how these events affected the national mood. People like Lewis were beginning to look like anachronisms to the generation that unabashedly honored the Confederate past.

Ultimately, the United Daughters of the Confederacy took over the coordination of fund-raising for the monument and collected a targeted $75,000 to pay for the statuary contracted through Moses Ezekiel. The ladies memorial associations remained part of the effort, but they clearly took a back seat to the new powerhouse for the women's side of the Confederate tradition. The cornerstone was laid in 1910, with William Jennings Bryan providing the keynote address. Within four years the thirty-two-foot-high monument, New South, appeared, topped by the figure of a woman facing south. Inclined shields supported the plinth; each one had the coat of arms of one of the states of the Confederacy. The African American figures all supported the notion of the happy darkie willing to sacrifice and care for the master. The message of the monument attested to a cause that appealed to not a few northerners:

Not Lured By Ambition
Or Goaded By Necessity,
But In Simple
Obedience To Duty
As They Understood It
These Men Suffered All
Sacrificed All
Dared All—And Died.[73]

There were still veterans and other northerners who did not appreciate certain elements of this southern resurgence, which Woodrow Wilson learned quickly enough when he refused the invitation of the GAR to speak on Memorial Day. Members of that organization met with friends of Wilson on May 24 to impress upon him how this act could ruffle sectional feathers. Congress was particularly sensitive to the GAR, which remained a strong lobbying force. Up to the White House went Thomas Pence, secretary of the Democratic congressional committee, who carried word to Wilson that GAR camps across the country had decided to express their resentment of the president's slight at Memorial Day celebrations around the country. Posts besieged Congress by telegraph to see if the president had changed his mind before delivering the speeches that conveyed their dismay. When it was announced that Wilson would attend the GAR function at Arlington, the White House staff issued a statement denying what everyone still assumed were the real reasons: that he had miscalculated the sentiment of the GAR and that Champ Clark, a political rival, had decided to go. "The president reconsidered his refusal," stated Wilson's secretary, "because he felt that a deliberate attempt had been made to distort his reasons. He had believed it would be inadvisable to talk about war at a time like this, when the Mexican situation was under consideration, and in view of the fact that it would be hard to avoid that topic the President had preferred to make his Arlington speech under different circumstances."[74]

When the day arrived, the tumultuous cheers that greeted Clark subsided only after an estimated five or six minutes, while the crowd gave the president a much cooler reception. The introduction itself, performed by an officer of the GAR, was noticeably perfunctory: "I have the honor to present the President of the United States." Wilson claimed he had come without preparing a speech, but that does not seem likely. He lavishly praised the efforts of the Union veterans, claiming they had a "peculiar privilege" in restoring the Union. He tried to stress the peace that had been achieved, rather than the war that had been fought, as he paid tribute to the sacrifice both of the men in the ground and of those who stood before him. Most importantly, he did not say a word about the Confederacy or the southern soldiers who lay in the same confines. That could wait another five days.[75]

Americans usually forgive someone who does public penance. The GAR attended the dedication of the Confederate monument at Arlington; no one mentioned Wilson's gaffe. Enduring the ceremony on Union Memorial Day apparently had been the act of contrition that restored the president to grace. Thousands turned out for the Confederate affair, which featured some blue mingling with the preponderance of gray. The grandson of Robert E. Lee was among the attendees. Hilary Herbert of Confederate Veterans Camp 171 pulled the cords that released the draperies. The Stars and Stripes were draped along with the Confederate flag over the monument. The president asked his listeners to forget the past and concentrate on the future. He also believed that a ceremony that celebrated a divisive civil war could only have happened in a democracy. He then proposed, "This chapter in the history of the United States is now closed, and I can bid you turn with me your faces to the future, quickened by the memories of the past, but with nothing to do with the contests of the past, knowing, as we have shed our blood upon opposite sides, we now face and admire one another." Wilson's words had little chance to stir the crowd, mostly because they were interrupted by a brutal thunderstorm. As the president spoke, "torrents of wind-driven rain drenched the blue and gray veterans and women and children before they could reach shelter, and then there was a wild dash for automobiles and trolley cars, participants and spectators alike forgetting the almost finished program." Wilson hurried to his car with his two daughters and immediately left the cemetery for the White House.[76]

Perhaps the more interesting speech was delivered by Bennett Young, commander in chief of the United Confederate Veterans, whose theme created the headline "South's Cause Just; Nothing to Recall." He echoed Wilson in suggesting that a "republic alone could foster or permit those who lost in a great, prolonged struggle to erect in such a place as this a tribute to the dead, who for four years battled against the flag that floats above a place of sepulture like this." He added, "The sword said that South was wrong, but the sword is not necessarily guided by conscience and reason. The power of numbers and the longest guns cannot destroy principle nor obliterate truth. Right lives forever." Young added that accepting the rule of force was another proof of the grace and nobility of the southern people. Blessing the entire event, and also praising the valor of the soldiers in the Confederate section, was his opposite number, the commander in chief of the GAR.[77]

These words flew out over the graves and the white marble headstones of men who would have found them . . . confusing. The unity had not existed during the war, either between or within the sections. Gone was the venom of people who wanted to hurt one another and who had accomplished this task exceedingly well. Similarly, the portrayal of brave men courageously meeting their death and performing their duty may or may not have told the stories of the men in the ground. No one said whether the men had passed away from sickness contracted in camp rather than battlefield, had charged the enemy or had tried to flee, had hated their officers or had loved them, had embraced the cause or had created their own reasons for performing the gruesome work of a soldier. No one mentioned that the graves of these men had once lain with those of African Americans, or that they had come to this location with the blessing of a president who hoped to trade these bodies for overseas expansion and the support of African Americans who feared further massacre. Nor did the assembled people reflect on how the monument had come there. The graves no longer suggested disloyalty but were used as examples by a new generation of politicians to portray a particular kind of American character that would meet the international challenges of the moment. The Cities of the Dead had lost their immediacy as a spark for awakening sectional passions among white people, but they had not lost their utility for creating an idealized nation.

NOTES

ABBREVIATIONS

Duke   Perkins Library, Duke University, Durham, North Carolina
HL   Handley Library, Winchester, Virginia
HU   University Archives and University Museum, Hampton
        University, Hampton, Virginia
LC   Library of Congress, Washington, D.C.
LV   Library of Virginia, Richmond
MHS   Massachusetts Historical Society, Boston
MC   Museum of the Confederacy, Richmond, Virginia
NARA   National Archives and Records Administration, Washington,
        D.C.
UVA   Alderman Library, University of Virginia, Charlottesville
VHS   Virginia Historical Society, Richmond

INTRODUCTION

1. Hobsbawm, "Mass Producing Traditions," 263–64. Some works by American scholars who have looked at public ceremonies include Waldstreicher, *In the Midst of Perpetual Fetes*; Davis, *Parades and Power*; Travers, *Celebrating the Fourth*; Kachun, *Festivals of Freedom*; Clark, "Celebrating Freedom."

2. Buck, *Road to Reunion*.

3. Osterweis, *Myth of the Lost Cause*; Wilson, *Baptized in Blood*; Foster, *Ghosts of the Confederacy*. Some histories of the South did contain hints of the importance of Confederate tradition for the road to segregation. See, for instance, Woodward, *Origins of the New South*, 51.

4. Van Zelm, "On the Front Lines of Freedom"; Clark, "Celebrating Freedom," 121 (quotation); Kachun, *Festivals of Freedom*.

5. Blight, *Race and Reunion*, 2.

6. Kousser, *Shaping of Southern Politics*, 28.

7. Hobsbawm makes this distinction of official and unofficial. See his "Mass-Producing Traditions," 263.

CHAPTER ONE

1. "Holidays," *North American Review* 84 (April 1857): 335.

2. For the use of ceremonies to support a ruling elite as part of a nation-state, see Hobsbawm and Rangers, *Invention of Tradition*, esp. 1–14. For the contested meaning of ceremonies, see Waldstreicher, *In the Midst of Perpetual Fetes*; Kachun, *Festivals of Freedom*; Rael, *Black Identity and Black Protest*, chap. 2; Shane White, " 'Proud Day' "; Travers, *Celebrating the Fourth*; Piehler, *Remembering War*, 35–36, 44–45.

3. Waldstreicher, "Rites of Rebellion, Rites of Assent."

4. Gilje, *Road to Mobocracy*, 23. For an extended analysis of the culture of plebeians and patricians, see Thompson, "Patricians and Plebs," in his *Customs in Common*.

5. Gilje, *Road to Mobocracy*, 42.

6. Baker, *Affairs of Party*, 292–302.

7. Genovese, *Roll, Jordan, Roll*, 573–76.

8. Ibid., 576; *Colored American* (Augusta, Ga.), January 13, 1866.

9. For the nonpartisan nature of pre-Constitutional ceremonies, see Green, "Listen to the Eagle Scream," 118. For harassment of Tories, see Travers, *Celebrating the Fourth*, 24.

10. Green, "Listen to the Eagle Scream," 123–24; Travers, *Celebrating the Fourth*, 41–54.

11. Cushing, *Oration*, 4–8 (quotation on 4).

12. Blassingame, *Frederick Douglass Papers*, 360 (first quotation), 368 (second quotation).

13. Ibid., 371.

14. *Colored American* (Augusta, Ga.), January 13, 1866.

15. *National Era*, June 24, 1847.

16. Sweet, "Fourth of July and Black Americans," 262–63.

17. Shane White, " 'Proud Day,' " 38; Sweet, "Fourth of July and Black Americans," 270.

18. Gregg D. Kimball, "African, American, and Virginian," in Brundage, *Where These Memories Grow*, 59–60, 62–63; Waddell, *Annals of Augusta County, Virginia*, 420.

19. Johnson, *William Johnson's Natchez*, 126, 183, 284, 337, 390, 533, 575, 621–22, 657.

20. *Wilmington Daily Journal*, July 3, 1856, in Green, "Listen to the Eagle Scream," 135.

CHAPTER TWO

1. *True Southerner*, April 19, 1866.

2. For a long time, historians who studied the public ceremonies of the postwar South stressed the use of these occasions for reconciliation while ignoring the conflict they caused as well as the political context. More recently, studies have begun to highlight the divisive nature of the celebrations. See

Blight, *Race and Reunion*; Clark, "Celebrating Freedom" and "History Is No Fossil Remains"; Kachun, *Festivals of Freedom*.

3. McPherson, review of *Race and Reunion*. McPherson did not use the term "Unionist," but he recognized that reunion and reconciliation were two different issues.

4. Blackett, *Thomas Morris Chester*, 288–94.

5. Boney, Hume, and Zafar, *God Made Man*, 16.

6. Looby, *Complete Civil War Journal*, 77. Also see the account of Charlotte Forten in *Atlantic Monthly*, June 1864, 668–69, and Stevenson, *Journals of Charlotte Forten Grimké*, 428–35.

7. *Colored American* (Augusta, Ga.), January 13, 1866.

8. Page, " 'Stand by the Flag,' " 285–301; Harding, *There Is a River*, 299; Reidy, *From Slavery to Agrarian Capitalism*, 178–79; *Staunton Spectator*, July 9, 1867.

9. *Richmond Times*, June 30, 1866.

10. Ibid., July 4, 1866.

11. Hollywood Memorial Association, minutes, July 2, 1866, MC.

12. Clark, "History Is No Fossil Remains," 31; *True Southerner*, December 14, 1865.

13. For a particularly rich analysis of black organizations in the urban South, see Rachleff, *Black Labor in Richmond*, 24–33. For organizations in Memphis, Tennessee, consult Page, " 'Stand by the Flag,' " 285–301; William Kennedy, "The Constitution of the Sons of Jacob" (n.d.), Kennedy Papers, VHS.

14. Report of John A. McDonnell, Assistant Commander of the 9th Subdistrict of Virginia, July 1, 1868, Freedmen's Bureau Papers, RG105, reel 32, M1048, NARA.

15. *True Southerner*, December 7, 14, 28, 1865; *Colored American* (Augusta, Georgia), January 6, 1866.

16. *Richmond Dispatch*, December 28, 1865.

17. Clark, "History Is No Fossil Remains," 34–35.

18. *Colored American* (Augusta, Ga.), January 13, 1866.

19. Fitzgerald, *Union League Movement in the Deep South*, 2–3; Eric Foner, *Reconstruction*, 110, 283.

20. Reidy, *From Slavery to Agrarian Capitalism*, 178–79; *Richmond Daily Dispatch*, April 9, 1866.

21. *Feliciana Ledger*, March 27, 1869.

22. Clark, "Celebrating Freedom," 121.

23. Ibid., 122–23; *True Southerner*, December 14, 1865 (quotation).

24. See, for instance, *Staunton Spectator*, June 5, 1877; *Valley Virginian*, May 11, 1880; van Zelm, "On the Front Lines of Freedom," 289–90. For the observation of the hierarchy of gender in black ceremonies, see Clark, "History Is No Fossil Remains," 55, and "Celebrating Freedom," 121–22.

25. Eric Foner, *Reconstruction*, 110–11.

26. Briscoe, "Ashes of Roses," VHS, 172; Purdue, Barden, and Phillips, *Weevils in the Wheat*, 244.

27. *Richmond Dispatch*, March 26, 1866.

28. Quotation in Elsa Barkley Brown, "Uncle Ned's Children," 20–21. See also O'Brien, *From Bondage to Citizenship*, 327–28, 334–42.

29. See, for example, *New York Times*, April 4, 1866.

30. *Petersburg Daily Index*, April 5, 1866.

31. Briscoe, "Ashes of Roses," VHS, 172.

32. *Richmond State*, March 31, 1866.

33. *Richmond Dispatch*, March 30, 1866; broadside no. 1866:13, VHS; Elsa Barkley Brown, "Uncle Ned's Children," 21.

34. *Petersburg Daily Index*, April 4, 1866.

35. O'Brien, *From Bondage to Citizenship*, 336–38; *Richmond Dispatch*, March 30, 1866.

36. *Petersburg Daily Index*, April 4 (quotation), 11, 1866.

37. *Richmond Dispatch*, April 9, 1866; Rachleff, *Black Labor in Richmond*, 39–40; O'Brien, *From Bondage to Citizenship*, 238–39, 339–42; William Kennedy, "The Constitution of the Sons of Jacob" (n.d.), Kennedy Papers, VHS.

38. *Richmond Daily Dispatch*, April 9, 1866.

39. *Petersburg Daily Index*, April 5, 1866.

40. *New York Times*, April 4, 1866.

41. O'Brien, *From Bondage to Citizenship*, 342; *Petersburg Daily Index*, April 11, 1866 (quotation).

42. For testimony from the coroner's inquest, see *Richmond Times*, April 19, 1866, and *Richmond Dispatch*, April 19, 1886. The rest of the account is compiled from the *Norfolk Virginian*, April 16, 17, 18, 1866; *Richmond Dispatch*, April 18, 21; *Richmond Times*, April 18, 24, 1866.

43. Lowe, *Republicans and Reconstruction in Virginia*, 64; *Richmond Dispatch*, August 1, 1866.

44. Lowe, *Republicans and Reconstruction in Virginia*, 31,

45. Maddex, *Virginia Conservatives*, 46; Eric Foner, *Reconstruction*, 412–15.

46. *Richmond Dispatch*, April 2, 1867.

47. Ibid., April 20, 22 (Lewis address), 1867.

48. Ibid., May 4, 1867.

49. Ibid., April 6, 1867 (emphasis in original).

50. *Richmond Times*, April 4, 1867; *Richmond Dispatch*, April 4, 1867.

CHAPTER THREE

1. John Preston Cooke, "Hollywood Memorial Association of Richmond Virginia" notes, folder 1, Hollywood Sketches, VHS, 9.

2. Buck calls Memorial Days "an agency of reconciliation" in his *Road to Reunion*, 119. Foster denies that Memorial Days provided a means of carrying on resistance. "Occasionally, a southerner attributed the emphasis on bereavement to federal opposition to other activities, but little evidence exists to support this claim" (*Ghosts of the Confederacy*, 44). Piehler also denies any

partisanship behind the creation of Memorial Days, especially in the case of John Logan calling for them in the North; see *Remembering War*, 58.

3. Janney and Janney, *Composition Book*; R. T. W. Duke, "Reminiscences," vol. 2, box 1, Duke Papers, UVA, 36–38; O'Brien, *From Bondage to Citizenship*, 102–3; Leigh, *Ten Years on a Georgia Plantation*, 68.

4. *Winchester Journal*, May 4, 1866.

5. Graf, *Papers of Andrew Johnson*, 669; [?] Parsons Jr. to General E. S. Molineaux, May 19, 1865, Adjutant General's Office, pt. 1, E 1732, NARA; *Southern Banner*, May 31, 1865. For the ban on wearing uniforms in South Carolina, see Simkins and Woody, *South Carolina during Reconstruction*, 31. For a general comment on the situation, see Worsham, *One of Jackson's Foot Cavalry*, 293–94.

6. *Army and Navy Journal*, excerpt reprinted in *New York Times*, September 16, 1866. For a list of sites, see *Richmond Dispatch*, March 29, 1867.

7. *Richmond Daily Examiner*, May 5, 1866.

8. *Norfolk Virginian*, March 31, 1866.

9. This and the following description of events in Richmond are taken from the *Richmond Dispatch*, May 11, 1866.

10. Avary, *Dixie after the War*, 41.

11. *Richmond Times*, May 12 (quotation), 14, 1866 (emphasis in original). For Jackson references, see *Richmond Dispatch*, May 11, 14, 1866.

12. *Richmond Dispatch*, May 11, 1866; entry May 10, 1866, Fife Diary, UVA, 87–88.

13. For this and the following descriptions about the Hollywood Memorial Day, see Mitchell, *Hollywood Cemetery*, 68; *Richmond Dispatch*, June 1, 1866; *Richmond Times*, June 1, 1866.

14. *Richmond Dispatch*, August 21, 1866.

15. O'Brien, *From Bondage to Citizenship*, 349; *New York Times*, June 28, 1866.

16. Avary, *Dixie after the War*, 408.

17. Harry T. Hays to John J. Williams, July 27, 1866, Williams Family Papers, HL; *History of the Confederate Memorial Associations of the South*, 119–20.

18. *Petersburg Daily Index*, April 27, 1867 (quotation), May 17, 1867.

19. *Richmond Enquirer*, May 27, 1867.

20. *Richmond Dispatch*, May 31, 1867.

21. Ibid., May 4, 1867; *Lynchburg Virginian*, May 11, 1867.

22. *Richmond Enquirer*, June 1, 1867; *Richmond Dispatch*, June 1, 1867; *Richmond Times*, June 1, 1867; James H. Gardner to Mary P. Gardner, June 1, 1867, Gardner Papers, VHS.

23. *New York Times*, June 3, 1867; Schofield assessment reprinted in the *Petersburg Daily Index*, June 6, 1867.

24. *Staunton Spectator*, June 16, 1868.

25. *Atlanta Daily Intelligencer*, May 12, 1868, quoted in *Richmond Examiner*, May 18, 1868.

26. *Valley Virginian*, May 15, 1867; *Richmond Enquirer*, May 21, 1867, June 17, 1868 (fire company quotation).

27. *Petersburg Daily Index*, June 10, 1868.

28. *Richmond Enquirer and Examiner*, June 17, 1868.

29. *Richmond Dispatch*, May 11, 1868.

30. Maddex, *Virginia Conservatives*, 47, 63; Lowe, *Republicans and Reconstruction in Virginia*, 76.

31. *Norfolk Virginian*, May 11, 1868; *Richmond Enquirer and Examiner*, May 8, 1868 (quotation); *Southern Opinion*, May 16, 1868.

32. Blight, *Race and Reunion*, 65 (quotation), 68–71.

33. *Richmond Dispatch*, May 29, June 1 (quotation), 1868.

34. Ibid., May 29, 1868; *Richmond Enquirer and Examiner*, June 1, 1868.

35. *New Orleans Semi-Weekly Louisianan*, June 1, 1871.

36. *Richmond Daily Dispatch*, June 1, 1868.

37. A. R. Calhoun statement quoted in *Petersburg Daily Index*, May 24, 1869.

38. *Staunton Spectator*, August 31, 1869.

39. *National Intelligencer*, June 2, 1869.

40. *Valley Virginian*, June 3, 1869.

41. *Richmond Daily Enquirer*, June 2, 1871.

42. J. E. Williams to Salmon P. Chase, June 4, 1869, frames 756–57, reel 38, Chase Papers, LC.

43. *Staunton Spectator*, June 8, 1869.

44. *Maryland, My Maryland*, 52. For a contemporary version, see *Staunton Spectator*, July 20, 1869.

45. Breckinridge, *Addresses in Memory of the Confederate Dead*, Southern Pamphlets, no. 373, Duke.

CHAPTER FOUR

1. *New York Times*, May 21, June 28, 1866; *Petersburg Daily Index*, April 7, 1868.

2. Faust, *Mothers of Invention*, 253.

3. Clark, "Celebrating Freedom," 119.

4. A number of scholars have placed the creation of memorial ceremonies in the South within the broader context of the redefinition of gender and with having an impact on the configuration of power. See, for instance, Faust, *Mothers of Invention*, 249–50; Whites, *Civil War as a Crisis in Gender*, 133–35; Brundage, "White Women and the Politics of Historical Memory," 117; Clark, "History Is No Fossil Remains." While David Blight acknowledges how these ceremonies could become political, he sees this happening after the ceremonies took root; see his *Race and Reunion*, 78–79. For a denial of these ceremonies as a subterfuge for celebrating the southern cause, see Foster, *Ghosts of the Confederacy*, 44.

5. Faust, *Mothers of Invention*, 252; Whites, *Civil War as a Crisis in Gender*, 167–68.

6. *Southern Opinion*, May 2, 1868.

7. Mitchell, *Hollywood Cemetery*, 84–90.

8. Records of the Memorial Society, May 6, 1866, LV.

9. For examples of organizational meetings, see ibid.; Ladies Memorial Association of Appomattox, Minute Book, May 18, 1866–May 10, 1870, VHS; Hollywood Memorial Association, minutes, folder Minutes, May 1866–May 1868, MC; "Hollywood Memorial Association of Richmond, Virginia," notes, John Preston Cocke, Hollywood Sketches, VHS; *Richmond Dispatch*, May 2, 1866 (for constitution and bylaws of Ladies Memorial Association of Oakwood Cemetery). For similarities in organizations across the Confederate South, see Foster, *Ghosts of the Confederacy*, 38–46.

10. *Richmond Dispatch*, April 19, 1866.

11. Ibid., May 15, 29, June 26, 1866.

12. *Southern Opinion*, May 2 (Vicksburg), January 9 (Georgia), 1868.

13. "To the Women of the South," VHS.

14. Dawson, *Reminiscences*, 162.

15. Foster, *Ghosts of the Confederacy*, 38–39; Charles H. Dimmock to Mrs. Dr. Bolton, June 28, 1867, Hollywood Memorial Association, VHS; *Richmond Dispatch*, May 27, 1868.

16. Whites, *Civil War as a Crisis in Gender*, 187–88.

17. *Richmond Dispatch*, May 29, 1866; Records of the Memorial Society, June 12, 1867, LV, 25.

18. Ladies Memorial Association of Appomattox, Minute Book, June 14, 28, 1866, Mss4 L1246a1, VHS; *Petersburg Daily Index*, June 10, 1868; Records of the Memorial Society, December 5, 1866, acc. no. 24254, LV, 17.

19. Hollywood Cemetery Company, Minute Book, Mss3 H7298a1, section 1, VHS; Ladies Memorial Association of Appomattox, Minute Book, June 29, July 28, 1866, Mss4 L1246a1, VHS; Whites, *Civil War as a Crisis in Gender*, 189; Records of the Memorial Society, May 7, 1868, acc. no. 24254, LV, 41 (quotation).

20. *Southern Opinion*, June 6, 1868; R. E. Lee to Genl. Thos. L. Rosser, December 13, 1866, Letterbook of Robert Edward Lee, VHS.

21. *Richmond Dispatch*, May 29, 1866.

22. See particularly Faust, *Mothers of Invention*, 252, and Whites, *Civil War as a Crisis in Gender*, 167–68.

23. *Richmond Times*, May 29, 1866.

24. *Richmond Dispatch*, March 27, 1866.

25. *Richmond Daily Dispatch*, May 30, 1866.

26. *Richmond Dispatch*, May 14, 1866.

27. Nina Silber, "Intemperate Men, Spiteful Women, Jefferson Davis," in Clinton and Silber, *Divided Houses*, 293–95, 304 (quotation).

28. *New York Times*, June 28, 1866.

29. *Springfield Republican* quoted in *Petersburg Daily Index*, April 7, 1868.

30. Quoted in *New York Times*, May 21, 1866.

31. Dawson, *Reminiscences*, 168, 163; *Richmond Times*, July 2, 1866.

32. *Richmond Times*, April 11, 1866.

33. *Richmond Examiner and Sentinel*, April 27, May 1, 11, 1867; *Richmond Dispatch*, June 18, 1867.

34. *Richmond Dispatch*, May 29, 1866; *Richmond Times*, May 29, 1866; Mrs. D. B. Comfort to Nancy Macfarland, June 10, 1870, Mss2 M1642b, Macfarland Papers, VHS.

35. Dennie, "One King, Two Burials," 2; Wills, *Lincoln at Gettysburg*, 41–62.

36. *Winchester Times*, October 31, 1866, in Mss1 As346a144, Ashby Family Papers, VHS.

37. Freeman, *Lee's Lieutenants*, 1:309; *Southern Illustrated News*, October 18, 1862.

38. Joseph Holmes Sherrard to Madam, August 22, 1866, Mss1 As346a219, Ashby Family Papers, VHS.

39. *Winchester Times*, October 31, 1866, in Mss1 As346a144, ibid.; Averitt, *Memoirs of General Turner Ashby and His Compeers*, 243–55.

40. *Richmond Daily Enquirer*, January 4, 1867. The newspaper reprinted the entire text of Wise's speech. Unless otherwise noted, the following quotations from the ceremony come from this source.

41. Unidentified clipping, Coalman Papers, VHS; *Winchester Times*, October 31, 1866, in Mss1 As346a144, Ashby Family Papers, VHS.

42. James H. Gardner to Mary P. Gardner, June 1, 1867, Gardner Papers, VHS; *Norfolk Virginian*, January 6, 1867.

43. Johnston, *Life of Gen. Albert Sidney Johnston*, 700–703. For other accounts of the incident, see Sefton, *United States Army and Reconstruction*, 97; Roland, *Albert Sidney Johnston*, 352–54.

44. Johnston, *Life of Gen. Albert Sidney Johnston*, 703–4.

45. Report from the *Louisville Courier* reprinted in *Richmond Enquirer and Examiner*, April 25, 1868.

46. *Jackson (Miss.) Clarion*, January 21, 1866, quoted in *Petersburg Daily Index*, February 9, 1866.

47. Mitchell, *Hollywood Cemetery*, 86; *Army and Navy Journal*, June 8, 1867, quoted in *Petersburg Daily Index*, June 26, 1867.

48. Mitchell, *Hollywood Cemetery*, 88–89; *Times* (London), July 12, 1872.

49. Du Bois, *Black Reconstruction in America*, 110; Jim Cullen, " 'I'se a Man Now': Gender and African American Men," in Clinton and Silber, *Divided Houses*, 77.

50. For the acceptance of more respectable behavior among young white men in the antebellum South, see Carmichael, "Last Generation"; for the stress on a tempered manliness, see Bederman, *Manliness and Civilization*.

51. *Colored American* (Augusta, Ga.), January 13, 1866.

52. Ibid.

53. Gilmore, *Gender and Jim Crow*, xix, 62–63; Clark, "History Is No Fossil Remains," 31–32; Edwards, *Gendered Strife and Confusion*, 148, 171–72.

54. Glenda Gilmore makes the same point. See her *Gender and Jim Crow*, 74.

55. Langston, *From the Virginia Plantation*, 240.

56. *Richmond Examiner and Sentinel*, April 4, 1867; *South Carolina Leader*, January 1, 1866, quoted in Kachun, *Festivals of Freedom*, 119.

57. *Greensboro Patriot*, July 9, 1868.

58. Van Zelm makes the observation that black women displayed a greater affinity for the government in these celebrations; see her "On the Front Lines of Freedom," 277–78.

59. *Richmond Examiner*, January 3, 1866.

60. Elsa Barkley Brown, "Negotiating and Transforming the Public Sphere," 107–46. For the cooperative traditions of black people under slavery, see Saville, *Work of Reconstruction*.

61. *Richmond Dispatch*, May 25, April 10, 1867.

62. Elsa Barkley Brown, "Negotiating and Transforming the Public Sphere," 125–26.

63. King, *Great South*, 630–31.

CHAPTER FIVE

1. *Lynchburg Virginian*, May 3, 1875; *People's Advocate*, July 8, 1876.

2. Blight, *Race and Reunion*, 202.

3. Woodward, *Origins of the New South*, 51; Perman, *Struggle for Mastery*, 10; Holt, "Change and Continuity in the Party Period," 106. On biracial politics, see Hahn, *Nation under Our Feet*, esp. 384–93.

4. Woodward, *Origins of the New South*, 51.

5. Buck observed, "The process of reconciliation was fatefully involved in this counterpurpose of party aims" (*Road to Reunion*, 73); see also Blight, *Race and Reunion*, 128.

6. Holt, "Change and Continuity in the Party Period," 107–9 (quotation on 109).

7. Chase, *Papers*, 156, 166 (quotation), 176, 183, 192.

8. *Southern Opinion*, July 4, 1868.

9. Van Deusen, *Horace Greeley*, 16–35.

10. Gerrit Smith to Chief Justice Chase, May 28, 1866, frames 490–92, reel 36, Chase Papers, LC.

11. Freeman, *R. E. Lee*, 4:373–77, 376 (quotation). Also see Fellman, *Making of Robert E. Lee*, 286–88; Thomas, *Robert E. Lee*, 390–91.

12. Maddex, *Virginia Conservatives*, 46.

13. Eric Foner, *Reconstruction*, 412–13.

14. Lowe, *Republicans and Reconstruction in Virginia*, 174, 176–77; Maddex, *Virginia Conservatives*, 80–81.

15. Maddex, *Virginia Conservatives*, 195.

16. *Staunton Spectator*, July 29, 1873.

17. *Richmond Enquirer and Examiner*, June 1, 1869.

18. *Staunton Spectator*, June 13, 1871; *Lynchburg Virginian*, May 10, 1871; *Richmond Enquirer*, May 25, 1871.

19. *Richmond Enquirer*, April 12, 1871.

20. *Staunton Spectator*, June 5, 12, 1877; *Valley Virginian*, June 14, 1877; *Staunton Spectator*, June 1, 1880.

21. *Staunton Spectator*, June 18, 1878.

22. Blight, *Race and Reunion*, 80–84. Also see Wilson, *Baptized in Blood*, 21–23, 186 n. 6; Maddex, *Virginia Conservatives*, 193.

23. J. L. Kemper to Genl. J. A. Early, October 26, 1875, Early Papers, LC (quotation); *Staunton Spectator*, October 26, 1875.

24. J. L. Kemper to Genl. J. A. Early, October 11, 26, 1875, Early Papers, LC.

25. *Times* (London), June 22, 1875; *Philadelphia Inquirer* quoted in *Lynchburg Virginian*, June 3, 1875.

26. King, *Great South*, 34.

27. *Staunton Spectator*, June 22, 1875.

28. Fitzhugh Lee to Gen. Early, July 6, 1875, Early Papers, LC.

29. Ibid., May 9, 1875.

30. *Valley Virginian*, December 2, 1875.

31. *Nation*, August 19, 1875, and *Chicago Tribune* quoted in Buck, *Road to Reunion*, 52–53.

32. *Times* (London), July 6, 1877.

33. *Charleston News and Courier*, July 4, 8, 1876; *Atlanta Constitution*, July 8, 1876; *Staunton Spectator*, July 18, 1876.

34. *Atlanta Constitution*, July 6, 7 (quotation), 1876.

35. Quoted in *Charleston News and Courier*, June 30, 1876.

36. Ibid., June 29, 1876; *Atlanta Constitution*, July 4, 1876.

37. *Charleston News and Courier*, July 4, 1876.

38. U.S. Centennial Commission, *Reports*, 2:163–64; *New Orleans Democrat*, May 14, 1876, quoted in W. Burlie Brown, "Louisiana and the Nation's First One-hundredth Birthday," 270.

39. U.S. Centennial Commission, *Reports*, 2:119, 125–26, 176–77.

40. For changes in the post-Reconstruction South, see, for instance, Foster, *Ghosts of the Confederacy*, 79–87; Ayers, *Promise of the New South*, 3–33; Woodward, *Origins of the New South*, 107–41; Hahn, *Roots of Southern Populism*, 137–69.

41. *Staunton Spectator*, January 9, 1872.

42. Dailey, *Before Jim Crow*, 2–3. Also see Moore, *Two Paths to the New South*; Pearson, *Readjuster Movement in Virginia*; Woodward, *Origins of the New South*, 92–98; Ayers, *Promise of the New South*, 45–47.

43. Dailey, *Before Jim Crow*, 2; Deglar, *Other South*, 269–70.

44. Pulley, *Old Virginia Restored*, 37.

45. W. H. Payne to Early, November 22, 1879, Early Papers, LC; for South Carolina fears that Mahonism would spread, see Holden, " 'Is Our Love for Wade Hampton Foolishness?,' " 67.

46. *Lynchburg Virginian*, May 12, 1875.

47. Mrs. J. M. Wyche to General Mahone, May 8, 1878, folder for Blandford Cemetery, box 173, Mahone Papers, Duke.

48. *Staunton Spectator*, December 9, 1879.

49. Ibid., June 14, 1880.

50. "Address of Gen. Early," *Winchester Times Extra*, June 7, 1889, in Early Papers, LC.

51. Charles M. Blackford to Captain R. Taylor Scott, August 16, 1899, Mss1 Sco855a4, Scott Papers, VHS.

52. *Staunton Spectator*, June 14, 1881; Holden, " 'Is Our Love of Wade Hampton Foolishness?,' " 69–71.

53. Lewis E. Horace to General W. Mahone, March 21, 1880, folder March 21–31, box 18, Mahone Papers, Duke.

54. Dailey, *Before Jim Crow*, 2–3. See also Hahn, *Nation under Our Feet*, 384–93.

55. For the debate over the slave past and other controversies within the black community, see Kachun, *Festivals of Freedom*, 148–50, 175–76.

56. *People's Advocate*, June 10, September 2, 1876.

57. *Staunton Spectator*, June 5, 1877; *Valley Virginian*, May 11, 1880; *Richmond Planet*, May 24, 1890, May 30, 1896.

58. *Staunton Spectator*, June 5, 1883; Kachun, *Festivals of Freedom*, 178.

59. Elsa Barkley Brown, "Negotiating and Transforming the Public Sphere," 125; *Southern Workman*, June 1872; *Petersburg Lancet*, January 17, 1885.

60. *Southern Workman*, February 1886, 17; *People's Advocate*, April 14, 21, 1883.

61. *Southern Workman*, February 1878, 16.

62. Kachun, *Festivals of Freedom*, 118.

63. Wiggins, "Juneteenth," 238–40.

64. Jervey, *Elder Brother*, 68; O'Leary, *To Die For*, 113.

65. Blight, *Race and Reunion*, 134.

66. For overviews of the massacre, see Eric Foner, *Reconstruction*, 571–72; Drago, *Hurrah for Hampton!*, 7–8; Simkins and Woody, *South Carolina during Reconstruction*, 486–88; *Charleston News and Courier*, July 10, 1876; *Congressional Record*, 44th Cong., 1st sess., 4641–46.

67. Quoted in Philip S. Foner, "Black Participation in the Centennial of 1876," 534; Savage, *Standing Soldiers, Kneeling Slaves*, 87.

68. Kachun, "Before the Eyes of All Nations," 314.

69. Langston quoted in Blight, *Race and Reunion*, 133.

70. *People's Advocate*, April 1, 1882.

71. *Southern Workman*, February 1886, 17; *Petersburg Lancet*, January 17, 1885.

72. *Petersburg Lancet*, October 13, 1883.

73. Kachun also asserts the growing partisanship of these occasions. See his *Festivals of Freedom*, 190.

74. *People's Advocate*, January 17, 1880.

75. Paige, *Twenty-Two Years of Freedom*, 10.

76. *New York Globe*, April 28, 1883.

77. Paige, *Twenty-Two Years of Freedom*, 42–43.

78. Ibid., 44–45, 57–58.

79. Ibid., 46–47, 48.

80. Foster, *Ghosts of the Confederacy*, 66, 74; Marian Adams to Father, March 5, 1885, reel 599, Adams Family Papers, MHS; Wiggins, *O Freedom!*, 112.

CHAPTER SIX

1. *Richmond Planet*, June 7, 14, September 27, 1890; Blight, *Race and Reunion*, 267–72; Foster, *Ghosts of the Confederacy*, 100–103; *New York Times*, May 29, 1890.

2. *Richmond Dispatch*, October 17, 1890; Litwicki, *America's Public Holidays*, 58–66.

3. New work complicates the notions of accommodation, showing that uplift ideology could contain strains of resistance. See, for instance, Gaines, *Uplifting the Race*; Rael, *Black Identity and Black Protest*. The otherwise subtle and enduring work of August Meier denied the political connection to uplift. While tracing the disenchantment with the Republican Party, Meier said this caused black people to emphasize economic development at the expense of politics. He shows disillusionment with political activity in general that seems at odds with the themes of many Emancipation Day speakers. See Meier, *Negro Thought in America*, 26.

4. *Richmond Dispatch*, October 16, 1890.

5. *Richmond Planet*, June 7, 1890; Blight, *Race and Reunion*, 271.

6. *Petersburg Lancet*, January 20, 1883.

7. On uplift ideology, see Gaines, *Uplifting the Race*, xiv; for shame over the slave past, see Kachun, *Festivals of Freedom*, 239–40; on Crummel and the disagreement with Frederick Douglass over remembering the slave past, see Moses, *Alexander Crummel*, 226–28.

8. Boney, Hume, and Zafar, *God Made Man*, 135.

9. Ibid., 136–37.

10. *Weekly Echo*, January 20, 1884. On the most vocal advocates of independent voting, see *Washington Bee*, August 18, 1883. For background on black dissent, especially against the Chester A. Arthur administration, see De Santis, "Negro Dissatisfaction," 151–54.

11. Kachun, *Festivals of Freedom*, 203–4.

12. *Washington Bee*, August 18, 1883.

13. *Palmetto Press* (Charleston, S.C.) quoted in *People's Advocate*, May 12, 1883; *Washington Bee*, May 12, 1883.

14. Blight, *Race and Reunion*, 307–9; Meier, *Negro Thought in America*, 29; *People's Advocate*, October 6, 1883; De Santis, "Negro Dissatisfaction," 155–56.

15. Meier, *Negro Thought in America*, 29; *People's Advocate*, October 6, 1883.

16. Quoted in *Southern Workman*, July 1884, 30.

17. Ibid.

18. Kousser, *Shaping of Southern Politics*, 28.

19. D. B. Williams, *Sketch of Capt. R. A. Paul*, 62, 64–66.

20. Ibid., 67–68.

21. The *Call* (San Francisco), February 23, 1895, in Frederick Douglass Papers,

LC, online, Politics, folder 3, <http://memory.loc.gov/cgi-bin/ampage?
collId=mfd&fileName=19/19009/19009page.db&recNum=1&item Link=/
ammem/doughtml/dougFolder2.html&linkText=7> (accessed March 7,
2004).

22. Emmanuel K. Love, *Oration Delivered on Emancipation Day, Jan. 2, 1888*,
Pamphlets, Daniel A. P. Murray Collection, LC, online, p. 5, <http://
memory.loc.gov/cgi-bin/query/D?aap:12:./temp/~ammem_UVEA::>
(accessed March 7, 2004). Also see Kachun, *Festivals of Freedom*, 180.

23. *Washington Bee*, January 18, 1890.

24. Blight, *Race and Reunion*, 267–71; Foster, *Ghosts of the Confederacy*, 103. For
another work showing Lee becoming a northern hero, see Connelly, *Marble
Man*, esp. chap. 4.

25. *New York Times*, May 30, 1890; *Commercial Gazette* quoted in *New York Age*,
May 30, 1890.

26. *Detroit Plaindealer*, June 6, 1890; *State Capital* (Springfield, Ill.) and
Champion (Louisville, Ky.) quoted in *Richmond Planet*, June 14, 1890.

27. *Richmond Planet*, June 7, 1890.

28. Ibid.

29. See, for example, the statements of a former police official of Richmond
in the *New York Times*, May 28, 1890.

30. Ibid., April 15, 1890.

31. Ibid., April 13, 1890 (quotations); for reference to southern birth, see ibid.,
April 20, 1890.

32. Ibid., April 13, 1890.

33. *Southern Workman*, November 1899, 447–48 (emphasis in original).

34. *New York Times*, May 30, 1890.

35. *New York Age*, June 7, 1890.

36. *Washington Bee*, May 31, 1890.

37. Kousser, *Shaping of Southern Politics*, 32.

38. For biographical information on Mitchell, see the Library of Virginia
website, <http://www.lva.lib.va.us/whoweare/exhibits/mitchell/index
.htm> (January 23, 2004); *New York Times*, March 4, 1890.

39. *Richmond Planet*, June 14, September 6, 27 (quotation), 1890. For a good
overview of the convention and Mitchell's role, see Litwicki, *America's Public
Holidays*, 58–66.

40. *Richmond Planet*, October 11, 1890.

41. Ibid., September 27, 1890.

42. Ibid., October 11, 1890.

43. All comments in ibid., September 27, 1890.

44. *Richmond Dispatch*, October 16, 1890. For the observation of political
assertiveness, see Litwicki, *America's Public Holidays*, 61.

45. *Richmond Dispatch*, October 16, 1890.

46. *Richmond Planet*, October 18, 1890.

47. *Richmond Dispatch*, October 16, 1890.

48. *Richmond Planet*, October 18, 1890; Litwicki, *America's Public Holidays*, 61; *Richmond Dispatch*, October 17, 1890.

49. *Richmond Planet*, October 25, 1890; *Richmond Dispatch*, October 18, 1890.

50. Washington, *Papers*, 3:383, 496; *Southern Workman*, February 1898, 38.

51. *New York Globe*, June 9, 1883.

52. For emancipation celebrations, see, for instance, the descriptions of Washington and San Antonio events in the *New York Globe*, April 19, 1884, and the *New York Age*, July 12, 1890.

53. *Richmond Planet*, January 9, 1892, January 11, 1896; for Thomas's net worth, see *Colored People*, pamphlet 871, Peabody Collection, HU, 13.

54. W. T. B. Williams, "Colored Public Schools" and "Community Work at Colored Schools."

55. *Richmond Planet*, January 8, 1898.

56. *Southern News*, October 15, 1892.

57. W. S. Scarborough, "Co-operation Essential to Race Unity," *Proceedings of the Hampton Negro Conference Number VI* (July 1902): 60–65 (quotations on 61, 62), HU.

CHAPTER SEVEN

1. *National Tribune*, May 30, 1914; *Washington Post*, May 31, 1914; *New York Times*, May 31, 1914.

2. *New York Times*, May 31, 1914.

3. *Washington Post*, June 5, 1914.

4. *Washington Herald*, June 5, 1914, in folder 2, "clippings," box 14, Lewis Papers, VHS.

5. McGerr, *Decline of Popular Politics*, 5–7.

6. Kachun has done a particularly good job of linking the devolution of Emancipation Days to broader political and cultural trends. See his *Festivals of Freedom*, 243 (quotation). Blight's *Race and Reunion* gives little attention to the class divisions among black people in the demise of freedom celebrations.

7. Elias M. Greene to Maj. Genl. S. P. Heintzelman, May 5, 1863, and to Brg. Genl. M. C. Meigs, May 7, 1863, both in box 49, Arlington Estate, Quartermaster General Records, NARA.

8. Gibbons, *Life*, 372; *Washington Daily National Intelligencer*, January 15, 1867.

9. M. C. Meigs to Edwin M. Stanton, June 15, 1864, Quartermaster General Records, item 11 of 12, box 8, E576, NARA; Weigley, *Quartermaster General of the Union Army*, 296; *OR*, ser. 3, 4:1212.

10. Unidentified Report to the Secretary of War, n.d., Quartermaster General Records, item 4 of 12, box 7, E576, NARA.

11. *Washington Daily National Intelligencer*, November 15, 1866 (emphasis in original).

12. *Washington Chronicle* report in *New Orleans Semi-Weekly Louisianan*, June 15, 1871; *New Orleans Semi-Weekly Louisianan*, June 22, 1871.

13. *Washington Daily National Intelligencer*, June 1, 1868.

14. Wm. W. Belknap to John J. Patterson, May 24, 1874, and unidentified newspaper clipping, n.d., both in Quartermaster General Records, item 3 of 12, box 6, E576, NARA.

15. Mrs. C. P. Culver to W. Wm. Belknap, January 9, 1875; Oscar A. Mack to Eppa Hunton, December 19, 1874; Oscar A. Mack to Mrs. C. P. Culver, January 18, 1875; Eppa Hunton to W. W. Belknap, January 11, 1875, all in Quartermaster General Records, box 6, E576, NARA; *New York Times*, January 29, 1875.

16. *New York Tribune*, May 28, 1877; "Arlington," *Appleton's Journal*, November 14, 1874, 620.

17. For the Spanish-American War as the ultimate turning point for reconciliation and a new patriotism, see Buck, *Road to Reunion*, 306–7; Woodward, *Origins of the New South*, 369; Foster, *Ghosts of the Confederacy*, 146–53; Ayers, *Promise of the New South*, 304; Blight, *Race and Reunion*, 153.

18. Gilmore, *Gender and Jim Crow*, 78–79; Ayers, *Promise of the New South*, 328–29; Foster, *Ghosts of the Confederacy*, 146–49.

19. J. Bryan to Jno. P. Branch, July 2, 1898, sec. 34, Bryan Letterbook, VHS; Foster, *Ghosts of the Confederacy*, 150.

20. Ayers, *Promise of the New South*, 332; *Washington Post*, December 16, 1898. For the clearest articulation of McKinley as a sentimentalist, see Woodward, *Origins of the New South*, 462. For other historians who have connected McKinley's conciliation with the president's desire to cultivate the southern white congressional delegation for support of the treaty with Spain, see Haley, "Race, Rhetoric, and Revolution," 211–12; Perman, *Struggle for Mastery*, 118–19.

21. *New York Times*, December 15, 1898; *Washington Post*, December 15, 1898.

22. *Washington Post*, December 18, 1898.

23. "A Resolution," John D. Little and others, Georgia State Legislature, December 14, 1989, reel 64, McKinley Papers, LC.

24. Smith quotation in J. C. Shaffer to Mr. Kohlsaat, December 28, 1898, reel 5, ibid.; R. M. Barton Jr. to William McKinley, December 16, 1898, reel 64, ibid.; *Washington Post*, December 16, 1898.

25. John S. Kountz to Mr. President, December 19, 1898, reel 64, McKinley Papers, LC; *New York Times*, December 29, 1898.

26. *Richmond Enquirer and Examiner*, June 2, 1869; J. K. Ohl to Mr. Cortleyou, December 22, 1898, reel 85, McKinley Papers, LC.

27. *New York Times*, December 17, 1898; John S. Kountz to Mr. President, December 19, 1898, reel 64, McKinley Papers, LC.

28. William Wigman to William McKinley, December 20, 1898, reel 64, McKinley Papers, LC; William McKinley to My Dear Holden, December 29, 1898, reel 5, ibid. The president sent the editor the badge to show that it was innocuous and said that he "felt especially pleased at the warm reception

extended to me by ex-Confederates on my trip throughout the South. The only possible criticism I could make on the badge would be that it contains a rather poor picture of myself."

29. *Richmond Planet*, December 10, 1898; Waddell quotation in Cecelski and Tyson, *Wilmington Race Riot of 1898*, 4.

30. *Richmond Planet*, December 17, 24, 1898; *Washington Post*, December 18, 1898.

31. *Washington Post*, December 16, 1898.

32. Perman sees McKinley's silence on racial issues as a "conscious policy of conciliation." See his *Struggle for Mastery*, 118–19.

33. Booker T. Washington, "The Story of My Life and Work," in Washington, *Papers*, 1:127–29. For other petitions from black institutions, see Harriet E. Giles to William McKinley, December 3, 1898, and D. G. Purse to John Addison Porter, December 11–12, 1898, both in reel 64, McKinley Papers, LC.

34. *Washington Post*, December 17, 1898; *New York Times*, December 17, 1898; Washington, *Papers*, 1:131; Booker T. Washington to President William McKinley, December 22, 1898, reel 64, McKinley Papers, LC.

35. *Washington Post*, December 17, 1898.

36. Dodge, "Arlington National Cemetery's Confederate Burials," 28–29; [Lewis] to Capt. Julian G. Moore, April 15, 1901, box 10, Lewis Papers, VHS.

37. Lewis to Joseph Wheeler, February 22, 1899, box 10, Lewis Papers, VHS.

38. "Arlington," an address dated May 18, 1903, box 11, ibid.

39. *New York Times*, May 2, 1901.

40. Extract of comments by Janet H. W. Randolph, September 27, 1900, folder 1, box 10, Lewis Papers, VHS.

41. H. A. Herbert to Samuel Lewis, February 6, 1901, box 10, ibid.

42. Committee of Five to Elihu Root, March 28, 1901, Quartermaster General Records, E635, NARA.

43. *New York Times*, May 2, 1901.

44. Lizzie Pollard to General John B. Gordon, printed in *History of the Confederate Memorial Associations of the South*, 28. Although it began with only thirteen societies, by 1903 the group had embraced more than fifty memorial associations, with an average membership of seventy-five in each. See ibid., 32.

45. [Lewis] to Capt. Julian G. Moore, April 15, 1901, box 10, Lewis Papers, VHS.

46. Samuel Lewis to Mrs. W. J. Behan, March 3, 1902, ibid.

47. *New Orleans Picayune*, March 20, 1902; undated memoranda, box 11, Lewis Papers, VHS. Although this became an important time for celebrations, June 3 did not always work for practical reasons. In the beginning, celebrants of the Confederate South tended to hold commemorations on the first Sunday after Davis's birthday.

48. Kachun, *Festivals of Freedom*, 233–37. Kachun characterizes the period between 1900 and 1920 as a time of dissolution for freedom celebrations. See his chap. 7.

49. *Washington Bee*, April 25, 1891. For a detailed analysis of this, see Kachun, *Festivals of Freedom*, chap. 6.

50. P. H. Bethea to Mrs. Mary Church Terrell, August 2, 1891, frame 394, Terrell Papers.

51. Theo. C. Ray, past colonel, Robert G. Shaw Command No. 4, Union Veterans' Union, Department of Potomac, to Mary Church Terrell (president, Bethel Literary and Historical Association), April 26, 1893, frame 365, reel 3, container 4, Terrell Papers; Wedin, *Inheritors of the Spirit*, 129–30.

52. Quoted in *New York Age*, January 4, 1900, in frame 393, reel 3, container 4, Terrell Papers.

53. Washington, *Papers*, 10:250–52, 262; *Christian Recorder*, February 8, April 11, 1912, in clippings no. 273, Peabody Collection, HU, 1:2.

54. Washington, *Papers*, 12:112–13.

55. *New York Age*, May 22, June 19, in Tuskegee Clipping File, frames 822, 828, reel 240, HU; Washington, *Papers*, 12:112–13.

56. Tuskegee Clipping File, frame 823, reel 240, HU; *Richmond Planet*, January 4, 1913.

57. Giles B. Jackson to H. C. Stuart, September 8, 1915, folder Colored Industrial, box 7, Stuart Papers, LV.

58. Frank, "Negro Exhibition," 410.

59. "Remarks of Thomas A. Martin, of Virginia, and Others," July 8, 1914, in pamphlet 66, Peabody Collection, HU, 1–8 (quotation on 3).

60. Ibid., 7.

61. Giles B. Jackson to Henry C. Stuart, December 16, 1914, and Henry C. Stuart to Giles B. Jackson, December 18, 1914, both in folder Colored Industrial, box 7, Stuart Papers, LV; *Norfolk Virginia Pilot*, July 6, 1915, in clippings no. 2u74, Peabody Collection, HU, 49.

62. Tuskegee Clipping File, frame 859, reel 240, HU; "A Proclamation," dated July 2, 1915, in Link, *Papers of Woodrow Wilson*, 33:464.

63. *Richmond Times-Dispatch*, July 5, 1915.

64. Ibid., July 10, 1915.

65. Tuskegee Clipping File, frame 869, reel 240, HU.

66. *Richmond Planet*, August 14, 1915, in ibid., frame 866.

67. [Illegible] to H. C. Stuart, Commissioners for National Negro Exposition, August 6, 1915, folder Colored Industrial, box 7, Stuart Papers, LV.

68. Samuel E. Lewis to General Marcus J. Wright, October 28, 1905, and Samuel E. Lewis to Virginia Faulkner McSherry, December 15, 1910 (quotation), both in folder 1, box 14, Lewis Papers, VHS.

69. H. A. Herbert to General Stephen D. Lee, December 3, 1906, ibid.

70. Stephen D. Lee to Dr. Lewis, November 13, 1906, ibid.

71. Public Resolution No. 38, E703, NARA; *New York Times*, February 7, 1908.

72. Samuel E. Lewis to General Wm. E Mickle, September 27, 1905, folder 1, box 14, Lewis Papers, VHS.

73. Dodge, "Arlington National Cemetery's Confederate Burials," 31–35.
74. *National Tribune*, May 30, 1914; *Washington Post*, May 31, 1914.
75. Link, *Papers of Woodrow Wilson*, 30:111.
76. *New York Times*, June 5, 1914; *Washington Post*, June 5, 1914.
77. *Washington Post*, June 5, 1914.

BIBLIOGRAPHY

PRIMARY SOURCES

Manuscript and Archival Materials

Alderman Library, University of Virginia, Charlottesville
  R. T. W. Duke Papers
  Sarah Strickler Fife Diary
Handley Library, Winchester, Virginia
  Philip Williams Family Papers
Library of Congress, Washington, D.C.
  Salmon P. Chase Papers, microfilm
  Jubal Anderson Early Papers
  William McKinley Papers, microfilm
  Daniel A. P. Murray Collection
  Mary Church Terrell Papers, microfilm
Library of Virginia, Richmond
  Executive Papers, Governor's Office, Henry Carter Stuart
  Records of the Memorial Society of the Ladies of the City of Petersburg,
      1866–1912
Massachusetts Historical Society, Boston
  Adams Family Papers, microfilm
Museum of the Confederacy, Richmond, Virginia
  Hollywood Memorial Association, minutes
  United Daughters of the Confederacy Papers
National Archives and Records Administration, Washington, D.C.
  Adjutant General's Office, RG 393
  Bureau of Refugees, Freedmen, and Abandoned Lands, RG 105, microfilm
  Quartermaster General Records, RG 92
    Arlington Estate
    Cemeterial Records, 1828–29 (561)
    Correspondence etc., Marcus J. Wright (585)
    General Correspondence, National and Post Cemeteries (576)
    Letters Sent, Relating to Cemeteries (564)

Letters Sent, Reports Received by Cemeteries (569)

Press Copies, Letters Sent to Secretary of War (565)

Quartermaster General Orders, National Cemeteries (590)

Perkins Library, Duke University, Durham, North Carolina

Mahone Papers

Southern Pamphlets

No. 373. William C. P. Breckinridge. *Addresses in Memory of the Confederate Dead*. Lexington Observer & Reporter, 1869.

University Archives and University Museum, Hampton University, Hampton, Virginia

Hampton Bulletin

Norfolk Virginia Pilot

Peabody Collection

Pamphlet 66. *Exposition to Celebrate the 50th Anniversary of Emancipation*. 1914.

Pamphlet 620. Christian Fleetwood. *The Negro as a Soldier*. 1895.

Pamphlet 871. *The Colored People, "Weighted in the Balance" with other Nations, Are not alone "Found Wanting." Oration Delivered at Eastville, Virginia, January 1st, 1890*. Hampton, Va.: Normal School Steam Press, 1890.

Pamphlet 872. Frederick M. Burrows. *Not as a Colored Man, but as a Man. A Speech Delivered at the Celebration of the Emancipation Proclamation, Eastville, Va*. January 1, 1891.

Proceedings of the Hampton Negro Conferences. 1897–1909.

Tuskegee Clipping File

Virginia Historical Society, Richmond

Ashby Family Papers

Briscoe, Marion Goode. "Ashes of Roses." Typescript of memoir, ca. 1950, Mss5 1B7744:1.

Broadside no. 1866:13, dated April 2, 1866

Henry Clay Brock Papers, 1862–72

Daniel Coalman Papers

Confederate Memorial Association, Joseph Bryan Letterbook

Charles Henry Dimmock Papers, 1850–73

James Henry Gardner Papers, 1826–67

Hollywood Cemetery Company, Richmond, Minute Books, 1847–68 and 1868–92

Hollywood Cemetery Company Records, 1856–1963

Hollywood Sketches, Mss1 C6458d FA2

Hutton Family Papers

William Kennedy Papers

Ladies Memorial Association of Appomattox, Appomattox Court House, Minute Book

Ladies Memorial Society of Petersburg

Letterbook of Robert Edward Lee, in Lee Family Papers, 1824–1918
Samuel Edwin Lewis Papers
Nancy MacFarland Papers
Robert Taylor Scott Papers
"To the Women of the South." Broadside, Hollywood Memorial
    Association, Mss1 L51b65.

Newspapers and Periodicals

Appleton's Journal
Atlanta Constitution
Charleston News and Courier
Colored American (Augusta, Ga.)
Colored American (New York, N.Y.)
Feliciana Ledger
Greensboro Patriot
Indianapolis Freeman
Lynchburg Virginian
Nation
National Era
National Intelligencer
National Tribune
New Orleans Democrat
New Orleans Picayune
New Orleans Semi-Weekly Louisianan
New York Age
New York Times
New York Globe
New York Tribune
Norfolk Virginian
North American Review
People's Advocate (Alexandria, Va.)
Petersburg Daily Index
Petersburg Lancet
Richmond Daily Dispatch
Richmond Daily Enquirer

Richmond Daily Examiner
Richmond Dispatch
Richmond Enquirer
Richmond Enquirer and Examiner
Richmond Examiner
Richmond Examiner and Sentinel
Richmond Planet
Richmond State
Richmond Times
Richmond Times-Dispatch
South Carolina Leader
Southern Banner
Southern Illustrated News
Southern News (Richmond, Va.)
Southern Opinion
Southern Workman
Staunton Spectator
Times (London)
True Southerner
Valley Virginian
Virginia Star
Washington Bee
Washington Daily National Intelligencer
Washington Post
Weekly Echo (Savannah, Ga.)
Winchester Journal

Books

Avary, Myrta Lockett. *Dixie after the War*. Boston: Houghton Mifflin, 1937.
Blackett, R. J. M., ed. *Thomas Morris Chester, Black Civil War Correspondent: His Dispatches from the Virginia Front*. Baton Rouge: Louisiana State University Press, 1989.
Blassingame, John W., ed. *The Frederick Douglass Papers*. Ser. 1, Speeches,

Debates, and Interviews. Vol. 2, *1847–1854*. New Haven: Yale University Press, 1982.

Boney, F. N., Richard L. Hume, and Rafia Zafar, eds. *God Made Man, Man Made the Slave: The Autobiography of George Teamoh*. Macon, Ga.: Mercer Press, 1990.

Chase, Salmon P. *The Salmon P. Chase Papers*. Vol. 5, *Correspondence, 1865–1873*. Edited by John Niven. Kent, Ohio: Kent State University Press, 1998.

Congressional Record: Proceedings and Debates of the . . . Congress. Washington, D.C.: GPO, 1873– .

Cushing, Caleb. *An Oration Pronounced at Boston Before the Colonization Society of Massachusetts, on the Anniversary of American Independence, July 4, 1833*. Boston: Lyceum Press—G. C. Light and Co., 1833.

Dawson, Francis W. *Reminiscences of Confederate Service, 1861–1865*. 1882. Reprint, Baton Rouge: Louisiana State University Press, 1980.

Drago, Edmund. *Hurrah for Hampton! Black Red Shirts in South Carolina during Reconstruction*. Fayetteville: University of Arkansas Press, 1998.

Gibbons, Abigail Hopper. *Life of Abby Hopper Gibbons: Told Chiefly through Her Correspondence*. Vol. 2. Edited by Sarah Hopper Emerson. New York: G. P. Putnam's Sons, 1896.

Graf, Leroy P., ed. *The Papers of Andrew Johnson*. Vol. 7, *1864–1865*. Knoxville: University of Tennessee Press, 1986.

History of the Confederated Memorial Associations of the South. New Orleans: L. Graham Co., 1903.

Jervey, Theodore D. *The Elder Brother*. New York: Neale, 1905.

Johnson, William. *William Johnson's Natchez: The Ante-Bellum Diary of a Free Negro*. Edited by William Ransom Hogan and Edwin Adams Davis. Baton Rouge: Louisiana State University Press, 1951.

King, Edward. *The Great South*. Edited by W. Magruder Drake and Robert R. Jones. Baton Rouge: Louisiana State University Press, 1972.

Langston, John Mercer. *From the Virginia Plantation to the National Capitol: The First and Only Negro Representative in Congress from the Old Dominion*. 1894. Reprint, New York: Bergman, 1969.

Leigh, Frances Butler. *Ten Years on a Georgia Plantation Since the War*. London: Richard Bentley and Son, 1887.

Link, Arthur S., ed. *The Papers of Woodrow Wilson*. Vol. 30. Princeton: Princeton University Press, 1979.

———. *The Papers of Woodrow Wilson*. Vol. 33. Princeton: Princeton University Press, 1980.

Looby, Christopher, ed. *The Complete Civil War Journal and Selected Letters of Thomas Wentworth Higginson*. Chicago: University of Chicago Press, 2000.

Maryland, My Maryland, and Other Poems: By James Ryder Randall. Baltimore: John Murphy Co., 1908.

Paige, T. F. *Twenty-Two Years of Freedom*. Norfolk: Barron's, 1885.

Stevenson, Brenda, ed. *The Journals of Charlotte Forten Grimké*. New York: Oxford University Press, 1988.

U.S. Centennial Commission. *Reports of the International Exhibition, 1876.* 9 vols. Washington, D.C.: GPO, 1880–94.

U.S. War Department. *War of the Rebellion: The Official Records of the Union and Confederate Armies.* 128 vols. Washington, D.C.: GPO, 1880–1901.

Waddell, Joseph A. *Annals of Augusta County, Virginia, 1726 to 1871.* 2nd ed. 1902. Reprint, Harrisonburg, Va.: C. J. Carrier Co., 1986.

Washington, Booker T. *The Booker T. Washington Papers.* 14 vols. Edited by Louis R. Harlan. Urbana: University of Illinois Press, 1972–89.

Williams, D. B. *A Sketch of the Life and Times of Capt. R. A. Paul.* Richmond: Johns and Goolsby, 1885.

Worsham, John H. *One of Jackson's Foot Cavalry: His Experience and What He Saw During the War, 1861–1865.* New York: Neale, 1912.

SECONDARY SOURCES

Books

Averitt, Rev. James B. *The Memoirs of General Turner Ashby and His Compeers.* 1867. Reprint, Baltimore: Selby and Dulany, 1984.

Ayers, Edward L. *The Promise of the New South: Life after Reconstruction.* New York: Oxford University Press, 1992.

Baker, Jean. *Affairs of Party: The Political Culture of Northern Democrats in the Mid-Nineteenth Century.* New York: Fordham University Press, 1998.

Bederman, Gail. *Manliness and Civilization: A Cultural History of Gender and Race in the United States, 1880–1917.* Chicago: University of Chicago Press, 1995.

Blight, David. *Race and Reunion: The Civil War in American Memory.* Cambridge, Mass.: Belknap Press, 2001.

Brundage, W. Fitzhugh, ed. *Where These Memories Grow: History, Memory, and Southern Identity.* Chapel Hill: University of North Carolina Press, 2000.

Buck, Paul S. *The Road to Reunion, 1865–1900.* Boston: Little, Brown, 1937.

Cecelski, David S., and Timothy B. Tyson, eds. *Democracy Betrayed: The Wilmington Race Riot of 1898 and Its Legacy.* Chapel Hill: University of North Carolina Press, 1998.

Clinton, Catherine, and Nina Silber, eds. *Divided Houses: Gender and the Civil War.* New York: Oxford University Press, 1992.

Connelly, Thomas L. *The Marble Man: Robert E. Lee and His Image in American Society.* New York: Alfred A. Knopf, 1977.

Dailey, Jane. *Before Jim Crow: The Politics of Race in Postemancipation Virginia.* Chapel Hill: University of North Carolina Press, 2000.

Dailey, Jane, Glenda Elizabeth Gilmore, and Bryant Simon, eds. *Jumpin' Jim Crow: Southern Politics from Civil War to Civil Rights.* Princeton: Princeton University Press, 2000.

Davis, Susan G. *Parades and Power: Street Theater in Nineteenth-Century Philadelphia.* Philadelphia: Temple University Press, 1986.

Deglar, Carl N. *The Other South: Southern Dissenters in the Nineteenth Century.* New York: Harper and Row, 1974.

Du Bois, W. E. B. *Black Reconstruction in America, 1860–1880.* New York: Atheneum, 1935.

Edwards, Laura. *Gendered Strife and Confusion: The Political Culture of Reconstruction.* Urbana: University of Illinois Press, 1997.

Faust, Drew Gilpin. *Mothers of Invention: Women of the Slaveholding South in the American Civil War.* Chapel Hill: University of North Carolina Press, 1996.

Fellman, Michael. *The Making of Robert E. Lee.* New York: Random House, 2000.

Fitzgerald, Michael. *The Union League Movement in the Deep South: Politics and Agricultural Change during Reconstruction.* Baton Rouge: Louisiana State University Press, 1989.

Foner, Eric. *Reconstruction: America's Unfinished Revolution, 1863–1877.* New York: Harper and Row, 1988.

Foster, Gaines M. *Ghosts of the Confederacy: Defeat, the Lost Cause, and the Emergence of the New South, 1865 to 1913.* New York: Oxford University Press, 1987.

Freeman, Douglas Southall. *Lee's Lieutenants: A Study in Command.* 3 vols. New York: Charles Scribner's Sons, 1944.

———. *R. E. Lee.* 4 vols. New York: Charles Scribner's Sons, 1935.

Gaines, Kevin K. *Uplifting the Race: Black Leadership, Politics, and Culture in the Twentieth Century.* Chapel Hill: University of North Carolina Press, 1996.

Genovese, Eugene D. *Roll, Jordan, Roll: The World the Slaves Made.* New York: Pantheon, 1972.

Gilje, Paul. *The Road to Mobocracy: Popular Disorder in New York City, 1763–1834.* Chapel Hill: University of North Carolina Press, 1987.

Gilmore, Glenda Elizabeth. *Gender and Jim Crow: Women and the Politics of White Supremacy in North Carolina, 1896–1920.* Chapel Hill: University of North Carolina Press, 1996.

Hahn, Steven. *A Nation under Our Feet: Black Political Struggles in the Rural South from Slavery to the Great Migration.* Cambridge, Mass.: Belknap Press, 2003.

———. *The Roots of Southern Populism: Yeoman Farmers and the Transformation of the Georgia Upcountry, 1850–1890.* New York: Oxford University Press, 1983.

Harding, Vincent. *There Is a River: The Black Struggle for Freedom in America.* New York: Harcourt Brace Jovanovich, 1981.

Hobsbawm, Eric, and Terence Rangers, eds. *The Invention of Tradition.* Cambridge: Cambridge University Press, 1983.

Janney, Asa Moore, and Werner Janney. *The Composition Book: Stories from the Old Days in Lincoln, Virginia.* N.p., 1973.

Johnston, William Preston. *The Life of Gen. Albert Sidney Johnston: Embracing His Services in the Armies of the United States, the Republic of Texas, and the Confederate States.* New York: Appleton, 1878.

Kachun, Mitch. *Festivals of Freedom: Memory and Meaning in African American*

Emancipation Celebrations, 1808–1915. Amherst: University of Massachusetts Press, 2003.

Kousser, J. Morgan. *The Shaping of Southern Politics: Suffrage Restriction and the Establishment of the One-Party South, 1880–1910.* New Haven: Yale University Press, 1974.

Litwicki, Ellen M. *America's Public Holidays, 1865–1920.* Washington, D.C.: Smithsonian Institution Press, 2000.

Lowe, Richard G. *Republicans and Reconstruction in Virginia, 1856–1870.* Charlottesville: University Press of Virginia, 1991.

Maddex, Jack P., Jr. *The Virginia Conservatives, 1867–1879: A Study in Reconstruction Politics.* Chapel Hill: University of North Carolina Press, 1970.

McGerr, Michael. *The Decline of Popular Politics: The American North, 1865–1928.* New York: Oxford University Press, 1986.

Meier, August. *Negro Thought in America, 1880–1915: Racial Ideologies in the Age of Booker T. Washington.* Ann Arbor: University of Michigan Press, 1964.

Mitchell, Mary H. *Hollywood Cemetery: The History of a Southern Shrine.* Richmond: Virginia State Library, 1985.

Moore, James Tice. *Two Paths to the New South: The Virginia Debt Controversy.* Lexington: University Press of Kentucky, 1974.

Moses, Wilson. *Alexander Crummel: A Study of Civilization and Discontent.* New York: Oxford University Press, 1989.

O'Brien, John Thomas, Jr. *From Bondage to Citizenship: The Richmond Black Community, 1865–1867.* Studies in Nineteenth-Century American Political and Society History, edited by Ronald P. Formisano. New York: Garland, 1990.

O'Leary, Cecilia Elizabeth. *To Die For: The Paradox of American Patriotism.* Princeton: Princeton University Press, 1999.

Osterweis, Rollin G. *The Myth of the Lost Cause, 1865–1900.* Hamden, Conn.: Archon Books, 1973.

Pearson, Charles Chilton. *The Readjuster Movement in Virginia.* New Haven: Yale University Press, 1917.

Perman, Michael. *Struggle for Mastery: Disfranchisement in the South, 1888–1908.* Chapel Hill: University of North Carolina Press, 2001.

Piehler, Kurt G. *Remembering War the American Way.* Washington, D.C.: Smithsonian Institution Press, 1995.

Pulley, Raymond H. *Old Virginia Restored: An Interpretation of the Progressive Impulse, 1870–1930.* Charlottesville: University Press of Virginia, 1968.

Purdue, Charles L., Thomas E. Barden, and Robert K. Phillips, eds. *Weevils in the Wheat: Interviews with Virginia Ex-Slaves.* Charlottesville: University Press of Virginia, 1976.

Rachleff, Peter. *Black Labor in Richmond, 1865–1890.* Urbana: University of Illinois Press, 1989.

Rael, Patrick. *Black Identity and Black Protest in the Antebellum North.* Chapel Hill: University of North Carolina Press, 2002.

Reidy, Joseph P. *From Slavery to Agrarian Capitalism in the Cotton Plantation*

South: Central Georgia, 1800–1880. Chapel Hill: University of North Carolina Press, 1992.

Roland, Charles P. *Albert Sidney Johnston: Soldier of Three Republics*. Austin: University of Texas Press, 1964.

Savage, Kirk. *Standing Soldiers, Kneeling Slaves: Race, War, and Monument in Nineteenth-Century America*. Princeton: Princeton University Press, 1997.

Saville, Julie. *The Work of Reconstruction: From Slave to Wage Laborer in South Carolina, 1860–1870*. New York: Cambridge University Press, 1996.

Sefton, James E. *The United States Army and Reconstruction, 1865–1877*. Baton Rouge: Louisiana State University Press, 1967.

Simkins, Francis Butler, and Robert Hilliard Woody. *South Carolina during Reconstruction*. Chapel Hill: University of North Carolina Press, 1932.

Travers, Len. *Celebrating the Fourth: Independence Day and the Rites of Nationalism in the Early Republic*. Amherst: University of Massachusetts Press, 1997.

Thomas, Emory. *Robert E. Lee: A Biography*. New York: Norton, 1995.

Thompson, E. P. *Customs in Common: Studies in Traditional Popular Culture*. New York: Norton, 1991.

Van Deusen, Glyndon G. *Horace Greeley: Nineteenth-Century Crusader*. Philadelphia: University of Pennsylvania Press, 1953.

Waldstreicher, David. *In the Midst of Perpetual Fetes: The Making of American Nationalism, 1776–1820*. Chapel Hill: University of North Carolina Press, 1997.

Wedin, Carolyn. *Inheritors of the Spirit: Mary White Ovington and the Founding of the NAACP*. New York: John Wiley and Sons, 1998.

Weigley, Russell F. *Quartermaster General of the Union Army: A Biography of M. C. Meigs*. New York: Columbia University Press, 1959.

White, William W. *The Confederate Veteran*. Confederate Centennial Studies, no. 22. Tuscaloosa, Ala: Confederate Publishing Co., 1962.

Whites, LeAnn. *The Civil War as a Crisis in Gender: Augusta, Georgia, 1860–1890*. Athens: University of Georgia Press, 1995.

Wiggins, William H., Jr. *O Freedom! Afro-American Emancipation Celebrations*. Knoxville: University of Tennessee Press, 1987.

Wills, Garry. *Lincoln at Gettysburg: The Words That Remade America*. New York: Simon and Schuster, 1992.

Wilson, Charles Reagan. *Baptized in Blood: The Religion of the Lost Cause, 1865–1920*. Athens: University of Georgia Press, 1980.

Woodward, C. Vann. *Origins of the New South, 1877–1913*. History of the South Series, vol. 9. Baton Rouge: Louisiana State University Press, 1951.

Articles, Essays, Dissertations, and Theses

"Arlington Cemetery." *American Architect*, July 23, 1904, 31.

Brown, Elsa Barkley. "Negotiating and Transforming the Public Sphere: African American Political Life in the Transition from Slavery to Freedom."

In *The Black Public Sphere*, edited by the Black Public Sphere Collective, 107–46. Chicago: University of Chicago Press, 1995.

——. "Uncle Ned's Children: Negotiating Community and Freedom in Postemancipation Richmond, Virginia." Ph.D. diss., Kent State University, 1994.

Brown, W. Burlie. "Louisiana and the Nation's First One-hundredth Birthday." *Louisiana History* 18, no. 3 (Summer 1977): 261–75.

Brundage, W. Fitzhugh. "White Women and the Politics of Historical Memory in the New South, 1880–1920." In *Jumpin' Jim Crow: Southern Politics from Civil War to Civil Rights*, edited by Jane Dailey, Glenda Elizabeth Gilmore, and Bryant Simon, 115–39. Princeton: Princeton University Press, 2000.

Carmichael, Peter S. "The Last Generation: Sons of Virginia Slaveholders and the Creation of Southern Identity, 1850–1865." Ph.D. diss., Pennsylvania State University, 1996.

Clark, Kathleen. "Celebrating Freedom: Emancipation Day Celebrations and African American Memory in the Early Reconstruction South." In *Where These Memories Grow: History, Memory, and Southern Identity*, edited by W. Fitzhugh Brundage, 107–32. Chapel Hill: University of North Carolina Press, 2000.

——. "History Is No Fossil Remains: Race, Gender, and the Politics of Memory in the American South, 1863–1913." Ph.D. diss., Yale University Press, 1999.

Dennie, Garrey. "One King, Two Burials: The Politics of Funerals in South Africa's Transkei." University of the Witwatersrand, African Studies Institute, African Studies Seminar Paper presented October 1990.

De Santis, Vincent P. "Negro Dissatisfaction with Republican Policies in the South, 1882–1884." *Journal of Negro History* 36 (April 1951): 148–59.

Dodge, George W. "Arlington National Cemetery's Confederate Burials," pt. 2. *Arlington Historical Magazine*, October 1994, 22–38.

Foner, Philip S. "Black Participation in the Centennial of 1876." *Negro History Bulletin* 39, no. 2 (1976): 533–37.

Frank, Lucy Brown. "The Negro Exhibition of the Jamestown Ter-Centennial Exposition of 1907." *Negro History Bulletin* 38, no. 5 (1975): 408–13.

Green, Fletcher. "Listen to the Eagle Scream: One Hundred Years of the Fourth of July in North Carolina, 1776–1876." In *Democracy in the Old South and Other Essays by Fletcher Melvin Green*, 111–56. Nashville: Vanderbilt University Press, 1969.

Haley, John. "Race, Rhetoric, and Revolution." In *Democracy Betrayed: The Wilmington Race Riot of 1898 and Its Legacy*, edited by David S. Cecelski and Timothy B. Tyson, 207–24. Chapel Hill: University of North Carolina Press, 1998.

Hobsbawm, Eric. "Mass Producing Traditions: Europe, 1870–1914." In *The Invention of Tradition*, edited by Eric Hobsbawm and Terence Rangers, 263–308. Cambridge: Cambridge University Press, 1983.

Holden, Charles J. " 'Is Our Love for Wade Hampton Foolishness?': South
Carolina and the Lost Cause." In *The Myth of the Lost Cause and Civil War
History*, 60–88. Bloomington: Indiana University Press, 2000.

Holt, Michael. "Change and Continuity in the Party Period: The Substance
and Structure of American Politics, 1835–1885." In *Contesting Democracy:
Substance and Structure in American Political History, 1775–2000*, 93–115.
Lawrence: University Press of Kansas, 2001.

Kachun, Mitch. "Before the Eyes of All Nations: African-American Identity and
Historical Memory at the Centennial Exposition of 1876." *Pennsylvania
History* 65, no. 3 (Summer 1998): 300–323.

McPherson, James M. Review of *Race and Reunion*, by David Blight. *Civil War
History* 47 (December 2001): 348.

Page, Brian D. " 'Stand by the Flag': Nationalism and African-American
Celebrations of the Fourth of July in Memphis, 1866–1887." *Tennessee
Historical Quarterly* 59 (Winter 1999): 285–301.

Sweet, Leonard. "The Fourth of July and Black Americans in the Nineteenth
Century: Northern Leadership Opinion within the Context of Black
Experience." *Journal of Negro History* 61 (July 1976): 256–75.

van Zelm, Antoinette G. "On the Front Lines of Freedom: Black and White
Women Shape Emancipation in Virginia, 1861–1890." Ph.D. diss., College of
William and Mary, 1998.

Waldstreicher, David. "Rites of Rebellion, Rites of Assent: Celebrations, Print
Culture, and the Origins of American Nationalism." *Journal of American
History* 82 (June 1995): 37–61.

Warren, Charles. "Fourth of July Myths." *William and Mary Quarterly*, 3rd ser.,
2 (July 1945): 237–72.

White, Shane. " 'It Was a Proud Day': African Americans, Festivals, and
Parades in the North, 1741–1834." *Journal of American History* 81 (June 1994):
13–50.

Wiggins, William H., Jr. "Juneteenth: A Red Spot Day on the Texas Calendar."
In *Juneteenth Texas: Essays in African-American Folklore*, edited by Francis
Edward Abernethy, Patricia B. Mullen, and Alan B. Govenar, 237–52.
Publications of the Texas Folklore Society 54. Denton: University of North
Texas Press, 1996.

Williams, W. T. B. "Colored Public Schools in Southern Cities." *Hampton
Bulletin*, September 1905, 15–37.

——. "Community Work at Colored Schools." *Hampton Bulletin*, September
1909, 46.

INDEX

Arlington National Cemetery, 7, 8, 171–93, 201–7; Confederate grave decoration in, 73–75, 112, 177–78; Confederate monument in, 171–72, 201–7; inception of, 174–75, 179; segregated graves in, 175–76; Confederate section of, 179, 187–93, 201, 202, 203
Army of Northern Virginia, 23, 25, 34, 82, 160
Arthur, Chester A., 150
Ashby, Richard, 91
Ashby, Turner, 90–94
Ashby Brigade, 91, 92
Atlanta, Ga., 65, 80, 181
Atlanta Constitution, 125–26
Atlanta Peace Jubilee (1898), 179, 182–84, 186, 188
Augusta, Ga., 30–31, 99, 125
Ayers, Edward L., 181

Baldwin, John B., 66, 116
Baltimore, Md., 89
Baptists, 29, 81
Battle Grove Cemetery (Ky.), 76
Beauregard, P. G. T., 44
Beecher, Henry Ward, 53
Belknap, William, 177
Belle Isle (Va.) cemetery, 53
Bethea, P. H., 194
Big Bethel, battle of, 60
Biracial coalitions, 8–9, 108, 114, 129–30, 134; decline of, 146
Black codes, 35, 51
Blackford, Charles, 132
Black nationalism, 147, 169
Blaine, James G., 124, 151, 161
Blight, David, 3–4, 70, 109, 111, 139
Border states, 89
Botts, John Minor, 44
Bragg, Braxton, 95
Breckinridge, William C. P., 76
Briscoe, Marion Goode, 34, 36
Bristow, Joseph, 172

Britain, 19, 20, 121
Brown, Elsa Barkley, 102–3
Brown, John, 26, 27, 111
Browne, W. W., 164
Bryan, J., 181
Bryan, William Jennings, 204
Buck, Paul, 2, 50, 109
Buckner, Simon Bolivar, 95
Butler, M. C., 138, 144

Calhoun, John C., 21
Calhoun, Stephen, 63
Calhoun Colored School (Ala.), 168
Camp Saxton (Sea Islands), 26
Caribbean area, 19, 20
Carpetbaggers, 44, 51, 178, 180
Carson, Perry, 193
Cemeteries: Confederate, 22, 50–62, 79–97; as contested ground, 52–53; Confederate women's maintenance of, 65, 77–78, 79–87; segregation of Union and Confederate dead in, 87–88, 89–90. *See also* Grave decoration; National cemeteries; Reburials; *specific names*
Centennial, U.S., 107, 120–26, 138, 158
Centennial Exposition (1876; Phila.), 124–25, 126; African American exclusions from, 138–39
Charleston, S.C., 51, 54, 125, 126
Charlottesville, Va., 51, 59, 61, 91
Chase, Calvin P., 193–94
Chase, Salmon P., 4, 74–75, 110–12, 114
Chicago Tribune, 88, 124
Christmas season, 15–16, 28–29, 30
Civil Rights Act of 1866, 34, 39, 42
Civil War, 3, 8–9, 14, 93; and slavery, 3, 4–5, 43, 75, 89; postwar interpretations of, 3–5, 24, 75, 76, 121, 155, 173; surrender dates of, 23, 25, 137; surrender celebrations, 34–42; Confederate losses in, 49; effect on southern white males of, 78–79,

Kachun, Mitch, 3
Kelley, William D., 106
Kemper, James, 119–20, 197
King, Edward, 121
Knights of Pythias, 136
Knights Templar, 117
Kousser, J. Morgan, 5, 152, 161
Ku Klux Klan, 148

Labor: and southern white males, 86–87, 93, 104; and African Americans, 104, 136–37; and racial discord, 128. *See also* Free labor
Labor organizations, 29, 38, 136–37, 186
Ladies Confederate Memorial Association, 62
Ladies' memorial societies, 61–63, 65, 78, 79–97, 189; male agents of, 82, 84; importance of, 94; and Arlington Cemetery, 189–90, 191; increased irrelevance of, 203, 204
Ladies Memorial Society of Petersburg, 80–81, 131
Ladies Southern Relief Society, 191, 193
Langston, John Mercer, 100–101, 139, 141, 146, 147
Lee, Fitzhugh, 121–23, 125, 155, 180, 189
Lee, Mary Custis, 73, 174, 179
Lee, Richard Henry, 124
Lee, Robert E., 79, 89, 121, 137, 142, 155, 156, 177, 205; burial site of, 8; unveiling of monument to, 9, 144–45, 146, 154–61, 162; surrender of, 34, 163; effigies of, 37; Confederate Memorial Day toasts to, 57; rejection of memorial events by, 73, 85; confiscated home of, 73, 174–75, 179, 202; and prescription for reunion, 113
Lee, Rooney, 142
Lee, Stephen D., 190, 202–3
Lewis, Samuel, 188–90, 192, 202–4

Lewis, Wyatt, 45
Lincoln, Abraham, 31, 42, 43, 45, 75, 92, 164; and emancipation, 16, 35, 110, 111, 140, 145, 162, 163, 197; African American honoring of, 27
Lincoln Clubs, 27, 32
Lindsay, Lewis, 46–47
Literacy, 141, 195
Logan, John A., 70, 71
Longstreet, James, 95, 144
Lost Cause, 2–3, 8, 58, 60, 131, 183; meaning of, 2, 173; toasts to, 57; rationale of, 92; women's perpetuation of, 94, 105; and crippled veteran metaphor, 127; changed meaning of, 154–55; and Confederate monument, 202
Louisiana, 9, 54, 72, 126, 137
Louisville convention (1883), 140, 150–51
Love, Emmanuel K., 153
Lovejoy, Elijah, 14
Loyal Leagues. *See* Union Leagues
Loyalty oaths, 51, 68
Lynchburg, Va., 34, 45, 64, 117, 132
Lynching, 161, 169

Macon, Ga., 31–32
Maddex, Jack, 114
Mahone, William, 129, 130–31, 133
Manhood: and Confederate cemetery movement, 78–79, 85–87; military service as defining, 98; African American qualities of, 99–101, 105; African American vs. Confederate images of, 104–5
"Marching through Georgia" (song), 143
Martin, Thomas S., 197–98
"Maryland, My Maryland" (song), 75
Massachusetts, 121–22
McKinley, William, 10, 179–88, 189, 191, 193
Meier, August, 154

Meigs, Montgomery C., 175–76

Memorial Days, 1–10, 29–30, 49–76; and national healing, 2, 121, 122, 172; expanded meaning of, 7, 173; and African Americans, 22, 134, 135–36, 176; at national cemeteries, 33, 171–72, 177; and politics, 171–72, 173. *See also* Confederate Memorial Days; Union Memorial Days

Memphis, Tenn., 62–63

Methodists, 81

Mexican War, 21

Middle class, 14, 30; African American, 100, 101, 167, 194–95. *See also* Respectability

Militias, 17; African American drills, 42, 138, 167; and Confederate Memorial Days, 55–60; African American women's ceremonial, 104, 167

Missouri, 44, 89

Mitchell, John, Jr., 9, 162–64, 185–86

Mobs, 12, 14, 16, 19, 23–24, 30, 138

Morgan, John Hunt, 95

Morton, Oliver P., 120

Mosby, John Singleton, 92

Mount Vernon, Va., 21–22

Mount Vernon Ladies Association, 21–22

"My Country 'tis of Thee" (song), 26

Natchez, Miss., 20–21

National Association of Colored Women, 195

National cemeteries, 8, 22, 33, 49, 50, 52–53, 76, 79, 171–72; treatment of Confederate graves in, 49–50, 52–53, 64, 71, 73–75, 76, 79, 182–84, 185–88, 201–3; denial of Confederate burial in, 64; Union Decoration Days at, 69, 71, 73; design and upkeep of, 70–71; burial of Confederate dead in, 87–88; at Gettysburg, 92; significance of, 177.

See also Arlington National Cemetery

National Colored Convention (1883), 140, 150–51

National Era, 18–19

Negro Conference, 168

Negro Development and Exposition Company, 197

Negro Historical and Industrial Association, 197

New Departure movement. *See* Conservative Party

New Jersey, 196

New Orleans, La., 51, 62, 95, 106, 121, 192

New South, 3, 127–34

New South (monument), 204

New Year's Day. *See* January 1

New York, 19, 20, 151, 152, 158, 196; civic commemorations, 11, 14, 19; and emancipation semicentennial, 199, 200

New York Age, 147, 149, 151, 160–61

New York Times, 35, 41, 62, 64–65, 87, 151, 155, 156, 160

New York Tribune, 111, 178–79

Norfolk, Va., 26, 41–42, 53, 68, 94, 141–42

Norfolk Light Artillery Blues, 121

Norris, Thomas, Jr., 141–42

North: and reconciliation, 69, 74–75, 109–15, 120–24, 155; views of ex-Confederate women's mourning rituals, 87–90, 93–97; and benefits of reunion, 120; reactions to Lee memorial unveiling in, 145, 155–59; impact of African American vote in, 152; changed meaning of Lost Cause in, 155; as Republican Party base, 161; continued sectionalism of, 172, 177, 184; and proliferation of ex-Confederate symbols, 184

North American Review, 11

North Carolina, 21, 25, 54, 152, 163

6, 64–65, 75–76, 105–7, 118–19; and racism, 10, 113; and ex-Confederate voting rights, 43–44; and Conservatives, 44–46, 113–15, 120; and Union Memorial Days, 69, 70, 72–74; in North, 69, 74–75, 109–15, 121–24, 155; and Arlington Cemetery grave tending, 73–75, 178–79; ex-Confederate view of, 107–8, 111, 113, 115–27; former abolitionists as, 109–11; politics of, 109–15, 179–80; and Democratic presidential victory, 142–43; and Lee monument unveiling, 158–59; and Confederate monument, 171–72, 201–7; and Spanish-American War, 180, 181; and McKinley policy, 182–84, 187. *See also* Reunion

Reconstruction, 4, 5–6, 9, 39–48; end of, 9–10, 107, 108, 119, 139; and July Fourth celebrations, 27–28; and Emancipation Days, 29–30, 34–35; and public violence, 30, 114; and military occupation, 42, 62, 68; and Memorial Days, 49–51, 55–76, 84, 97; and African Americans, 62, 101, 102, 103, 104; underground resistance to, 62–69; and open meetings, 68; and women's maintenance of Confederate legacy, 77–87, 105; and Confederate funeral oration, 92–93

Reconstruction Acts of 1867, 42, 62, 63, 69

Redeemer governments, 127–28

Republican Party, 5–6, 107–8, 172; and African Americans, 4, 5, 9, 25, 27, 31, 39–40, 42–43, 45–48, 51, 68, 69, 103, 108, 115, 134, 136, 138–42, 146–54, 158, 161, 165, 169, 176–77, 185; and Reconstruction, 9, 39–40; and Emancipation Day, 24, 35, 46–47; organization in South, 39–40; and reconciliation, 43, 109–10, 113, 139,

182–86; as emancipation party, 45, 46, 103, 109; and Union Decoration Days, 50–51, 69, 71, 177; and Confederate Memorial Days, 57–58, 61–62, 118; southern wing of, 109–10, 148–54, 178; founding principles of, 110; Conservative opponents of, 113, 114, 116; white southern strategy against, 123, 133–34; corruption in, 148, 149; and Lee monument unveiling, 156; turn-of-the century changes in, 161; and government care of Confederate graves, 182–86, 189–90. *See also* Radical Republicans; Union Leagues

Respectability, 17, 72; and African Americans, 6, 12–15, 29–30, 48, 100–104, 134, 165

Reunion, 94, 115, 116, 120, 121, 142–43, 178; Lee monument unveiling as benchmark in, 154–61; and Spanish-American War, 180; and McKinley's southern speeches, 182

Revolutionary War. *See* American Revolution

Rhett, Robert Barnwell, 21

Richmond, Va.: Emancipation Days, 7, 168–69, 173; reburial campaigns, 8, 22, 89–90, 96–97; Lee monument unveiling, 9, 144–45, 146, 154–61, 162; antebellum black freedom events in, 20; date of black emancipation in, 25, 47; fall to Union Army of, 25; July Fourth parades, 32, 42; Evacuation Day, 35–41, 47, 101, 137, 163; national cemeteries, 53, 71, 73; Confederate Memorial Days, 54, 55–62, 94; Union Memorial Days, 71–72, 73; ladies memorial societies, 80, 81, 82, 83, 89, 189; unemployed white males in, 86–87; African American Republicans in, 103, 115, 146;